THE "WE" PASSAGES
IN THE ACTS OF THE APOSTLES

Society of Biblical Literature

Studies in Biblical Literature

Number 14

THE "WE" PASSAGES
IN THE ACTS OF THE APOSTLES
The Narrator as Narrative Character

William Sanger Campbell

THE "WE" PASSAGES
IN THE ACTS OF THE APOSTLES

The Narrator as Narrative Character

William Sanger Campbell

Society of Biblical Literature
Atlanta

THE "WE" PASSAGES
IN THE ACTS OF THE APOSTLES

The Narrator as Narrative Character

Library of Congress Cataloging-in-Publication Data

Campbell, William S.
   The we passages in the Acts of the Apostles : the narrator as narrative character / by William Sanger Campbell.
         p. cm.—(Society of Biblical Literature studies in biblical
         literature ; no. 14)
Includes bibliographical references and index.
ISBN 978-1-58983-205-3 (pbk. : alk. paper)
1. Bible N.T. Acts—Criticism, Narrative. I. Title.

BS2625.52.C36 2007
226'.6066—dc22   2007033812

14 13 12 11 10 09 08 07   5 4 3 2 1

Printed in the United States of America on acid-free, recycled paper conforming to ANSI/NISO Z39.48-1992 (R1997) and ISO 9706:1994 standards for paper permanence.

For J. W. Wolslager
and in memory of
Josephine S. Wolslager
κράτιστε Θεόφιλε *(Luke 1:3; Acts 1:1)*

Contents

Preface

I am accustomed to meeting puzzled expressions when people learn that I am writing about the "we" passages in Acts. More often than not, even those who consider themselves if not experts, at least not biblically illiterate, are at best minimally aware of the employment of the first-plural grammatical person in Acts. Despite the obscurity of first-person plural style and although it accounts for less than 15 percent of the total Acts narrative—most of the book is written in the third person—the influence of the "we" passages on the interpretation of Acts cannot be overstated.

I first encountered these enigmatic passages when I was assigned the task of leading a graduate seminar discussion on Acts 27–28. Like so many students of Acts before me, I became fascinated by the abrupt and unexplained change in grammatical person that occurs in these chapters and at several other points in the narrative. The question that it raised for me, however, was different than the concern of many of my predecessors. Instead of *who* the putative historical eyewitness might be, I wondered *how* the sudden shifts in grammatical person functioned in the narrative—what, in other words, is the narrative significance of first-person plural style in Acts? It was this question that I pursued in my doctoral dissertation. Although parts have been thoroughly reworked, the present study retains the thrust and many details of the argument presented in that earlier work.

In approaching the "we" passages as integral to the drama and attending to their narrative role, my study presents a wholly literary interpretation of the first-person plural passages in Acts. In so doing, it necessarily sets aside the historical question, although it does not ignore the issue. The book opens with a brief overview of the most influential interpretations of the "we" passages during the modern period, analyzing their strengths and weaknesses and lifting up the developing impulse within Acts scholarship of the narrative significance of first-person style. Following that, chapter 1 discusses the theoretical and methodological strategies employed in the study, namely, literary narrative and reader-response criticisms, conceiving the narrator as a character in the story rather than simply the agency of narration. Then chapter 2 analyzes grammatical practice among ancient historians and demonstrates that they were capable of employing grammatical person in ways not generally conceived of by modern scholars and for purposes other than claiming eyewitness presence at events. The heart of the book's proposal, detailed in chapters 3 and 4, is that intermittent first-person grammatical style in Acts represents a character in the narrative. Paralleling in significant ways the role of Barnabas, Paul's initial companion who departs from the story just before the "we" character enters, the "we" narrator appears at crucial moments in Paul's career, drawing attention to the issue of the apostle's credibility, reinforcing the congruence between the divine missionary instructions Paul receives and his activities, and reassuring characters and readers alike that, whatever Paul's circumstances, the divine directives will be accomplished as part of God's plan.

One thing that has not changed from dissertation to the present work is my gratitude to those who have encouraged and assisted me. Beverly Roberts Gaventa's contributions cannot be overemphasized. As dissertation advisor, her critical yet affirming guidance of that earlier work provided a firm foundation on which to build the current study. David Moessner first recognized the potential and nurtured my vision of the "we" passages in the graduate seminar on Acts mentioned a moment ago. Others who have read portions of the work in its present or earlier forms and offered helpful observations and criticisms include C. Clifton Black, the late Donald H. Juel, Pheme Perkins, J. Ross Wagner, Matthew L. Skinner, Elna K. Solvang, and Christine Roy Yoder. Judith A. Jones's careful reading of the complete draft of the manuscript prevented numerous errors and infelicities, and her insightful comments and suggestions have considerably strengthened the end product. I am grateful as well to Sharon H. Ringe, formerly New Testament editor of the SBL Studies in Biblical Literature series, who shepherded the proposal for this book through the review process, and to Bob Buller, SBL's Editorial Director, for his supervision of its publication. My greatest debt and deepest gratitude are owed to Therese, whose support, reassurance, and confidence seem inexhaustible. May it ever be so!

Abbreviations

AB	Anchor Bible
ABD	*Anchor Bible Dictionary*. Edited by David Noel Freedman. 6 vols. New York: Doubleday, 1992.
AJT	*American Journal of Theology*
ANRW	*Aufstieg und Niedergang der Römischen Welt: Geschichte und Kultur Roms im Spiegel der neueren Forschung*. Edited by Hildegard Temporini and Wolfgang Haase. Berlin: de Gruyter, 1972–.
ANTC	Abingdon New Testament Commentaries
AThR	*Anglican Theological Review*
BAGD	Bauer, Walter, William F. Arndt, F. Wilber Gingrich, and Frederick W. Danker, *A Greek English Lexicon of the New Testament and Other Early Christian Literature*. 2nd ed. Chicago: University of Chicago Press, 1979.
BeO	*Bibbia e oriente*
Bib	*Biblica*
BR	*Biblical Research*
BTB	*Biblical Theology Bulletin*
CBQ	*Catholic Biblical Quarterly*
ET	English Translation
EvQ	*Evangelical Quarterly*
ExpTim	*Expository Times*
FRLANT	Forschungen zur Religion und Literatur des Alten und Neuen Testaments
GBS	Guides to Biblical Scholarship
GTA	Göttinger theologischer Arbeiten
HDR	Harvard Dissertations in Religion
HTR	*Harvard Theological Review*
ICC	International Critical Commentary
IDB	*Interpreter's Dictionary of the Bible*. Edited by George A. Buttrick. 4 vols. Nashville: Abingdon, 1962.
Int	*Interpretation*
JBL	*Journal of Biblical Literature*
JSNT	*Journal for the Study of the New Testament*
JSNTSup	Journal for the Study of the New Testament Supplement Series

JSOTSup	Journal for the Study of the Old Testament Supplement Series
JSPSup	Journal for the Study of the Pseudepigrapha Supplement Series
JTC	*Journal for Theology and the Church*
JTS	*Journal of Theological Studies*
LCL	Loeb Classical Library
LEC	Library of Early Christianity
LSJ	*A Greek-English Lexicon.* Edited by Henry G. Liddell, Robert Scott, and Henry. S. Jones. 9th ed with revised supplement. Oxford: Clarendon, 1996.
NAB	New American Bible
NEB	New English Bible
Neot	*Neotestamentica*
NICNT	New International Commentary on the New Testament
NIV	New International Version
NJB	New Jerusalem Bible
NovT	*Novum Testamentum*
NovTSup	Supplements to Novum Testamentum
NT	New Testament
NTS	*New Testament Studies*
OBT	Overtures to Biblical Theology
OCD	*Oxford Classical Dictionary.* Edited by Simon Hornblower and Antony Spawforth. 3rd ed. Oxford: Oxford University Press, 1996.
PRSt	*Perspectives in Religious Studies*
PSB	*Princeton Seminary Bulletin*
RSV	Revised Standard Version
SBLAcBib	Society of Biblical Literature Academia Biblica
SBLDS	Society of Biblical Literature Dissertation Series
SBLMS	Society of Biblical Literature Monograph Series
SBLSBS	Society of Biblical Literature Sources for Biblical Study
SBLSP	Society of Biblical Literature Seminar Papers
SBLSymS	Society of Biblical Literature Symposium Series
SNTSMS	Society for New Testament Studies Monograph Series
SP	Sacra Pagina
SUNT	Studien zur Umwelt des Neuen Testaments
TLZ	*Theologische Literaturzeitung*
TNTC	Tyndale New Testament Commentaries
TSAJ	Texte und Studien zum Antiken Judentum
TynBul	*Tyndale Bulletin*
WC	Westminster Commentaries
WUNT	Wissenschaftliche Untersuchungen zum Neuen Testament
ZNW	*Zeitschrift für die neutestamentliche Wissenschaft und die Kunde der älteren Kirche*
ZTK	*Zeitschrift für Theologie und Kirche*

INTRODUCTION

"The Insoluble Riddle"

*We are like dwarfs, sitting on the shoulders of giants, in order that
we may see things more numerous and more distant than they
could see, not certainly, by reason of the sharpness of our own
vision or the tallness of our bodies, but because we are lifted and
raised on high by the greatness of the giants.*
—Bernard of Chartres

The term "we passages" refers to sections of the Acts of the Apostles
in which the style of narration changes from the third person ("she/he" or
"they") to the first person plural ("we"). The exact number of first-person
plural passages is a matter of debate, but broadly speaking they include Acts
16:10–17; 20:5–21:18; and 27:1–28:16.[1] The shift in grammatical person in
these passages presents interpretive problems because the narrator does not
provide an explanation for the change and the reason is not obvious from
the narrative context. That is, the narrator does not say that at these points
he has entered events personally, nor does the story itself suggest that this is
the case.[2] First-person plural narration simply appears at certain points in

---

1. Many consider 20:5–15 and 21:1–18 to be separate first person plural passages and,
therefore, count four "we" passages (e.g., Joseph A. Fitzmyer, *The Acts of the Apostles* [AB 31;
New York: Doubleday, 1998], 50; idem, *Luke the Theologian: Aspects of His Teaching* [New
York: Paulist, 1989], 3). Others argue for five passages, with separate passages in 27:1–29
and 28:1–16 as well as 20:5–15 and 21:1–18 (e.g., Stanley E. Porter, *The Paul of Acts: Essays
in Literary Criticism, Rhetoric, and Theology* [WUNT 115; Tübingen: Mohr Siebeck, 1999],
28–33).

2. Chapter 1 examines the literary relationship between narrator and author, but suffice it
to say that the two are not identical. Simply put, the author is the storywriter, and the narrator
is the storyteller. In other words, by "author" I mean the individual responsible for the overall
production of the Acts narrative, in all likelihood combining his own composition with his
work as redactor or editor of traditions and other sources. In adopting the masculine personal
pronoun of the author, I accept Loveday C. A. Alexander's (*The Preface to Luke's Gospel:
Literary Convention and Social Context in Luke 1.1–4 and Acts 1.1* [SNTSMS 78; Cambridge:
Cambridge University Press, 1993], 2 n. 2) assessment and qualification: "the author of the

1

the book, suddenly and seemingly out of nowhere, and then just as abruptly disappears. In Acts 16:10, for example, after "they" (Paul, Silas, and Timothy) have gone through Phrygia and Galatia in Asia Minor and "he" (Paul) has seen a vision, "we" decide that God has called "us" to preach in Macedonia. Over the years, scholars have suggested a number of solutions to the narrative's enigmatic application of first person plural. These proposals can be grouped into four general categories, although, as will become apparent, they occasionally overlap: (1) the author shifted his writing style to first person plural or added the first person to a source document to indicate that he was present at certain events (author-as-eyewitness); (2) the author retained first person plural from or added it to a source document because the source was present at those events (source-as-eyewitness); (3) the author wrote in first-person plural style, but neither he nor his sources were there (fictional eyewitness); or (4) the author adopted first person plural where literary considerations demanded it (conventional eyewitness).

Categories 1 and 2: Author-As-Eyewitness and Source-As-Eyewitness Solutions

The first two categories share the understanding that first person plural in various sections of Acts indicates the presence of a historical eyewitness at the events reported, either the author of the overall Acts narrative (author-as-eyewitness solutions) or the author of the source document (source-as-eyewitness solutions). They represent the most widely accepted interpretations of the "we" passages and, as such, have dominated discussion of them. This is not surprising considering, in the words of one commentator, the "*prima facie* inference" that first person indicates the writer's presence at events.[3] The issue that advocates of these solutions have addressed and attempted to resolve, therefore, is: Who was there—the author or his source?

The first to appeal to the "we" passages in support of the author's presence seems to have been Irenaeus in the late second century C.E. In refuting gnostic claims that there were secret teachings of Paul known only to them, Irenaeus pointed to the "we" passages as proof that the author of Acts was Paul's constant companion whose presence assured readers that the account of events in Acts represents the entirety of Paul's gospel as well as an ac-

---

two works is more likely to have been male than female. If this assumption is wrong, I beg her pardon." On the other hand, the narrator is a character in the story. I refer to the narrator in masculine terms because the masculine form of the participle παρηκολουθηκότι ("having followed") used in Luke 1:3 indicates that this character is indeed male; see Gregory E. Sterling, *Historiography and Self-Definition: Josephos, Luke-Acts and Apologetic Historiography* (NovTSup 64; Leiden: Brill, 1992), 326; Robert C. Tannehill, *Luke* (ANTC; Nashville: Abingdon, 1996), 34–35.

3. C. K. Barrett, *The Acts of the Apostles* (ICC; 2 vols.; Edinburgh: T&T Clark, 1994–1998), 2:xxv; 2:xxvii.

curate record of the apostle's travels and activities.[4] But which companion, since neither Acts nor the Gospel of Luke—the two books were undoubtedly written by the same person—discloses the author's name? By the time of Irenaeus, the tradition had settled on a certain Luke mentioned in letters written in Paul's name to Philemon, Timothy, and the Colossian church (Phlm 24; 2 Tim 4:11; Col 4:14), based in part on the perceived correspondence between Luke's affiliation with Paul's mission expressed in Paul's letters and the first-person accounts in Acts.

Irenaeus's understanding of the "we" passages was for many centuries the accepted interpretation of them. Indeed, there was no serious challenge to the author-as-eyewitness solution until the beginning of the modern period a millennium and a half later. Interpreters of Acts revisited the issue beginning in the eighteenth century, when critical methodologies were introduced into the analysis of biblical texts. Source criticism (which attempts to expose earlier documents by isolating inconsistencies in style, vocabulary, and narrative sequence or content, including repetitions, chronology, theology, and the like), form criticism (which is concerned with the genre and original application of preexisting units of material in preaching, teaching, or worshiping in the church) that followed a century or so later, and after that redaction criticism (which seeks to separate earlier traditions from the author's own contributions in an effort to discover the author's theological perspective and insights) were each interested in recovering written sources or traditions that may have been utilized in the production of biblical texts.

The inexplicable change in grammatical person made the "we" passages an obvious choice for source-critical analysis, and early on scholars concluded that they represented one of the sources incorporated into Acts. If the "we" passages were the work of someone other than the author of Acts, source critics reasoned, then whoever wrote the source document, and not the author of Acts as a whole, must have been the eyewitness at the events reported. Those who opted for the source-as-eyewitness solution were divided over who the source was. Some continued to hold to the tradition that Luke was the eyewitness and argued, therefore, that he was the author of the "we" passage sections instead of the overall Acts narrative. Others nominated different candidates as Paul's companion most likely responsible for the first-person source document (Timothy or Silas, for example). Still others concluded that the information was insufficient to determine the identity of the eyewitness source. Source critics were in agreement, however, that evidence from Acts itself eliminated the author of the book as the eyewitness to any of the events narrated. They argued that the Gospel preface identifies the author as a researcher and editor of eyewitness sources, not someone

---

4. Irenaeus, *Adversus haereses* 3.1–14, esp. 3.1.1 and 3.14.1.

personally involved in the affairs about which he wrote. Notwithstanding the correspondences that earlier scholars had claimed, source critics cited the irreconcilability of some episodes in Acts with information in Paul's letters and with historical data drawn from outside the New Testament to demonstrate the author's lack of firsthand knowledge about events. The critique by source critics of the historical value of parts of Acts was in line with historical-critical analysis, which had already shown that Acts "fulfilled in a very imperfect way the historical purpose which had been ascribed to it by tradition."[5]

The conclusion that the author was not an eyewitness to the events narrated compelled source critics to address the question of why the author would retain the first-person plural style from a source in an otherwise third-person narrative to describe events at which the author was not personally present, leaving the impression (intentional or not) that he had witnessed some of them. The initial response was that the author wished to reproduce all of his sources exactly, including the "we" source, and so incorporated them intact into the narrative. It was, therefore, the author's faithfulness to his sources that created the inconsistencies that enabled scholars to detect and identify such underlying materials.[6] Analysis of literary and grammatical structure established that the writing style and vocabulary are uniform throughout the narrative, however, and specifically that the "we" passages are consistent in style with the rest of Acts, except, of course, for the use of first person plural.[7] The logical conclusion of this analysis was that a single individual was responsible for the final manuscript. In light of this probabil-

---

5. A. C. McGiffert, "The Historical Criticism of Acts in Germany," in *Prolegomena II: Criticism* (ed. F. J. Foakes Jackson and Kirsopp Lake; vol. 2 of *The Beginnings of Christianity, Part 1: The Acts of the Apostles*; London: Macmillan, 1922), 363.

6. Bernhard Königsmann, "De fontibus commentariorum sacrorum, qui Lucae nomen praeferunt deque eorum consilio et aetate," in *Sylloge Commentationum Theologicarum* (ed. David J. Pott; Helmstadt: Fleckeisen, 1802), 3:230–33; cf. McGiffert, "Historical Criticism of Acts in Germany," 385–86; Jacques Dupont, *The Sources of Acts* (trans. Kathleen Pond; London: Darton, Longman & Todd, 1964).

7. Ernst Mayerhoff, "Über den Zweck, die Quellen und den Verfasser der Apostelgeschichte," in *Historisch-critische Einleitung in die petrinischen Schriften nebst einer Abhandlung über den Verfasser der Apostelgeschichte* (Hamburg: Perthes, 1835), 1–30; Adolf Harnack, *Lukas der Arzt: Der Verfasser des Dritten Evangeliums und der Apostelgeschichte* (vol. 1 of *Beiträge zur Einleitung in das Neue Testament*; Leipzig: Hinrich, 1906), 19–121; ET: "Special Investigation of the So-Called 'We' Account of the Acts of the Apostles," in *Luke the Physician: The Author of the Third Gospel and the Acts of the Apostles* (vol. 1 of *New Testament Studies*; trans. J. R. Wilkinson; 2nd ed.; London: Williams & Norgate, 1909), 26–120; and idem, *Neue Untersuchungen zur Apostelgeschichte und zur Abfassungszeit der Synoptischen Evangelien* (vol. 4 of *Beiträge zur Einleitung in das Neue Testament*; Leipzig: Hinrich, 1906), 1–29; ET: "The Identity of the Author of the 'We' Sections of the Acts of the Apostles with the Author of the Whole Work," in *The Date of the Acts and of the Synoptic Gospels* (vol. 4 of *New Testament Studies*; trans. J. R. Wilkinson; London: Williams & Norgate, 1911), 1–29.

ity, source critics acknowledged that the author had thoroughly revised and edited his sources to achieve a unified narrative.

Given his editorial skill, some source critics could not imagine why the author retained the first-person plural style from the source and concluded that it must have been inadvertent, an editorial oversight.[8] Most, however, considered the author's retention of the first person plural to be purposeful. For example, the nineteenth-century movement known as the Tübingen school proposed that the author utilized the "we" source to assist in his effort to mediate the conflict between two rival groups in the nascent church. F. C. Baur, the school's founder, argued that Jewish and Gentile factions loyal to the adversarial apostolic figures Peter and Paul (1 Cor 1:11) competed for dominance in the early church and that the friction between these parties continued into the postapostolic era.[9] According to the Tübingen hypothesis, Acts was written between 110 and 125 C.E. in an attempt to reconcile the opposing parties. The author hoped that the Acts narrative would persuade anti-Paulinist Jewish Christians to accept Paul, his mission, and his doctrine.[10] He had in his possession a first-person memoir penned by Luke, the physician and companion to Paul of Col 4:14, and he used this account to gain credibility for his version of the history of the primitive church. First, the author preserved the "we" style exactly as it was in the memoir in order to identify himself with Luke, a well-known Paulinist and eyewitness to Paul's mission. So strong was the author's desire to pass for this particular co-worker that he refused to edit grammatical person in order to avoid giving the impression of claiming presence with Paul at any other time or location than those in the memoir, even though elsewhere he freely abbreviated and augmented the source as he saw fit.[11] Then he falsely credited authorship of Acts and the Third Gospel to Luke.

By the beginning of the twentieth century, form criticism was on the rise. Eduard Norden, among the first to apply the new method to Acts, concluded that the second half of the narrative was constructed from journey

---

8. W. M. L. de Wette, *Lehrbuch der historisch kritischen Einleitung in die kanonischen Bücher des Neuen Testaments* (5th ed.; Berlin: Reimer, 1848), 225–31; ET: *An Historico-Critical Introduction to the Canonical Books of the New Testament* (trans. Frederick Frothingham; Boston: Crosby, Nichols, 1858), 215–28.

9. F. C. Baur, "Die Christuspartei in der korinthischen Gemeinde, der Gegenzatz des petrinischen und paulinischen Christenthums in der ältesten Kirche, der Apostel Petrus in Rom," in *Historisch-kritische Untersuchungen zum Neuen Testament* (ed. Klaus Scholder; Stuttgart: Frommann, 1963), 1–146; repr. from *Tübinger Zeitschrift für Theologie* 4 (1831); idem, *Paulus, der Apostel Jesu Christi: Sein Leben und Wirken, seine Briefe und seine Lehre* (Stuttgart: Becher & Müller, 1845); idem, *The Church History of the First Three Centuries* (trans. Allen Menzies; 3rd ed.; 2 vols.; London: Williams & Norgate, 1878–1879).

10. Eduard Zeller, *The Contents and Origin of the Acts of the Apostles Critically Investigated* (trans. Joseph Dare; 2 vols.; London: Williams & Norgate, 1875–1876).

11. Ibid., 2:319, esp. n. 2.

memoranda of an eyewitness other than the author.[12] Such memoranda often originated as reports of military expeditions. For instance, Julius Caesar's commentaries on the Gallic wars are expansions of official military reports that he submitted annually to the Roman senate, which combine his personal notes (in first person) with the reports of officers under his command about expeditions they conducted without his direct involvement (in third person). Norden argued that Paul's companion, in similar fashion, had drafted a mixed memoir of personal and secondhand experiences with the apostle, and the author of Acts incorporated the memoir into his narrative. Norden faced the same question as the source critics: Why did the author retain the first person plural when he was not there? Norden's response was that he kept it for aesthetic and generic reasons. First, the "we" style added drama, vividness, and excitement, qualities that were lacking in most histories. More important than aesthetics, however, the author patterned Acts on the genre of Jewish historiography exemplified by the Old Testament books of Ezra and Nehemiah.

By the second decade of the twentieth century, most Acts scholars were in agreement that the author had fashioned the narrative out of a variety of written sources. A number of them, however, did not accept the source-as-eyewitness solution to the "we" question. For example, Henry J. Cadbury, perhaps the foremost American Luke-Acts scholar of the modern period, was part of the author-as-eyewitness camp. He accepted the consensus view that Acts is largely a compilation of written sources edited into a coherent narrative but insisted that the "we" passages are the product of the author's writing and editing activity.[13] Cadbury argued that, like other ancient historians, the author of Acts carried forward and revised the work of predecessors for events of past eras, then added to the historical record by writing from firsthand knowledge about current events. First person plural represents the author's grammatical style for narrating the current events at which he was present, a style not uncommon in popular literature of the time. Cadbury

---

12. Eduard Norden, *Agnostos Theos: Untersuchungen zur Formengeschichte Religiöser Rede* (Leipzig: Teubner, 1913), 34–37, 311–32.

13. The hyphenated title "Luke-Acts" was coined by Cadbury (*The Making of Luke-Acts* [New York: Macmillan, 1927], 11) to communicate that the Third Gospel and Acts represent a single continuous work that became separated in antiquity and in the Bible. Until recently, Cadbury's position has been widely shared among Acts scholars. It has now been credibly challenged by Mikael Parsons and Richard Pervo, *Rethinking the Unity of Luke-Acts* (Minneapolis: Fortress, 1993). See also Cadbury, *The Style and Literary Method of Luke* (Cambridge: Harvard University Press, 1920); idem, "The Purpose Expressed in Luke's Preface," *Expositor* 21 (1921): 431–41; idem, "The Knowledge Claimed in Luke's Preface," *Expositor* 24 (1922): 411–17; idem, "Commentary on the Preface of Luke," and "The Greek and Jewish Traditions of History Writing," in Foakes Jackson and Lake, *Prolegomena II: Criticism*, 489–510 and 7–29; idem, *The Book of Acts in History* (London: Black, 1955); idem, " 'We' and 'I' Passages in Luke-Acts," *NTS* 3 (1956–1957): 128–32.

and others who maintained that first person plural came from the pen of the author faced a question of their own, however. Why did he employ grammatical person in such an unusual way? Why, that is to say, the abrupt and unexplained intrusion of the "we" style? Cadbury's response was that it reflected the author's distinctive manner of written expression, his personal writing style.

Martin Dibelius, another pioneer among New Testament form critics, also came to a different assessment than many source and form critics.[14] He distinguished two forms behind the "we" sections. One was an itinerary of the ports along Paul's route that had come into the author's possession, a journal probably kept by someone who accompanied the apostle during many of his missionary travels as a way of remembering the route and hosts for future journeys (13:4–21:18). The other form identified by Dibelius was a sea-voyage narrative, perhaps largely fictitious, that provided the model for drafting the account of the journey to Rome (27:1–28:16). According to Dibelius, Luke inserted first person plural in various sections of the itinerary where it was not included originally and employed it in the composition of the sea voyage in order to indicate those occasions at which he was present during Paul's travels. Dibelius considered Luke to be the author of the Third Gospel and Acts because, he reasoned, ancient dedicatory practice would have insisted that the author be named along with the dedicatee, in this case Theophilus.[15] Luke's name would have been temporarily lost because at first each community had only one written Gospel, eliminating the need to distinguish among authors, and readers did not appreciate the requirement of including the author's name in the title of dedicated works. Luke's Gospel, therefore, became known simply as the "Gospel of Jesus Christ." Later, when the church began to label its writings by author, Luke's name was easily recoverable in the tradition.

In the mid-twentieth century, redaction criticism emerged as another method for analyzing the biblical texts. Redaction criticism presupposes that biblical narratives postdate the era in which the events they purport to describe occur. The author of Acts, therefore, would not have been Paul's contemporary, but someone belonging to a later generation. Ernst Haenchen applied redaction analysis to the "we" passages. He agreed with Dibelius that the author had introduced first-person plural grammatical style into his sources when editing them for Acts but, unlike Cadbury and Dibelius, did not accept the author as the eyewitness to which they point.[16] Haenchen argued,

---

14. Martin Dibelius, *Studies in the Acts of the Apostles* (ed. Heinrich Greeven; trans. Mary Ling; London: SCM, 1956).

15. Ibid., 88–90, 103–4, 135–37, 145.

16. Ernst Haenchen, "'We' in Acts and the Itinerary," *JTC* 1 (1965): 65–99; idem, *The Acts of the Apostles* (trans. Bernard Noble and Gerald Shinn; Philadelphia: Westminster, 1971); idem, "The Book of Acts as Source Material for the History of Early Christianity," in *Studies*

instead, that in gathering material for Acts the author collected several types of eyewitness accounts, including written reminiscences of older members of communities that Paul had visited, recollections of traveling companions, and an itinerary. He inserted "we" as he was editing these sources to indicate that eyewitness authority stood behind the accounts. In other words, Haenchen supported the source-as-eyewitness solution while arguing that the "we" style was the author's innovation. The author's motives for calling attention to the eyewitness quality of his sources were theological and narratological rather than historical. Theologically, the eyewitness report guaranteed that at a critical moment in his career Paul did in fact turn to the Gentiles in accordance with God's plan. The narrative impact of first person plural was to draw readers into the story, to allow them to become personally involved in Paul's journeys and to feel connected directly with Paul's life. Indeed, the author was even willing to extend "we" style beyond the eyewitness testimony to accomplish this effect (16:16–17; 20:7).

The survey of historical eyewitness solutions presented here is not exhaustive. It is, however, representative of the proposals offered in the modern period, giving attention to scholars whose interpretations have had the greatest influence on the discussion of the "we" passages over the years. A glance at recent extended treatments of the "we" passages and commentaries demonstrates that, within biblical scholarship, solutions in the historical eyewitness traditions continue to be the most influential explanations for the first-person plural style in Acts. Of the two latest full-length studies on the "we" passages, for example, one argues that the first-person accounts came from Silas, a companion of Paul but not the author, and the other proposes that first-person narration was Luke's (Paul's companion and the author of Acts) method of communicating his participation in the events narrated.[17]

Categories 3 and 4: Fictional and Conventional Eyewitness Solutions

While author-as-eyewitness and source-as-eyewitness proposals have dominated the discussion of the "we" passages, solutions opposed to the notion of a historical eyewitness have also been proposed. In the mid-nineteenth century, Bruno Bauer concluded that the overall Acts narrative had

---

in Luke-Acts (ed. Leander E. Keck and J. Louis Martyn; Nashville: Abingdon, 1966), 258–78; idem, "Acta 27," in Zeit und Geschichte (ed. Erich Dinkler; Tübingen: Mohr Siebeck, 1964), 235–54.

17. Jürgen Wehnert, Die Wir-Passagen der Apostelgeschichte: Ein lukanisches Stilmittel aus jüdischer Tradition (GTA 40; Göttingen: Vandenhoeck & Ruprecht, 1989); Claus-Jürgen Thornton, Der Zeuge des Zeugen: Lukas als Historiker der Paulusreisen (WUNT 56; Tübingen: Mohr Siebeck, 1991). See also, Barrett, Acts of the Apostles; and Fitzmyer, Acts of the Apostles.

no historical foundation and, consistent with that premise, that the eyewitness suggested by the "we" style was a product of the author's imagination (fictional eyewitness).[18] Bauer argued that each eyewitness account accompanies a miracle story and, therefore, that the author created the "we" companion to give credence to the accuracy of events in his miracle-filled narrative. In reality, Bauer claimed, the ideal world, the events, and even many of the characters portrayed in Acts are inventions of the author.

In the 1970s Vernon Robbins offered a different explanation, but one that also eliminated a historical eyewitness. Robbins argued that at the time Acts was written sea-voyage narratives represented a distinct genre in Greco-Roman literature. He attempted to demonstrate that first person plural was the preferred grammatical style in such narratives whether or not the author actually participated in the voyage (conventional eyewitness).[19] According to Robbins, first person plural developed into the customary narrative style for sea voyages because it emphasized the cooperation among travelers that was required for a successful cruise and it added drama. As a competent writer of that period, the author of Acts adopted first-person plural style because it was the grammatical construction appropriate for sea voyages. To do otherwise would have been literarily unfashionable. In addition to sociological and dramatic implications, Robbins speculated that the author of Acts may also have wished to demonstrate solidarity with the early Christian leaders about whom he was writing by participating, if only through the narrative, in the experiences that shaped their historic endeavors.

Drawing on both fictional and conventional theories, Eckhard Plümacher proposed a third nonhistorical alternative. Ironically, he considered Acts to be an ancient history and argued that ancient history writing highly valued historians' eyewitness testimony and depth of personal experience about their subject matter.[20] The author of Acts, therefore, passed himself off as an eyewitness to the events narrated and as an experienced seafarer to meet the expectations of ancient historiography.

Problems and Possibilities

None of the proposed solutions to the problem of the "we" passages has proven entirely satisfactory. Author-as-eyewitness solutions have been unable to account for the unconventional application of the first person

---

18. Bruno Bauer, *Die Apostelgeschichte: Eine Ausgleichung des Paulinismus und des Judenthums innerhalb der christlichen Kirche* (Berlin: Hempel, 1850), esp. 125–32.

19. Vernon Robbins, "The We-Passages in Acts and Ancient Sea Voyages," *BR* 20 (1975): 5–18; idem, "By Land and by Sea: The We-Passages and Ancient Sea Voyages," in *Perspectives on Luke-Acts* (ed. Charles Talbert; Danville, Va.: Association of Baptist Professors of Religion, 1978), 215–42.

20. Eckhart Plümacher, "Wirklichkeitserfahrung und Geschichtsschreibung bei Lukas: Erwägungen zu den Wir-Stücken der Apostelgeschichte," *ZNW* 68 (1977): 2–22.

plural, that is, its sudden and unexplained appearance and equally abrupt disappearance. Source-as-eyewitness solutions have not provided a sustainable rationale for the author's preservation or introduction of the "we" style as a way of noting an eyewitness source in an otherwise third-person narrative about events at which the author himself was not present. In addition, Acts supplies neither names nor the number of "we" participants, nor their association with Paul or his mission, nor even an introduction of them into the story. As a result, the focus of the author- and source-as-eyewitness categories on "we" as a historical eyewitness is at odds with the narrative's apparent indifference toward the eyewitness's identity and, therefore, historical significance.[21]

Another problem with the historical eyewitness solutions has been their identification of the Luke mentioned in Paul's letters with the author of Acts or the source document. For one thing, "Luke" was a common name; therefore, it is quite possible that, if the author of the Third Gospel and Acts was named Luke, different persons are meant. For another, there is considerable uncertainty that Paul was responsible for writing two of the letters (Colossians and 2 Timothy) in which the name Luke appears. Admittedly, the process that led to the tradition of Lukan authorship is shrouded in obscurity, but a few brief and ambiguous references in questionable letters constitute an extremely "frail tissue of texts" on which to base the decision.[22] Moreover, critical scholarship—beginning with source criticism—has vigorously and with more than a little success challenged the historical reliability of Acts, raising doubts about the author's familiarity with Paul or his work. Today many scholars continue to refer to the author as "Luke" for the sake of convenience but express serious reservations about the historical correctness of this traditional designation. Even those who advocate for one of the historical eyewitness solutions concede that silence in both the narrative and historical records renders impossible a positive identification of the author. He may have been someone named Luke, but the evidence supporting this conclusion is fragile and inconclusive. Furthermore, a majority of scholars consider the inscrutability of the author's identity to be intentional; that is, the author of Luke's Gospel and Acts (as well as the authors of the other Gospels) wrote anonymously. If this is the case, the question becomes: Why would the author purposely conceal his identity throughout the Third Gospel and much of Acts and then make the effort in the last half of the

---

21. Susan Marie Praeder, "The Problem of First Person Narration in Acts," *NovT* 29 (1987): 198.

22. Beverly Roberts Gaventa, *The Acts of the Apostles* (ANTC; Nashville: Abingdon, 2003), 50.

narrative to reveal his historical presence through the introduction of first person plural in such an idiosyncratic and incomprehensible way?[23]

Although fictional and conventional eyewitness solutions are not subject to the problems associated with historical eyewitness proposals, they too have encountered serious objections. Fictional hypotheses of the kind put forward by Bauer have simply been too radical to be taken seriously in biblical circles. Not only did he propose that the "we" character was fictional, but he also argued that a number of other characters in Acts were imagined as well, including, for example, Barnabas, Timothy, Silas, and Philip's daughters.[24] In fact, Bauer came to a conclusion against the historical existence of Jesus.[25] The conventional eyewitness proposals advocating a sea-voyage genre (Robbins) or the customary practices of historiography (Plümacher) have been shown to lack sufficient clear parallels in ancient literature on which the arguments for them rely, a weakness that Plümacher himself acknowledges.[26]

Thus, each category of proposals has and continues to face weighty and to date insurmountable challenges, objections that prevent scholarly agreement from coalescing around any particular category or proposal and that prompted Cadbury to lament that the "we" passages are the "insoluble riddle" in Luke's work.[27] At the same time, insights concerning the literary features of Acts contained in several of the proposals offer promising possibilities for understanding the narrative's perplexing first-person plural style. Obviously, fictional and conventional eyewitness proposals stand out because of their focus on the literary reasons for first-person plural narration. Whether a creation of the author or a requirement of genre (sea voyage or historiography), these proposals recognize that the choice of grammatical person has more to do with literary than historical issues. Several historical eyewitness proposals (author-as-eyewitness and source-as-eyewitness), however, have also given attention to the literary dimensions of first-person plural style, reflecting an increasing appreciation for and attention to the literary character of biblical writings generally. Haenchen's redaction-critical proposal proceeds beyond the historical character of the "we" style to ad-

---

23. In deference to the author's deliberate anonymity, I prefer to use "author" or other descriptive terms instead of "Luke" for this person.

24. Bauer, *Die Apostelgeschichte*, 130–31.

25. Bruno Bauer, *Kritik der Evangelien und Geschichte ihres Ursprungs* (3 vols.; Berlin: Hempel, 1850–1851); Albert Schweitzer, *The Quest of the Historical Jesus: A Critical Study of Its Progress from Reimarus to Wrede* (2nd ed.; London: Black, 1911), 137–60.

26. Plümacher, "Wirklichkeitserfahrung und Geschichtsschreibung bei Lukas," 22; Praeder, "Problem of First Person Narration," 206–8, 210–14; idem, "The Narrative Voyage: An Analysis and Interpretation of Acts 27–28" (Ph.D. diss., Graduate Theological Union, 1980), 212–27; David E. Aune, *The New Testament in Its Literary Environment* (LEC 8; Philadelphia: Westminster, 1987), 122–24.

27. Cadbury, *Making of Luke-Acts*, 357.

dress its narrative and theological significance. According to him, the author manipulated the use of grammatical person—even extending "we" beyond eyewitness testimony—to connect readers personally to Paul's mission and the mission to the plan of God, a central theological concept in Acts and the Third Gospel.[28] Dibelius argued that Acts is unique among New Testament writings because the genre of ancient historiography required more literary sophistication, and unique to other ancient literature because of its explicitly theological purpose.[29] Norden considered "we" a stylistic device that transforms an otherwise dull history into an exciting and dramatic account of events. Cadbury argued that first-person narration was the custom in popular literature of that time and that its distinct application in Acts (unannounced and unexplained) reflects the peculiar writing style of the author.

Beyond these insights, the emergence of narrative criticism in biblical studies in the latter third of the twentieth century has brought added attention to the literary character of the "we" passages. From the perspective of narrative criticism, for example, Robert C. Tannehill concludes that first-person plural style allows readers to heighten their experience of Paul's journeys by identifying with the narrator and, in so doing, become participants in the narrative as Paul's traveling companions.[30] William Kurz argues that the "we" style gives readers a sense that they are hearing directly from an insider and, therefore, increases the immediacy and vividness of the event reported.[31] Finally, Beverly Roberts Gaventa suggests that "we" intensifies readers' "sense of the urgency" concerning the events narrated.[32]

Narrator as Narrative Character

This study adopts narrative criticism to analyze the role of the first-person plural narrator—the "we" narrator character—in Acts. The "we" narrator replaces Barnabas in the story as Paul's trustworthy companion called upon at key moments in the apostle's mission to draw attention to the issue of Paul's credibility, to witness that Paul's missionary journeys and activities are in fact in response to divine initiative and in compliance with divine instruction, and to offer reassurance that the divine directives will be

---

28. John T. Squires, *The Plan of God in Luke-Acts* (SNTSMS 8; Cambridge: Cambridge University Press, 1993); idem, "The Plan of God in the Acts of the Apostles," in *Witness to the Gospel: The Theology of Acts* (ed. I Howard Marshall and David Peterson; Grand Rapids: Eerdmans, 1998), 19–39. For additional information, see appendix A.

29. Dibelius (*Studies in the Acts*, 183) actually considered the author more of a preacher than a historian.

30. Robert C. Tannehill, *The Narrative Unity of Luke-Acts: A Literary Interpretation* (2 vols.; Minneapolis: Fortress, 1990), 2:247.

31. William Kurz, *Reading Luke-Acts: Dynamics of Biblical Narrative* (Louisville: Westminster John Knox, 1993), 112–13.

32. Gaventa, *Acts of the Apostles*, 230.

followed and accomplished despite the circumstances in which Paul finds himself. The character of Barnabas acts in this capacity from the time he first meets and defends Paul until they argue and separate (Acts 9:27–15:39). Once Paul and Barnabas's partnership dissolves and Barnabas's presence can no longer be summoned for this purpose, the task falls to the "we" character through the utilization of first-person plural narration. The role that Barnabas and the "we" narrator character assume is an important one because of the suspicion and resistance that Paul's character encounters as a result of his reversal of position with respect to the Jesus movement.

This understanding of the "we" passages builds on the literary possibilities noted previously by exploring the narrative significance of the occasional use of first person plural in Acts. It addresses the question of how the "we" style meaningfully fits and contributes to the overall storyline. In attending to the literary character of the "we" passages, the study sets aside the issue of a historical eyewitness, either author or source. In any event, questions of whether the events described in the "we" sections of Acts are historical and whether Luke or his source/s witnessed them are unanswerable on the basis of the evidence currently available, as even the staunchest defenders of historicity and eyewitnessing acknowledge.[33] More important, the fact that Acts provides no information and, indeed, by writing anonymously and constructing an anonymous observer, actually withholds information about a putative historical eyewitness, suggests that first person plural in Acts has to do with narrative, not historical, eyewitnessing. That is to say, the function of the first-person plural style in the story rather than its potential reference to historical person or persons would seem to hold the key for understanding the "we" passages in Acts and, therefore, for solving Cadbury's "insoluble riddle."

---

33. For example, Colin J. Hemer, *The Book of Acts in the Setting of Hellenistic History* (WUNT 49; Tübingen: Mohr Siebeck, 1989), 330–31.

1

Stories, Storytellers, and Readers

The writer writes in a language and in a logic whose proper system, laws, and life his discourse by definition cannot dominate absolutely. He uses them only by letting himself, after a fashion and up to a point, be governed by the system. And the reading must always aim at a certain relationship, unperceived by the writer, between what he commands and what he does not command of the patterns of the language that he uses.

—Jacques Derrida

Before undertaking a detailed analysis of the "we" passages, it is worthwhile to examine the theoretical and methodological strategies on which the analysis depends, namely, narrative theory (narratology) and reader-response criticism. As Stephen D. Moore points out, narrative theorists (narratologists) "analyze texts mainly to develop theories," whereas narrative critics "utilize theory mainly to explicate texts."[1] In a literary narrative investigation of the "we" passages, therefore, the reason for such a discussion is not that theoretical issues are important in themselves. Rather, the conclusions drawn from critically reading the "we" passages, that is, reading characterized by careful analysis and evaluation—and that is the objective of this study—are dependent upon the principles and approaches applied in the investigation. Understanding the theory and method on which the study's conclusions are based is helpful for evaluating these conclusions.

Modern literary theory must be applied with caution to ancient writings because, even though the preface to the Third Gospel refers to the account that follows (including Acts) as a διήγησις (the Greek term for "narrative"), differences surely exist between ancient and modern concepts of narrative. For example, readers of the New Testament have often puzzled over

---

1. Stephen D. Moore, *Literary Criticism and the Gospels: The Theoretical Challenge* (New Haven: Yale University Press, 1989), 51.

such narrative problems as the unsatisfying endings in Mark's Gospel and the Acts of the Apostles and the relationship between Acts and the Gospel of Luke, questions that arise from modern assumptions about narrative unity (what constitutes a complete story with a definite beginning, middle, and end). One difficulty in determining whether writings even qualify as narratives is that literature is by nature an unstable entity variously constructed in accordance with prevailing ideologies and associated standards of value. That being the case, one reader's literature may well be another's uncultured drivel.[2] Another danger Moore warns against is the tendency of modern readers and critics to "overnaturalize" ancient written narratives. For Moore, this is a matter of concentrating on the features that written narratives share with more familiar "scenic narratives" (theater, television, and film), especially plot and character, while neglecting traits unique to written narratives, in particular the centrality of the narrator as mediator and point of view.[3] I would state the danger of overnaturalizing more broadly, namely, that even careful and experienced modern readers approach ancient texts with modern expectations and, therefore, are at risk of overlooking in their reading and analyses the differences that inevitably exist between modern and ancient narrative writing and reading. Care must be exercised, therefore, not to force literary styles or structures used in ancient texts to conform to modern norms. One useful technique for avoiding this tendency is to compare ancient narrative forms that are difficult to interpret with structures in other ancient narratives to determine if and how the practice might be explained within its own historical, cultural, and literary context.

Despite differences between ancient and modern narratives, however, both tell stories, and stories then and now are structured expressions of human experience. In other words, stories (whether fiction or nonfiction) "give experience both a form and a meaning, a linear order with a shapely beginning, middle, end, and central theme."[4] This understanding of narrative goes back at least as far as Aristotle in the fourth century B.C.E., who in *Poetics* examined the unfolding of plot in narratives. As a διήγησις, therefore, Luke and Acts, like other ancient narratives, may be presumed to present a comprehensive story from beginning to end.[5] In addition, although Moore's admonishment against overnaturalizing ancient texts is instructive, it is also

---

2. Terry Eagleton, *Literary Theory: An Introduction* (Minneapolis: University of Minnesota Press, 1983), 1–16. See also Stanley Fish, *Is There a Text in This Class? The Authority of Interpretive Communities* (Cambridge: Harvard University Press, 1980), 10–11.

3. Moore, *Literary Criticism and the Gospels*, 39–40.

4. J. Hillis Miller, "Narrative," in *Critical Terms for Literary Study* (ed. Frank Lentricchia and Thomas McLaughlin; Chicago: University of Chicago Press, 1990), 69.

5. Joseph A. Fitzmyer, *The Gospel according to Luke* (2 vols.; AB 28–28A; Garden City, N.Y.: Doubleday, 1981–1985), 1:173; see also his discussion of the term's use in other ancient literature on 1:173–74, 292. Chapter 4 will take up the relationship of Luke's two volumes.

the case that, despite the difficulties inherent in reading ancient texts through the lens of modern narratology, readers will continue to read only if they can make sense of what they are reading, if, that is, they are able to "reduce its strangeness so that it speaks to us in an idiom we can understand."[6]

Readers

Readers are essential to the narrative process in that they are the ones responsible for constructing characters, including the narrator. In fact, readers decide whether a composition is a work of literature at all and, if they conclude that it is, determine its genre. Indeed, texts themselves do not exist as independent entities but "emerge as the consequence of [readers'] interpretive activities."[7] In other words, readers through their reading activities are "the source of texts, facts, authors, and intentions."[8] Reading, however, is a subjective, idiosyncratic experience. No two readers are identical, so no two readers bring the same considerations to or get the same meaning from a literary work. Differences in gender, age, social, cultural, religious, philosophical, and educational backgrounds, economic status, and geographical location necessitate that reading experiences, practices, and agendas be inherently individual activities.[9] This makes it difficult—some would say impossible—to speak of readers in a general sense. Nonetheless, readers within specific communities usually share to an extent reading conventions and dynamics that permit, at least tentatively, collective assertions.[10] For example, a majority of American readers would likely agree on several characteristics as being common to novels (defined generally as works of fiction, often realistic in their portrayal of characters and situations, written in narrative form) and would for the most part share reading assumptions, approaches, and expectations when confronted with this genre. That such agreement is not absolute, however, is made clear by the current furor concerning the historicity of the narrative claim in the hugely successful novel *The Da Vinci Code* that Jesus was married to Mary Magdalene. The argument over this assertion rages in spite of the admission by the book's author that the work is meant to be a novel and despite his explicit inclusion of the list of items in the story for which he claims status as "fact"—a list that is quite minimal and contains nothing about Jesus or Mary Magdalene.[11]

---

6. Jonathan Culler, "Making Sense," *Twentieth Century Studies* 12 (1974): 30; see also Edgar V. McKnight, "A Biblical Criticism for American Biblical Scholarship," in *Society of Biblical Literature 1980 Seminar Papers* (SBLSP 19; Chico, Calif.: Scholars Press, 1980), 123.

7. Fish, *Is There a Text*, 13.

8. Ibid., 16.

9. John A. Darr, "Narrator as Character: Mapping a Reader-Oriented Approach to Narration in Luke-Acts," *Semeia* 63 (1993): 46–47.

10. Fish, *Is There a Text*, 1–17; Darr, "Narrator as Character," 46–48.

11. Dan Brown, *The Da Vinci Code* (New York: Doubleday, 2003), vii and 1.

In the reading communities presupposed for this study, readers build readers.[12] On one hand, readers read for a reason or, perhaps, a variety of reasons, including enjoyment, entertainment, information, and/or edification. On the other hand, they seek explicitly or intuitively to become competent readers, that is, readers who possess what in their view is the requisite linguistic, generic, historical, verbal, and grammatical knowledge for understanding what they are reading. An example of improving reading competency is a student who, while reading another of Dan Brown's novels, *Angels and Demons,* emailed to ask if the Catholic Church allowed priests to be adoptive parents, her question prompted by a priest with an adopted daughter in the novel.[13] Another example would be students who, before reading a collection of poems, undertake to learn something about poetry (metrics, figurative language, versification, imagery, etc.) in order to enhance their understanding of and appreciation for the poems they intend to read. Such efforts at increasing reading competency are attempts by readers to shape themselves into readers that they imagine reflect the intended audience in order to correlate the cognitive and affective experience of reading from their current contexts in a way that is consonant with the contexts of targeted readers. It is impossible, of course, to shed one's own cultural framework or to assume or, for that matter, understand with any degree of certainty other cultural contexts. This is especially the case with respect to ancient contexts because of the distance between ancient and modern readers and because much of the evidence from antiquity, cultural and otherwise, has been lost to history. That is to say, readers today are always twenty-first-century readers speculating to a greater or lesser degree about the circumstances of ancient audiences. That is not to suggest that information about ancient readers is nonexistent. Linguistic, cultural, religious, philosophical, educational, and geographical expectations in antiquity may be constructed from textual clues in the narrative together with general information gained from historical resources, as long as it is accepted that these construals must be tentative and speculative. In addition, the competency that readers try to attain depends on their particular interests and purposes for reading. Because of the focus of this study on the "we" passages in Acts, for example, chapter 2 will examine in detail the use of grammatical person in antiquity to determine what practices might have been familiar and comfortable to ancient audiences and to compare those practices with the use of person, especially first person plural, in Acts of the Apostles.

---

12. Based upon, but not identical to, Darr's assertion that "readers build characters, and critics build readers" ("Narrator as Character," 46).

13. Dan Brown, *Angels and Demons* (New York: Pocket Books, 2000).

Stories and Storytellers

As stories, narratives structure fictional or nonfictional human experience into a particular form. Specifically, narrative may be defined as a verbal communication process representing a succession of events.[14] *Verbal communication process* consists of an addresser who transmits the story through language and an addressee who receives it. "Verbal" can include any medium or combination of media employing language in the communications process, whether visual (plays or film) or nonvisual (lyricized music, for example). *Succession of events* indicates more than one incident related through explicit or implicit causation.[15] "The king died, and then the queen died of grief" is an example of explicit causation in that the second event is said to be a consequence of the first.[16] Implicit causation lacks this cause-and-effect relationship among events. In the statement "the king died, and then the queen died," for example, the only express relationship is temporal, that is, the second event occurred subsequent to the first, but not explicitly because of it. Although either is possible in narrative, explicit causation is more common because it involves the rise and resolution of conflict (defined as the opposition of "actions, ideas, desires, or wills" among characters in the narrative) that many theorists and critics consider a requisite of narrative structure.[17] It may be said, therefore, that narrative re(-)presents events in two ways: (1) it attempts to portray events through verbal discourse; and (2) it is discourse in the preterit, recounting events that occurred—actually or fictively—at some point in the past.

This understanding of narrative has implications for the narrator or storyteller. The past-tense quality of narrative undercuts the widely accepted concept of an omniscient narrator who knows everything, can relate events happening simultaneously at different locations or concerning characters who seem to be alone, and even appears to have the ability to read characters' minds.[18] Since storytellers are actually retelling events that have already occurred, their so-called omniscience is nothing more than already knowing the story they are narrating and how matters turn out and attributing to characters thoughts and emotions in light of events and their aftermath. Some narratologists argue that narration can precede events, but they are

---

14. Shlomith Rimmon-Kenan, *Narrative Fiction: Contemporary Poetics* (New York: Methuen, 1983), 2–5.

15. Ibid., 17.

16. E. M. Forster, *Aspects of the Novel* (New York: Harcourt, Brace, 1927; repr., Harmondsworth, U.K.: Penguin, 1963), 93.

17. Mark Allan Powell, *What Is Narrative Criticism?* (Minneapolis: Fortress, 1990), 42; Rimmon-Kenan, *Narrative Fiction*, 135 n. 12.

18. Rimmon-Kenan, *Narrative Fiction*, 95. While she affirms the relevance of the characteristics of narrators signified by omniscience, Rimmon-Kenan concedes that the term is an exaggeration.

referring principally to second-level narration, about which more will be said momentarily.[19] At the first level of narration, however, the event always precedes the telling.[20] In addition, the narrator, whether more or less intrusive, is indispensable in narrative as the mediating presence between narrated events and the recipients of the narration. Some literary theorists view the narrator as optional, but as the narratologist Shlomith Rimmon-Kenan argues,

> there is always a teller in the tale, at least in the sense that any utterance or record of an utterance presupposes someone who has uttered it. Even when a narrative text presents passages of pure dialogue, manuscript found in a bottle, or forgotten letters and diaries, there is in addition to the speakers or writers of this discourse a "higher narratorial authority" responsible for "quoting" the dialogue or "transcribing" the written records.[21]

Although narrators are identified with the author in many narratives, ancient and modern, they are not identical to the author. Most literary theorists agree that authors are barely discoverable, if at all, in their writings. This insight led to the concept of an implied author as the "ideal, literary, created, version" of the real author construed by readers from the text.[22] The difference between the author and the implied author, as Rimmon-Kenan explains, is that

> [a]n author may embody in a work ideas, beliefs, emotions other than or even quite opposed to those he has in real life: he may also embody different ideas, beliefs and emotions in different works. Thus while the flesh-and-blood author is subject to the vicissitudes of real life, the implied author of a particular work is conceived as a stable entity, ideally consistent with itself within the work.[23]

In other words, authors may project different selves in their writings than is the case in reality, not unlike the contrast between public and private selves that most people display. The relationship among the real author, implied

---

19. Gérard Genette, *Narrative Discourse: An Essay in Method* (trans. Jane E. Lewin; Ithaca, N.Y.: Cornell University Press, 1980), 216–17; Mieke Bal, *Narratology: Introduction to the Theory of Narrative* (trans. Christine van Boheemen; Toronto: University of Toronto Press, 1985), 135; Rimmon-Kenan, *Narrative Fiction*, 89–91.

20. Genette, *Narrative Discourse*, 219–20.

21. Rimmon-Kenan, *Narrative Fiction*, 88. See also Seymour Chatman, *Story and Discourse: Narrative Structure in Fiction and Film* (Ithaca, N.Y.: Cornell University Press, 1978), 146–47, 151, who acknowledges that what he calls "nonnarrated" may in fact be "minimally narrated."

22. Wayne C. Booth, *The Rhetoric of Fiction* (2nd ed.; Chicago: University of Chicago Press, 1983), 75.

23. Rimmon-Kenan, *Narrative Fiction*, 87.

author, and narrator is illustrated in Seymour Chatman's well-known chart of participants in the communication process:[24]

Narrative

Real author ····› Implied author → (Narrator) → (Narratee) → Implied reader ····› Real reader

As the chart indicates, the narrator is distinct from both the author and the implied author. The narrator is the only one of the communicators character-ized in the narrative (indicated by parentheses) and so able to be constructed to any degree by readers. When the narrator is a participant in events, it is the narrator character, not the author or implied author, about whom read-ers are learning. The distinction between narrator and author is especially pronounced in Acts because the narrative was written anonymously; that is to say, the author's identity is never disclosed.

Storytelling and Storytellers

Narration or narrating is the process of textual production, the produc-tion of narrative action or, simply, the act of storytelling.[25] Narratologists distinguish a hierarchy of narration and narrators in the text, generally referred to as "narrative levels." Narrative levels attempt to differentiate between narration *in* the story and the narration *of* the story.[26] The nar-ration of the story occurs at the primary narrative level and is considered outside the narrative. This level of narration is often called extradiegetic, from the Greek διήγησις (meaning "narrative," as previously mentioned). The story that the extradiegetic narrator tells is the first-level narrative. In other words, a narrator outside the story tells the story. In addition, narra-tologists recognize narrative levels within the story, that is, internal levels of narration, as Rimmon-Kenan explains:

> A character whose actions are the object of narration [by the outside nar-rator] can himself in turn engage in narrating a story. Within his story there may, of course, be yet another character who narrates another story, and so on in infinite regress. Such narratives within narratives create a stratifica-tion of levels whereby each inner narrative is subordinated to the narrative within which it is embedded.[27]

Narratives may contain, therefore, internal levels of narration that are sub-ordinate to the extradiegetic level. The hierarchical relationship between external and internal narrative levels does not diminish the value of internal narration, but neither are the levels of equal status. Internal narration has

---

24. Chatman, *Story and Discourse*, 151.
25. Genette, *Narrative Discourse*, 27; Rimmon-Kenan, *Narrative Fiction*, 3–4.
26. Genette, *Narrative Discourse*, 228–29; Rimmon-Kenan, *Narrative Fiction*, 91–92.
27. Rimmon-Kenan, *Narrative Fiction*, 91.

a dependent relation to external narration similar to the dependence of a subordinate clause to the main clause of a sentence. Moreover, as Rimmon-Kenan notes, there may be any number of internal levels of narration, each of which is superior to the narrative level below it and subordinate to the level above. Thus, the first intradiegetic narrator, as internal narrators are called, tells a second-level story, that is, one level below the level of narration of the extradiegetic (outside) narrator, and the second intradiegetic narrator tells a story at the third level, and so on.

An example from Acts helpfully illustrates this model of narrative. Acts 21:27–22:21 tells of Paul's difficulties when he arrives in Jerusalem at the completion of his last missionary journey and the defense that he offers to the leaders there. In general, from 21:27 to 21:40 the extradiegetic or outside narrator reports the events leading up to Paul's arrest and speech (first-level story). Then in his speech, Paul (the first intradiegetic or internal narrator) recalls his upbringing, his experience on the way to Damascus, and subsequent events in Damascus and Jerusalem (second-level story). Within Paul's narration, Ananias (22:14–15), the Lord (22:18, 21), and Paul himself (22:19–20) become additional intradiegetic narrators at the third level who relate other incidents that Paul has or will encounter.

Despite widespread acceptance among theorists, this understanding of narration contains several problems. The distinction between the narration *of* the story and narration *in* the story is founded on the premise that narrative content (the story) is separable, at least theoretically, from the act of narrating (telling the story, or narration). This assumption is the basis for Chatman's formative work on narrative. After proposing two necessary components of narrative—story (consisting of the chain of events, characters, and setting) and discourse (the means of communicating the events), the what and how of narrative—he argues that the transferability of the story to various media and languages demonstrates its independence from narration.[28] Others have used Chatman's understanding to argue that the extradiegetic narrator belongs to the narration, the act of telling the story, and thus is excluded from the story itself. The flaw in this reasoning, however, is that if fails to consider that many times the narrator is or becomes explicitly a character participant in the story, which is the case with the "we" passages in Acts. Severing the narrator from the story has led to the depersonalization and depersonification—the decharacterization, if you will—of the narrator among literary theorists as the voice inscribed in the text as the speaker of the text, that is, as the agency of narration. Narratologist Mieke Bal, for example, introduces the narrator into her discussion with the following comment, "When . . . I discuss the narrative agent, or *narrator,* I mean the linguistic subject, a function and not a person, which expresses

---

28. Chatman, *Story and Discourse*, 19.

itself in the language that constitutes the text. . . . In order to keep this distinction in mind, I shall refer to the narrator as *it,* however odd this may seem."[29] Reduction of narrator to "its" functional aspects, however, is a misconception of the narrator's role as storyteller and the complex of potential character traits attributable to such a character. The narrator might not be a participant in the events narrated but is nonetheless always a character in the story. To be sure, the narrator's role as the storyteller is distinct from the roles of other characters, but like them the narrator wholly belongs to and is inseparable from the story. At the same time, as the character responsible for telling the story, the narrator may not be separated from narration either. Still, the narrator is not simply the bridge between story and narration, the narrative voice, if you will. Rather, the narrator's act of narrating is as integral to the story as the actions of any other character.

Characterizing the Storyteller

Characters are constructed by readers from evidence offered in the text. Readers designate personality traits for characters by gathering information about them in the reading process. Rimmon-Kenan's explanation of characterization is helpful in this regard. Character traits, she maintains, "may or may not appear as such in the text. How, then, is the construct [of character] arrived at? By assembling various character-indicators distributed along the text-continuum and, when necessary, inferring the traits from them."[30] It is the reader's interpretation of what characters say and do, how they interact with other characters, what is said to and about them and done to them, their setting in the narrative, and the like, that transforms characters from mere textual information into person-like figures, that is, individuals. Readers gather these traits and construct the narrator character just as they do for any other character.

Narratologists traditionally have used "point of view" (perspective) with reference to authors, in effect emptying the narrator's character of any content. Moore, for instance, describes point of view as "the rhetorical activity of an author as he or she attempts through the medium of a narrator . . . to impose a story-world upon a reader."[31] It is more accurate, however, to speak of point of view as an element of the narrator's characterization. Interpretive theory (known also as hermeneutics) has come to the recognition that all speaking subjects communicate from "multiple, contingent, and frequently contradictory" social locations and, thus, that all texts, including narra-

---

29. Bal, *Narratology,* 119 (emphasis original). See also Rimmon-Kenan, *Narrative Fiction,* 3–4, 87.
30. Rimmon-Kenan, *Narrative Fiction,* 59.
31. Moore, *Literary Criticism and the Gospels,* 26.

tives, should be regarded as perspectival.[32] As the storyteller, the narrator
is the primary speaking subject in the narrative; therefore, the perspective
gleaned in reading the story belongs to the characterization of the narrator. Rimmon-Kenan's discussion of narration and focalization might help
clarify this. She argues that, although the activities of narrating (speaking)
and focalizing (perspective) may be attributed to the same person, this need
not be the case because a narrative agent "is also capable of undertaking to
tell what another person sees or has seen."[33] Using the opening of Joyce's *A
Portrait of the Artist as a Young Man*, she attempts to illustrate the possibility of such a divided perspective in narrative:

> Once upon a time and a very good time it was there was a moocow coming
> down along the road and this moocow that was coming down along the
> road met a nicens little boy named baby tuckoo. . . .[34]

Rimmon-Kenan argues that the language is that of a child (specifically the
character Stephen as a child) but that the sentence structure betrays a more
mature narrator.[35] In contrast to Rimmon-Kenan's conclusion, however, the
language does not represent Stephen's grammar and vocabulary as a child,
but the narrator's interpretation of the youngster character's perception and
how he might communicate it. That is to say, narratives are told from the
narrator character's perspective, and nothing escapes the narrator's ideological lens. What is said and done, who says or does it, and how it is said
or done are all filtered through the narrator's perspective, regardless of how
much or little the narrator intrudes in the story.

Conclusions: Narrator and Narrative Levels

With the narrator properly understood as a character in the narrative,
specifically the storyteller, infinite multiple narrative levels become unnecessary and may be condensed. Narratives may be considered to exist on a single
plane with two levels of discourse. Primary or first-level narration focuses
on the story, the succession of events with which the narrator is concerned.
The narrator, and this conceptualization has only one narrator, relates the
events of the story using a variety of techniques, including the discourse of
other characters. This level may be designated the "event level" because it
deals with telling the narrative events. The secondary level, which has to do
with telling about the storytelling, may be designated the "narrator level."
This level contains many of the narrator's explicit character-indicators. At
this level, through nonevent commentary, what the narrator thinks, believes,

---

32. Rajeswari Sunder Rajan quoted in George Aichele et al., *The Postmodern Bible* (New
Haven: Yale University Press, 1995), 5.
33. Rimmon-Kenan, *Narrative Fiction*, 72.
34. Ibid.
35. Ibid., 73.

or is certain of concerning the narrative, why this particular tale is being told as well as the narrator's qualifications for doing so, and other matters about the narrator and narration, are often reported. Because of the centrality of storytelling to the narrator's role, however, narrator-level narration, while revealing the narrator's character as narrator, is at the same time related to or concerned with event-level narration. This two-level interdependent narrative structure properly locates the whole of the narrative action—events and narrator commentary—*inside* the narrative. Under this narrative model, the example from Acts 21:27–22:21 previously discussed is understood as all on the same narrative level, namely, the event level. The narrator employs the techniques of character discourse (Paul) and subdiscourse (Ananias, the Lord, and Paul) in the narration. The preface to Luke's Gospel (Luke 1:1–4), on the other hand, typifies the narrator level. Rather than the events of the story, this opening section discusses the narrator, the source of information for the narrative, the narrator's investigation into events, and the reason for writing the story.

To summarize, narratives generally have one—and only one—narrator, not an omniscient but contentless cipher outside the narrative through which the author voices the narrative but a character in the narrative from whose limited and interested perspective the story is told and whose characterization as storyteller readers construct from character-indicators found mostly, but not entirely, at the narrator level of narration. As a character, the narrator may participate in the narrative at the event level. In addition, narratives consist of two narrative levels (event and narrator) that distinguish interdependent foci *inside* the narrative. Thus, comments, asides, and other techniques employed at the narrator level contribute to event-level discourse as they simultaneously reveal the narrator's character.

2

The Narrator as "He," "Me," and "We"

THE USE OF GRAMMATICAL PERSON IN ANTIQUITY

*We refer to ourselves sometimes by proper name and other times
by common expressions such as "when I said this" or again "when
we assented." . . . [I]t is necessary to alter our self-designations
so that we not offend by continuously repeating our name, nor
fall unintentionally into a boorish rhetorical style by constantly
interjecting "of me" or "on account of me."*

—Polybius

The New York Public Library Writer's Guide to Style and Usage offers the following comments concerning the use of grammatical person in
writing: "Many fiction writers use the first person . . . to tell a story from
the point of view of one of the characters. . . . Most professional writing
[however]—whether fiction, nonfiction, journalistic, or business—uses third
person. . . . Mixing person within a manuscript is usually considered bad
form."[1] Modern standards of grammatical style, therefore, prefer third-
person constructions and discourage commingling grammatical person,
regardless of genre. The same literary conventions did not govern ancient
authors, however. In fact, in antiquity the use of grammatical person differed
significantly from these modern guidelines. Ancient writings refer to their
narrators in the first (singular and plural) and third persons for both event-
and narrator-level narration.[2] This assortment of grammatical constructions
for the narrator, so cacophonous to the modern (literary) ear, reflects acceptable literary practice in antiquity. The present chapter explores the literary
character of grammatical person, especially first-person plural style, in the

---

1. *The New York Public Library Writer's Guide to Style and Usage* (ed. Andrea J. Sutcliffe
et al.; New York: HarperCollins, 1994), 127.
2. See the discussion of narrative levels in chapter 1.

work of several ancient writers to assist in gaining an understanding of the literary dimensions of the "we" passages in Acts.

The texts selected for analysis include the Greek histories of Thucydides and Polybius and the two prominent works of the Jewish historian Josephus, *Jewish War* and *Jewish Antiquities*. The choice of these three historians does not imply that Acts is historiography. Indeed, generic studies suggest that Acts draws upon several ancient genres, including historiography, historical monograph, biography, and romance.[3] In addition, the nature of genre is itself somewhat artificial. None of the generic categories listed exists in a vacuum, and it is fair to say that there is a degree of overlap and interdependence among them. For example, Richard Pervo, an articulate advocate for classifying Acts as an ancient novel, specifies it as a "*historical* novel," that is, fiction that utilizes historiographical conventions to "heighten its appearance of authenticity . . . to give [the] work credibility and 'tone.'"[4] The fact that Acts is often categorized as historical in form, content, or both has influenced the choice of texts for comparative analysis, but the decision is prompted primarily by three factors. First, the compositions selected are third-person narratives (like Acts) with which Acts undeniably shares a number of literary features. Second, their standing as literature is uncontested. Third, they represent antiquity from the late fifth century B.C.E. (Thucydides) to the mid-second century B.C.E. (Polybius) to the mid- to late first century C.E. (Josephus), when Acts was most likely written.

Thucydides

Thucydides of Athens (ca. 460–398 B.C.E.), considered by many scholars to be the dean of ancient historiography, wrote a history of the Peloponnesian War (431–404 B.C.E.) between Athens and the Spartan alliance in Peloponnese. His writing style is considered first rate: clear, direct, graphic, compact, and fast-moving.[5] Indeed, the speeches contained in his history have been praised as perhaps the best ever written.[6] When referring

---

3. Douglas R. Edwards, "Acts of the Apostles and the Graeco-Roman World: Narrative Communication in Social Contexts," *Society of Biblical Literature 1989 Seminar Papers* (SBLSP 28; Atlanta: Scholars Press, 1989), 362–77; Cadbury, *Making of Luke-Acts*, 127–39.

4. Richard Pervo, *Profit with Delight: The Literary Genre of the Acts of the Apostles* (Philadelphia: Fortress, 1987), 115–38, esp. 117–18 (emphasis added).

5. C. Forster Smith, introduction to Thucydides, *History of the Peloponnesian War* (trans. C. Forster Smith; 4 vols.; LCL; New York: Putnam, 1919), 1:vii–xxii, esp. 1:xvi; Michael Grant, *The Ancient Historians* (New York: Scribner, 1970), 69–121; *OCD*, s.v. "Thucydides (2)."

6. Thucydides did not duplicate speeches word for word, a practice he considered unreasonable. Instead, he sought to convey in general terms the sense of what speakers were attempting to say as he understood it, "the essence rather than the substance" (Grant, *Ancient Historians*, 90–91; see also Smith, introduction, xvii). In fact, some of the speeches may never have been delivered, and for those that were the historian felt free to select, add, or elaborate. Thus, while seeking to communicate the views of the assumed speakers, the sentence structure

to Thucydides himself, the narrative most often uses third-person style. For example, the history opens with the announcement that Thucydides is its author: "Thucydides, an Athenian, wrote the history of the war between the Peloponnesians and the Athenians while they were at war with one another, beginning immediately as it was breaking out" (Thucydides 1.1.1).[7] Thucydides is again noted as the author later in a preface to the second phase of his history (5.26.1).[8] In addition to the prefaces, the narrative often notes the war's anniversary dates with a formula that includes mention of Thucydides as author, as in, "These things happened in the winter, and so came to an end the second year in this war about which Thucydides wrote the history" (2.70.4).[9] These passages are at the narrator level, but Thucydides also becomes a third-person participant in the narrative in 4.102–107.

The use of the third person in reference to Thucydides at both the narrator and event levels distances the author/actor from the narrator or storyteller. The name "Thucydides" identifies the author/actor with the historical person who is credited with authorship of the history but separates the character as author/actor from the narrator character. Third-person references to Thucydides, therefore, effectively sever the narrator from the actor and dissociate the narrator and the author. As a result, the opening commentary ("Thucydides . . . wrote the history") gives the sense that the narrator is a character distinct from Thucydides narrating the history composed by Thucydides. Indeed, the sentence could be rephrased something like this: "Let me tell you the events as they have been recorded by a certain historian named Thucydides."

As Michael Grant argues, the effect of third-person self-reference is to increase the narrative's sense of historical objectivity, an impression that appears to have been important to the historian.[10] Early on, Thucydides establishes strict criteria for the historical reliability of the events of the war to be included, claiming a preference for those he observed personally or that were reported by eyewitnesses. In addition, recognizing that individual

---

and expressions in the speeches reported are those of Thucydides himself, regardless of speaker or situation. Thucydides' use of speech as a literary device was so effective that it became the model for subsequent ancient history writing.

7. For interested readers, major passages used in the analysis of grammatical person in this chapter are given in Greek and English in appendix B. I have translated the Greek as literally as possible—hopefully without losing the sense of the original—in order to manifest clearly the constructions of grammatical person under analysis.

8. According to the narrative, the combatants signed a treaty after ten years of fighting, but, after approximately seven years, war broke out again. With the resumption of hostilities, Thucydides decided to include the second phase of the conflict in his history (5.25–26; see also Grant, *Ancient Historians*, 82; Smith, *History of the Peloponnesian War*, 3:48 n. 1).

9. Similar notations are included at 2.103.2; 3.25.2; 3.88.4; 3.116.3; 4.51.1; 4.135.2; 6.7.4; 6.93.4; 7.18.4; 8.6.5; and 8.60.3.

10. Grant, *Ancient Historians*, 116.

memories of the same events are never identical and are affected by the biases of those remembering, he tells of his efforts to discover what really happened by comparing various eyewitness reports (1.22.2–3).[11] That is not to claim that Thucydides consistently adheres to the standards he set.[12] Testing the historical accuracy of the narrative, including Thucydides' actual participation in events, is beyond the scope of this analysis. Thucydides the author and actor of the story, however, insists on the unbiased and careful recording of events. Referring to himself in the third person is one method of rhetorically displaying objectivity.

Despite the concern to portray impartiality through the use of third-person references, at the narrator level the history also refers to Thucydides in the more personal first person singular that reconnects the author with the narrator.[13] The use of first person might seem in tension with the narrative's preoccupation with projecting historical detachment, but in Thucydides' writing it too supports claims of historical authenticity. First-person singular style emphasizes the author/narrator's knowledge and authority. Thucydides employs it in passages that defend the historical accuracy of the account by demonstrating his personal involvement in the events or his meticulous scrutinizing of evidence gathered from other sources. For example, in the second preface discussed a moment ago, grammatical person shifts from third to first person as Thucydides defends the correctness of his information about the war because he was able to observe the conflict closely from both sides: "I lived through all of it . . . devoting attention to it so that I would know it accurately . . . and being present at the affairs of both sides . . . learned better their events" (5.26.5–6; see also 2.48). In the opening chapter of the book, the initial preface also changes to first person singular when Thucydides mentions the quality of his research: "it was impossible to recover clearly events previous to these . . . because of the passage of time, but from the evidence which, after I examined it in the greatest depth, it turns out that I can trust, I do not consider them to have been important" (1.1.3). Elsewhere in his book Thucydides utilizes first person singular to assess the quality of sources and his use of them (1.20.1; 1.21.1), to take credit as the first to recognize and explain correctly the exact motives for the outbreak of the war (1.23.5–6), to justify his choice of events for inclusion in the history

---

11. These standards focus on contemporary events, and Thucydides confesses that the accuracy of prior historical events contained in his history is questionable (1.20.1–2). 1.22.1–2 are written in first person singular. See discussion below and appendix B.

12. Grant, *Ancient Historians*, 116–17.

13. The nature of Greek first person singular inflections makes a complete search for them impractical. I have, therefore, limited the analysis of first person singular style to personal pronouns, first person singular forms of the verb "to be" (εἰμι), and distinctively first-person verb forms (e.g., the middle/passive endings –ομαι, –ομην, and –αμην; for those unfamiliar with ancient Greek, verb suffixes indicate grammatical person).

(1.23.5; 1.97.2; 3.90.1; 3.113.6), to acknowledge gaps in available information (5.68.2; 6.2.1), to highlight the accuracy of his narrative (6.54.1; 6.55.1), and to summarize his historical method (1.22.1–2), all in an attempt to legitimate his version of events.[14]

Although used sparingly, first person plural also occurs in Thucydides' history. The five instances of first person plural style in nonspeech material are all at the narrator level, and in every case but one the first-person plural comment qualifies a grammatically superlative statement: "the earliest sea battle of those we know" (1.13.4); "the longest period of discord of those we know" (1.18.1); "the greatest event of the war of those we know" (7.87.5); "the worst earthquake of those we remember" (8.41.2).[15] The effect of this use of first-person plural style is that it simultaneously accentuates the authority of the narrator (similar to first person singular) while at the same time tempering it by including his experience with that of others through the use of the collective "we." In Thucydides' narrative, therefore, first person plural makes and at the same time moderates claims that may be open to challenge as exaggerated or excessive by others with different perspectives on or information about events.

Polybius

Two centuries after Thucydides, Polybius (ca. 200–118 B.C.E.) penned a history of the expansion of Rome's dominance in the Mediterranean region. Polybius was a native of Megalopolis in Arcadia (a region in Peloponnese) and was politically active in the confederation of Greek city states known as the Achaean League, which sometimes cooperated with and other times opposed Rome. He was deported to Rome with other Greeks suspected of being sympathizers of Macedonia, with which Rome was at war (168 B.C.E.; Polybius 31.23.1–31.25.1). During his detention he was under the protection of the Roman commander of the Macedonian campaign, Lucius Aemilius Paullus, and was befriended by his son, Scipio Aemilianus.[16]

Just as in Thucydides' history, Polybius's narrative usually prefers the

---

14. Other first person singular comments are sprinkled throughout the narrative, many of them formulaic expressions used to accentuate the narrator's view or to refer to a previous comment or event narrated (e.g., "it seems to me" [μοι δοκεῖ] or "I think" [οἶμαι]). The list includes 1.3.1; 1.3.2; 1.3.3; 1.9.1; 1.9.3; 1.10.4; 1.20.1; 1.21.1; 1.23.5; 1.93.7; 1.97.2; 2.17.2; 3.90.1; 3.113.6; 5.1.1.; 5.68.2; 6.2.1; 6.54.1; 6.55.1; 6.55.3; 6.94.1; 7.87.5; 8.24.4; 8.87.4.

15. The final first person plural comment defends the account of the myth of Alcmaeon that Thucydides summarizes as the tradition that "we have received" (παρελάβομεν; 2.102.6).

16. F. W. Walbank, *A Historical Commentary on Polybius* (3 vols.; Oxford: Clarendon, 1957), 1:1–37; H. J. Edwards, introduction to Polybius, *The Histories* (trans. W. R. Paton; 6 vols.; LCL; New York: Putnam, 1922–1927), 1:vii–xvi; Evelyn S. Shuckburgh, introduction to Polybius, *The Histories of Polybius* (trans. Evelyn S. Shuckburgh; 2 vols.; New York: MacMillan, 1889), 1:xvii–lx; Grant, *Ancient Historians*, 144–64.

third person when describing events that present Polybius himself as a participant. Again, I am speaking of Polybius as a character in the narrative, not assessing the historical reliability of the claims made concerning his personal involvement. Many of these passages are similar to what has been noted in Thucydides, and several are quite extensive. For example, 31.11.4–31.14.3 elaborates on the assistance Polybius provides to the Seleucid prince Demetrius in the prince's attempts to escape Roman custody.[17] Beyond that, the history reports speeches attributed to Polybius in the third person, something not found in Thucydides. In 28.7.8–13, for instance, Polybius helps settle a dispute over certain honors that were accorded to Eumenes II (of Pergamum) and subsequently revoked: "Polybius stood and made a longer speech. . . . He said, 'But, those around Sosigenes and Diopeithes . . . used this pretext to overturn all the honors of the king.'"[18] As with Thucydides, the effect of narrating Polybius's participation in events in the third person is to distance the author/actor from the narrator and, in so doing, to increase the sense of historical objectivity. Reporting Polybius's speeches in third-person style increases the distance between author and narrator. To gain a better appreciation for the separation produced by this literary technique, imagine quoting yourself in the third person when writing an essay (instead of "I said/wrote," use "she/he [or your name] said/wrote").

At the narrator level, first-person singular style is used frequently throughout Polybius's history. As in Thucydides, first person singular serves to identify the author and narrator and to underscore the knowledge and credibility of the author/narrator. For that reason, it is most often located in passages that highlight Polybius's personal involvement in affairs or defend his decisions concerning writing style or historical content, that is, to strengthen the justifications offered as to why he includes, excludes, or abbreviates certain events, his reasoning for the order of narration, and his views on the ethical lessons of history.[19] One passage, for instance, makes clear that Polybius was more than simply an eyewitness to the history he

---

17. Other passages narrating Polybius's activities in the third person include 12.4–6; 24.6.3–6 (see appendix B); 28.3.7–10; 28.6.8–9; 28.13.1–14; 29.23.2–5; 25.5–7; 31.23.3–31.25.1; 31.29.8; 32.3.14–17; and 36.11.1.

18. See appendix B for the full text of this passage. Other texts of direct or indirect discourse by Polybius include 29.24.1–9; 31.11.4–6; and 39.3.4–39.5.6.

19. Polybius also has a propensity for using the comment "it seems to me" (μοι δοκεῖ); see, e.g., 1.14.2; 1.15.6; 2.14.1; 2.55.8; 3.23.2; 4.6.6; 4.7.11; 4.17.11; 4.20.3; 4.21.1; 4.27.2; 4.30.4; 4.33.4; 4.34.2; 4.73.9; 5.38.10; 5.75.2; 5.84.6; 5.106.5; 6.3.6–7; 6.26.11; 6.45.2; 6.46.11; 6.48.2; 6.56.6–7, 9, 12; 7.7.6; 7.8.8; 7.11.2; 8.1.1; 8.8.2; 9.3.5, 9; 9.8.1; 9.22.7, 10; 9.24.1; 10.2.8; 10.15.5; 10.19.5; 10.26.8; 10.32.12; 10.41.6; 10.43.1; 12.4c.1; 12.4d.1; 12.8.5; 12.13.6; 12.23.7; 12.25.5; 12.25c.2, 4; 12.25e.4; 12.25f.1; 12.28.1; 13.5.4; 14.5.15; 15.4.9; 16.1.5; 16.12.6; 16.17.8; 16.20.1; 16.22a.2; 16.28.1, 7; 16.29.3; 18.14.11; 18.46.8; 21.26.14; 22.19.3; 23.11.8; 23.12.4; 27.9.2; 27.16.4; 28.10.2; 29.5.2; 29.8.2; 29.27.3, 13; 31.2.7; 33.6.3; 38.5.4; 38.6.1; 38.16.11; 38.18.8; 39.3.1.

is reporting; he was on occasion an important actor in these episodes: "be-cause of the significance of events . . . but most of all because I have been not only an eyewitness to most of them, but of some a participant and of others even an administrator, I was persuaded to write" (3.4.13). Another passage argues that the speeches included in his account are accurately reported (in contrast to Thucydides): "But I do not think it seemly . . . for historians to practice on their readers or make a show of their ability but, after inquiring closely into all such matters, to make clear what was actually said, and of these the things most timely and most related to the subject" (36.1.3–7).[20]

Thus far Polybius's use of grammatical person is not dissimilar to that of Thucydides, but it becomes apparent in reading Polybius's history how differently he employs first person plural. For one thing, first-person plural style occurs much more frequently in Polybius's narrative than in that of his predecessor (approximately 678 occurrences in nondiscourse material, as compared to the handful [five] noted for Thucydides).[21] Second, the his-tory opens in the first person plural and continues in this style throughout the preface (1.1.1–1.5.5).[22] Third, in addition to narrator-level commentary, Polybius's work contains two instances of first-person plural event-level pas-sages, representing the first known use of intermittent first-person narration in a third-person narrative.[23] Because of their correspondence to the "we" passages in Acts, it is worth pausing to examine these two texts in detail.

The first passage tells of Polybius's summons to Lilybaeum (36.11.1–4). The chapter begins with a third-person account of the consul Manilius's instructions to the Achaeans to send Polybius to the Sicilian coastal city and their decision to comply (36.11.1). In the following verse, the narrative sud-denly shifts to first person plural grammatical style as the narrator describes how "we" concurred in this decision and, therefore, set sail at the beginning of the summer. When the "we" group arrives at Corcyra, however, they read a letter informing the city's citizens of the Carthaginian surrender (in the Third Punic War). Assuming that the war is therefore over and "our" assis-tance no longer required, the "we" contingent returns home (36.11.2–4):

> 36.11.1 When instructions arrived in the Peloponnese from Manilius for the Achaeans that they would do well to send Polybius the Megalopolitan with haste to Lilybaeum, as there was need of him for affairs of state, the Achaeans resolved to send him in accordance with the petition of the con-sul. 36.11.2 We, thinking it our duty for many reasons to obey the Romans,

---

20. See also 29.21.8–9 (included in appendix B) and 4.31.3–8.

21. *Thesaurus Linguae Graecae*, version D (University of California, Irvine, 1992); see also *Thesaurus Linguae Graecae: Canon of Greek Authors and Works* (ed. Luci Berkowitz and Karl Squirtier; 3rd ed.; Oxford: Oxford University Press, 1990).

22. See also 1.2.1; 1.3.1, 5, 7b; 1.4.1, 2; 1.5.1.

23. Thornton, *Der Zeuge des Zeugen*, 182. "Intermittent" is a term used of the sudden and unexplained shift of grammatical person.

putting aside all other matters, set sail when summer began. 36.11.3 Arriving in Corcyra and finding there a letter from the consuls that had been sent to the Corcyraeans in which they made quite clear that the Carthaginians had already handed over the hostages to them and were prepared in every way to obey them, 36.11.4 thinking that the war had been brought to end and there was no further any need of us, we sailed back again to the Peloponnese.

At this point Polybius departs from his account to offer an explanation for the variety in grammatical person in his history, after which the narrative resumes in third-person style (36.12.1–36.13.1). I shall return to Polybius's explanation after examining the second intermittent event-level first-person plural passage, which is located in the history's epilogue. There the narrative shifts once more into first person plural (39.8.1) as it addresses Polybius's return from exile in Rome, then slips almost imperceptibly into first-person plural comments (narrator-level narration) as the narrator offers a prayer to the gods for continued good fortune in the future (39.8.2), followed by his summary of the entire history (39.8.3–8):

> 39.8.1 After accomplishing these things, then, we returned from Rome, having been successful, as it were, with respect to certain principal aims of the previous political activities, a favor worthy of the goodwill toward the Romans. 39.8.2 Therefore, we offer prayers to all the gods that the remaining part of life continues in these ways and on these paths, observing that fate, as much as it is good, is envious of humankind and is forceful especially against this instance, namely, insofar as anyone seems especially to have been blessed and to succeed in life. 39.8.3 And it turned out that these things happened in this way. And we, as we come to the end of the whole treatise, after recalling the beginning and the introduction that we composed when we committed the history to writing, wish to sum up the entire subject, reconciling the beginning to the end both over all and in particulars. . . .

First person plural is a complex and ambiguous style. The analysis of Thucydides demonstrated how this grammatical construction can be used to lift up the authority of the narrator even as it shields him somewhat from responsibility for what is said. First-person plural style is further complicated by the elasticity of its potential referents. Typically in narratives, "we" can include the narrator and any number of others, whether characters, noncharacter groups ("we Greeks," for example), or the narrator's audience. Narrative context does not always provide sufficient information for readers to identify clearly the referent or referents. In addition, referents can change from one instance of "we" to the next. For example, Polybius 1.3.7 uses first person plural twice, once of the narrator individually and a second time of the narrator and other Greeks.

The application of first person plural to an individual is not foreign to English speakers. Some academic disciplines, particularly within the sciences, prefer first-person plural grammatical style in argumentation. In addition, English speakers have encountered the royal "we" used by monarchs (and political, church, and other leaders) to refer to themselves in written and oral pronouncements and the editorial "we" employed by newspaper editorialists and other media commentators. In each case, first person plural refers to the speaker alone, but with broader referential implications in view. For academicians, first person plural is often favored over the impersonal third person ("one") as the appropriate grammatical style for presenting scholarly arguments in a dispassionate and unbiased manner. Heads of state and others in positions of authority use first-person plural style to associate themselves with the citizens or members of the communities that they lead. Editorialists and commentators speak of themselves as "we" in their role as public policy spokespersons for their employers or other groups.

It is impossible to determine whether wider referential inferences influenced the decision of ancient authors to use first person plural to refer to the narrator individually. Regardless of the reasons for employing it, however, first person plural suggests familiarity and a shared purpose. Readers sense that they know or should recognize who "we" are and, in addition, that at some level they are part of the collective voice. Even when the narrative context explicitly defines or limits referents, readers experience a connection to the "we," whether it be the narrator only, other characters or narrative participants, or other persons or groups with which the narrator might be associated. Even when the precise identity of "we" is unclear, the sense of personal involvement with first-person referents that readers experience often engenders a more sympathetic disposition toward first-person plural referents, and that can lead to a more empathetic reading perspective.

The argument here is not that ancient authors set out to achieve these effects. Without clarification on their part or guidance from rhetorical handbooks, the literary strategies of ancient authors are often impenetrable. As mentioned, however, Polybius does offer an explanation for his use of grammatical person (36.12.1–5):

> 36.12.1 One need not be surprised if we refer to ourselves sometimes by proper name and other times by common expressions such as "when I said this" or again "when we assented." 36.12.2 For since we have been much involved in the events to be recorded hereafter, it is necessary to alter our self-designations so that we not offend by repeating what is said in continuously mentioning the name nor, again, that we should fall into a boorish rhetorical style without being aware by constantly interjecting "of me" or "on account of me." 36.12.3 But by making use of all these and substituting always what is fitting at the time, we should avoid as much as possible the exceeding offensiveness of speaking about ourselves, 36.12.4 since by nature such expression is unacceptable but is often necessary when what is being represented cannot be signified in a different way. 36.12.5 It has been some support to us for this matter, by accident as it were, that no one

up to our time has inherited a proper name identical to ours, at least as far as we know.

Polybius's stated reason for varying references to himself—sometimes using his name, other times first person singular, and still other times first person plural—has to do with literary and rhetorical aesthetics. He is in a difficult situation. On one hand, self-reference was generally considered inappropriate at that time.[24] On the other hand, it is unavoidable in Polybius's situation, given his claims of personal involvement in the affairs reported. In his view, constantly referring to himself as "Polybius" would be offensive, but substituting for that option the incessant repetition of "I/me" would be equally obnoxious. Polybius's solution is to include the first person plural as an additional and, apparently, in his view, more tasteful self-reference, in effect softening the boorishness of copious personal references by alternating among the three possibilities ("Polybius," "I/mine/me," and "we/our/us"). Polybius's liberal application of first person plural as a reference to himself—he even employs it in this explanation of his grammatical choices—and the fact that it is not mentioned with first person singular or naming himself as an objectionable grammatical practice could indicate that he had a preference for first-person plural style. Indeed, Polybius's partiality for first person plural may have led to the innovation of intermittent first-person plural narration. His digression to explain his use of grammatical person immediately following the initial instance of first person plural at the event level and his remark that readers "need not be surprised" at his usage suggest that the way he employs first person plural is something of a novelty.[25]

It is surely an oversimplification to accept at face value Polybius's justification that his use of grammatical person of himself, particularly the adoption of first-person plural style for this purpose, reflects a literary technique selected to make acceptable to readers his voluminous self-references. Nevertheless, several passages in which he combines grammatical person in an assortment of ways, including first person singular and plural, first person and third person, and first person singular and plural with third person, would appear to support at least partially his assertion. A representative example of multiple-person style is the story of Polybius's friendship with

---

24. Consistent with the view expressed by Polybius, George Lyons (*Pauline Autobiography: Toward a New Understanding* [Atlanta: Scholars Press, 1985], 53–60) has argued that the "decorum of autobiographical remarks as a rhetorical exercise was problematic" among ancient philosophers and rhetoricians, appealing for support to Aristotle's recommendation in *Rhetoric* that speakers who must refer to themselves "use the third rather than the first person." See also Beverly Roberts Gaventa, "Galatians 1 and 2: Autobiography as Paradigm," *NovT* 28 (1986): 324–26.

25. Along this line, Thornton (*Der Zeuge des Zeugen*, 175–76) suggests that Polybius was compelled to offer an explanation because of the unusual nature of the intermittent first-person plural narration that he introduces in 36.11.2–4.

Scipio, the son of the Roman commander, narrated in 31.23.1–31.25.1. The account opens with a short introduction (31.23.1–4) that begins by using both first person singular and plural (31.23.1), followed by first- and third-person comments about Polybius (31.23.2–3). As the story moves into the narrative proper, a first-person plural comment gives way to third-person narration about Polybius and Scipio that continues for the remainder of the story. In this excerpt, therefore, grammatical person fluctuates according to Polybius's outline, referring to the narrator within five verses as "Polybius," "them" (with Scipio), "I," and "we":

> 31.23.1 Since the plan and the state of affairs in the narrative have called our attention to this family, I wish to fulfill for the sake of those who would enjoy hearing what was left as a promise in the previous book. 31.23.2 For I promised before to describe in detail why and how the fame of Scipio in Rome advanced so much and burst forth more quickly than was his due 31.23.3 and with this how it happened that Polybius grew in friendship and intimacy with the aforementioned person to such an extent that, not only did the report about them extend as far as Italy and Greece, but their conduct and companionship also became well-known in more distant regions. 31.23.4 We have, therefore, indicated in what has been said previously that the beginning of the friendship between the aforementioned men came out of a certain loan of books and the conversation about them. 31.23.5 But as intimacy increased, and when those who had been summoned were sent out to the cities, Fabius and Scipio, the sons of Lucius, strongly recommended to the praetor that Polybius remain in Rome.[26]

Josephus

The first-century C.E. Hellenistic Jewish historian Josephus authored two major histories, *Jewish War* and *Jewish Antiquities,* both of which were written during the same period as Acts.[27] Examining both volumes provides

---

26. Other multiple-person passages include 36.1.1–7; 36.11.1–4 (the intermittent first-person plural passage just examined); and 38.20.1–38.21.3. Polybius 38.21.1 contains the only occurrence that I have been able to uncover in Polybius's history of intermittent first person singular (see appendix B). It is very brief, perhaps owing to the textual problems in this section. All of 38.20.11 and the beginning of 38.21.1 have been damaged beyond restoration, making it impossible to determine the exact extent of the first-person references in this passage (see Walbank, *Commentary on Polybius*, 3:722–24).

27. *Jewish War* was probably published in the mid-70s C.E., and *Jewish Antiquities,* which purports to chronicle the history of the Jews from creation to the period just before the war, in the mid-90s C.E. From among the many helpful resources on Josephus's biography and writings, the following have been most useful: Per Bilde, *Flavius Josephus between Jerusalem and Rome: His Life, His Works, and Their Importance* (JSPSup 2; Sheffield: Sheffield Academic Press, 1988); Louis H. Feldman, *Josephus and Modern Scholarship (1937–1980)* (New York: de Gruyter, 1984); H. St. J. Thackeray, introduction to *Josephus* (trans. H. St. J. Thackeray, Ralph Marcus, and Louis H. Feldman; 9 vols.; LCL; Cambridge: Harvard University Press, 1926–1965); Sterling, *Historiography and Self-Definition*; and Mireille Hadas-Lebel, *Flavius*

insights into how an author might employ grammatical person differently in different narratives. Josephus was commissioned as military commander in Galilee at the outbreak of the first Jewish-Roman War in 66 C.E. As a prisoner of war following his capture during Vespasian's Galilean campaign, he found favor with the Roman commander. After the war he settled in Rome under the patronage of Vespasian, who had become Roman emperor in 69 C.E. and who granted Josephus freedom, Roman citizenship, and a pension.[28]

Large sections of *War* are devoted to Josephus's involvement in the conflict, and once again, as was the case in Thucydides and Polybius, event-level passages with Josephus as a character—indeed the main character and protagonist—are narrated in the third person. One brief example is the account of his appointment as commander of Galilee: "John, son of Ananias, was appointed commander of Gophna and Acrabetta, and Josephus, son of Matthias, of each of the two Galilees" (*War* 2.568). The following lengthy narrative detailing his activities in that region (*War* 2.569–647) consistently employs third-person style, referring to Josephus by name and with third-person pronouns and verb forms. Moreover, this section does not exhaust the third-person references to Josephus in *War*. Other narrative blocks in which Josephus is a primary character all speak of him in the third person as well.[29] To illustrate how Josephus adapts grammatical person to suit different narratives, consider the autobiographical apologia for his conduct during combat (*The Life*) that he wrote approximately thirty years after *War*. In significant part, that work parallels the storyline dealing with Josephus's activities in *War* 2.562–3.34.[30] As might be expected of an autobiography, however, it narrates events entirely in the first person singular.[31]

Josephus: Eyewitness to Rome's First-Century Conquest of Judea (New York: Macmillan, 1993).

28. The circumstances surrounding Josephus's diplomatic and personal alliance with the Romans are murky. His autobiography (*The Life*) tells of the respect he gained for Rome's rulers and military power on a previous visit to Rome in 64 C.E.; that when upon his return he could not persuade other Jews against the planned revolt, he attempted to keep matters calm, hoping that the Roman procurator Gessius Florus would be able to put down the rebellion before it gathered momentum; and that early on he was suspected of disloyalty and treachery by a number of Jewish dissidents. *War*, which also describes the suspicions of other Jews toward Josephus, claims that he was spared execution after his capture through the intercession of Titus, Vespasian's son, who admired his bravery and was moved by his youth. According to the narrative, Vespasian's leniency was also influenced by Josephus's ability and willingness to forecast the commander's destiny to be emperor (*War* 3.392–408).

29. For additional examples, including several speeches by Josephus, see *War* 3.59–408; 3.432–442; 4.622–629; 5.361–420; 5.541–547; and 6.93–129. See *War* 3.142–144 in appendix B.

30. *Life* 28–411.

31. It is worth noting that in another of Josephus's writings, *Against Apion*, he admits to using assistants to help with the Greek language in his translation of *War* from Aramaic,

First-person singular narrator-level comments occur only sporadically in *War,* but one extensive first-person singular section is the preface.[32] As it begins, the narrative explicitly identifies the narrator and the author by introducing Josephus as author/narrator:

> I, Josephus, a priest from Jerusalem, son of Matthias, having myself fought the Romans at the beginning and present at events afterwards out of compulsion, propose to relate to those under Roman rule, after translating into the Greek language, what I originally composed in my native language and sent to the barbarians inland. (*War* 1.3)

First person singular continues throughout the remainder of the preface (*War* 1.1–30) to support grammatically Josephus's insistence that his account will be factual, in contrast to earlier inadequate histories of the war, and that although his feelings for the Jewish people will be evident, he will neither exaggerate their deeds to offset disparagement of the Jews by other historians nor diminish the responsibility of Jewish revolutionaries for the defeat and destruction suffered at the hands of the Romans. In addition, he defends the importance of contemporary history and his decision to focus on the events of the recent war because of his personal connection to it.

First-person plural references to the narrator individually are rare as well and consist mostly of comments that call attention to events the narrator has or will report elsewhere ("as we said," "as we have said previously," etc.).[33] This appears to be a conventional literary construction, since *War* never uses first person singular for these expressions even in passages that otherwise employ first person singular of the narrator (e.g., *War* 2.114). The ending also contains a passage in first person plural, but on this occasion the collective first-person plural voice gives way to the individual first person singular as the narrator moves to defend the veracity of his account:

> Here is the end of the history by us, which we promised to convey with total accuracy to those wishing to learn how this war by the Romans against the Jews was waged. How it has been expressed, let it be left to the readers to judge. But concerning the truth, I would not hesitate to say with confidence that I endeavored after this throughout the entire composition. (*War* 7.454–455)

---

the language in which it was originally composed (*Against Apion* 1.50; *War* 1.3). Although they certainly influenced grammatical constructions in *War,* Josephus is responsible for its final shape and for the decision not to adopt its third-person style when composing *Life* (for which, as far as is known, he did not utilize Greek collaborators).

32. *War* contains the occasional "it seems to me" (μοι δοκεῖ), similar to Thucydides and Polybius (e.g., *War* 2.156; 2.191; 5.354; 5.489; 6.373) and a few other instances of first person singular (e.g., *War* 6.81; 7.274).

33. *War* 1.33; 1.182; 1.344; 1.365; 1.406; 1.411; 1.418; 1.610; 1.668; 2.114; 2.557; 2.651; 3.47; 4.153; 4.208; 4.353; 4.611; 5.1; 5.140; 5.152; 5.162; 5.183; 5.227; 5.232; 5.237; 5.251; 5.445; 5.550; 6.400; 6.433; 7.96; 7.215; 7.244; 7.253; 7.293; 7.304.

One additional multiple-person passage occurs in the preface, where, as noted, the narrator employs first person singular to assure readers that he is going to chronicle events factually ("I decided not to exaggerate the deeds of my race but am relating the actions of both sides with accuracy") but acknowledges that his emotions will color his presentation ("while giving the accounts about the events, I am imparting my own feelings as well as my emotions to lament over the misfortunes of the homeland" [*War* 1.9]). He then shifts to first person plural as he appeals to readers who might object to the introduction of personal views into a historical work ("should anyone criticize that we might say such things . . . or lament over our homeland's misfortunes, let him make allowance" [*War* 1.11]). Finally, he moves to the third person, asking those who remain critical of him for including his personal views to separate fact from feeling in the narrative, to attribute to the history the events recounted and to him the emotions revealed in his narrative ("should anyone be a harsher judge of compassion, let him adjudge the facts to history, the lamentations to the writer" [*War* 1.12]). The shifts in grammatical person in *War* do not seem to fit Polybius's literary aesthetics explanation. Rather, *War* consistently utilizes the third person for the author/narrator when he takes part in events and, generally speaking, first person singular in passages dealing with the factuality of the history and first person plural for conventional and other comments concerning the acts of narrating.

The first noticeable difference in grammatical person between *War* and *Antiquities* is that the latter writing never refers to Josephus by name or in the third person. It is not surprising that *Antiquities* contains no third-person accounts about Josephus, since the narrative's concern is with matters that predate his entrance into the public arena; he is not a participant in the events narrated. Still, it seems odd that, instead of identifying Josephus in the preface as author/narrator as *War* does ("I Josephus"), the unnamed narrator of *Antiquities* specifies that he is also the author of *War*: "for, understanding from experience the war that we Jews waged against the Romans, the events in it and what end resulted, I was compelled to describe it in detail because of those who in their writing were defiling the truth" (*Ant.* 1.4).

First person singular in *Antiquities* often serves to distinguish the author/narrator individually from first-person plural references close at hand that associate him with the Jewish people.[34] Sometimes the connection to other Jews is explicit, as in the passage just cited ("we Jews"); other times it must be determined from the narrative context. This pattern is quite prominent in the preface and conclusion but is present as well in other parts of

---

34. In a few rare instances, "we" connects Josephus to other constituencies. For example, first person plural in *Ant.* 1.21 links him with humanity in general. For association with other groups, see *Ant.* 1.156; 6.186; 6.342.

Antiquities.[35] For example, the narrative's final chapter includes the following comment:

> Here will end my account of ancient history, after which I began to write about the war. This encompasses, from the beginning of humankind's creation up to the twelfth year of Nero's reign, the tradition of the things that have happened to us Jews in Egypt and Syria and Palestine, how much we have suffered under the Assyrians and Babylonians, how the Persians and Macedonians have treated us, and after them the Romans. For I believe I have compiled all things with accuracy. (*Ant.* 20.259–260)

This passage illustrates that, besides separating the author/narrator from his compatriots, first-person singular style continues to promote the factual quality of the historian's work.[36] Comparable first-person singular assurances can be found in the narrative's conclusion, as in "I have described without error the succession of the kings" (*Ant.* 20.261) and "I assert that no one else . . . could have delivered to the Greeks this treatise so accurately" (*Ant.* 20.262). Earlier in the book the author/narrator defends his fidelity to Hebrew sources used in *Antiquities*:

> Let no one criticize me for reporting throughout the treatise all of these events as I find them in the ancient books. For even at the beginning of the history, I safeguarded myself against those who would seek or find fault with something about the facts by saying that I was only translating the Hebrew books into the Greek tongue and by promising to set forth these matters without adding to or subtracting from the events on my own. (*Ant.* 10.218)

Antiquities also employs first person plural to refer to the narrator individually. Formulaic comments about subjects covered elsewhere in the narrative are quite popular.[37] In addition, periodically multiple instances

---

35. Other occurrences of "I" (narrator individually) and "we" (narrator and other Jews) include 1.9; 1.10; 1.11–12; 1.15; 1.18; 1.23–24; 1.129; 2.176–177; 3.248; 8.155; 8.159; 12.325; 14.189; 16.174–178; 18.29; 19.15; 20.263–264; 20.267; 20.268.

36. There are a number of formulaic first-person singular constructions in *Antiquities* similar to those encountered in the other texts treated. Since I have commented on them previously, I simply list the occurrences in *Antiquities*: μοι δοκεῖ ("it seems to me") in *Ant.* 3.186; 3.257; 6.346; 10.210; 10.280; 11.68; 13.72; 16.159; and 17.192; μοι δεδήλωται ("it has been disclosed by me") and variants in *Ant.* 1.108; 1.136; 1.203; 3.187; 3.201; 9.280; 14.467; 18.142; and 19.123; διέξειμι ("I go through in detail") in *Ant.* 1.160; 3.213; 15.371; and 18.142; ἐπάνειμι ("I shall return") in *Ant.* 6.350; 8.298; 8.393; 16.178; and 18.80; τρέψομαι ("I shall turn [to]") in *Ant.* 1.129 and 3.218.

37. The most prevalent expressions used to note events discussed elsewhere in *Antiquities* are (without nearly exhausting the possibilities): various tenses of δηλόω ("to relate") in *Ant.* 1.137; 1.175; 2.177; 3.74; 3.158; 3.257; 3.295; 4.74; 5.89; 5.231; 6.105; 6.322; 7.89; 7.105; 7.244; 7.330; 7.344; 7.393; 8.1; 8.159; 8.224; 8.229; 9.28; 9.158; 9.183; 9.266; 10.80; 10.107; 10.148; 10.151; 11.184; 11.341; 12.237; 12.238; 12.244; 12.257; 13.1; 13.11; 13.36; 13.61; 13.80; 13.108; 13.112; 13.119; 13.256; 13.275; 13.285; 13.288; 13.372; 14.9; 14.267;

of first person plural occur that both specify the narrator individually and identify him collectively with other Jews. An illustration of this is the brief discussion of Mosaic food regulations in *Ant.* 3.259:

> Whenever an occasion for writing about these matters presents itself to us [narrator individually], we [narrator individually] shall relate them in detail, giving as well the reasons why he [Moses] was moved to recommend to us [narrator and other Jews] that some of them were to be eaten but ordered to abstain from others.[38]

On other occasions, first person singular and plural are used in the same passage to designate the narrator individually, as in, "I could say still more things about Saul and his courage, which furnishes abundant material for the purpose. But in order that we do not appear vulgar in declaring his praises, I am returning from where I digressed into these matters" (*Ant.* 6.350).[39] Finally, a few passages contain an even more complex commingling of grammatical person, combining the collective first person plural (narrator with all Jews), the individual first person plural (narrator individually), and first person singular (narrator). An example is found in the preface as the narrator introduces remarks about Moses:

> Since almost everything depends upon the wisdom of Moses, our [narrator and other Jews] lawgiver, it is necessary for me [narrator] to speak briefly about him lest any of the readers be at a loss about how it happens that the book by us [narrator individually], while having in so much of it the description of laws and practices, is also concerned with an inquiry into the causes and phenomena of nature.[40] (*Ant.* 1.18)

Josephus offers no explanation for his complex and, at least for the modern reader, potentially confusing application of grammatical person. Some shifts are explainable on the basis of formulaic phrases (in first person singular or plural) or assertions of the narrator's credibility (first person singular). The reason for others, however, is unclear and, in these cases, may reflect the need for variety in referring to the narrator, as Polybius claimed; in other words, for literary aesthetics.

14.388; 15.1; 15.240; 15.254; 16.206; 20.53; 20.102; 20.157; 20.199; 20.237; and 20.248; ἐρῶ ("to tell") in *Ant.* 1.133; 1.142; 2.195; 2.198; 3.62; 3.143; 3.218; 3.230; 3.247; 3.264; 5.343; 6.1; 7.70; 7.103; 7.230; 7.243; 7.311; 7.333; 7.364; 8.130; 8.141; 8.175; 8.178; 8.190; 8.246; 9.1; 9.95; 9.112; 10.36; 10.81; 10.142; 10.230; 12.66; 12.189; 13.62; 13.297, 13.320; 13.347; 14.1; 14.5; 14.78; 14.176; 15.2; 15.181; 16.73; 18.134; 19.366; 20.239; εἶπον ("to say") in *Ant.* 8.325; 9.29; 12.387; 15.39; 20.9, 20.187; see as well other terms for "to say," viz., λέγω (*Ant.* 4.302; 8.56) and φημί (*Ant.* 5.235; 14.267; 14.323; 20.199; 20.227).

38. See also *Ant.* 3.247; 8.175; 14.77–78 (see appendix B); 14.323; 16.161.

39. See also *Ant.* 1.25; 3.218; 4.159; 10.151; 13.297; 13.347; 16.187; 20.154–157. See appendix B for 1.25, 10.151, and 16.187.

40. See also *Ant.* 8.55–56; 8.159; 14.265–267 (see appendix B).

Review and Results: Summary of Findings

The analysis of grammatical person in these four ancient histories reveals that, although their classification as third-person narratives is well deserved, each exhibits variety in the choice of grammatical person. In addition to the third person, the narratives utilize in some measure the first person (singular and plural) to refer to the narrator. The three accounts that portray the author as an actor in events overwhelmingly employ third-person style when narrating the episodes in which he is a participant. The effect of third-person style in these histories is to foster a sense of objectivity by distancing the authors as participants from their roles as narrators. Thucydides' *History of the Peloponnesian War* extends this practice by referring to the author at the narrator level in the third person (by name or other third-person constructions), while Polybius's *Histories* and Josephus's *Jewish War* and *Jewish Antiquities* use primarily first-person style for narrator-level commentary.

Although Josephus's *Antiquities* sometimes employs first person singular to distinguish the narrator individually from first-person plural references to the narrator and others, first person singular is most often used by these historians in passages that seek to strengthen the author/narrator's case for his version of events. The author/narrator frequently attempts to establish his trustworthiness by lifting up his personal involvement in or thorough research and critical assessment of the subject matter. Making the argument in the narrator's own voice for his integrity and the accuracy of his account projects personal confidence in his knowledge and authority to tell the story at hand and, in so doing, increases his personal credibility and the believability of his account. An analogous example from the twenty-first century of the persuasive potential of first-person testimony might be the system of criminal jurisprudence in the United States. By law, defendants are not required, and so may not be compelled, to testify at their trials. Given the risks of submitting to cross-examination, deciding whether to assert the privilege not to testify is a key issue in any defense strategy. In practice, however, there is general agreement among legal analysts that juries are biased in favor of defendants who take the witness stand in their own defense.[41] For a variety of reasons having to do with the inclination to attach greater weight to personal disclosures, jurors are more likely to accept the defense's version of events if they hear it from the defendant personally rather than from other

---

41. For perspectives on this issue in view of two recent high-profile criminal cases in the United States, see Julie Hilden, "Should Martha Stewart's Lawyer Have Strongly Advised Her to Testify? Assessing the Defense in the Stewart Case, Part One," *FindLaw Legal News and Commentary* (15 March 2004): n.p. [cited 3 August 2006]; online: http://writ.news.findlaw.com/hilden/20040315.html; Joseph J. Aronica, "Big Mouths," *Legal Times* 29/23 (5 June 2006): n.p. [cited 7 August 2006]; online: http://www.duanemorris.com/articles/static/aronicalegaltimes060506.pdf.

defense witnesses, so long as they consider the defendant trustworthy. In other words, jurors want to hear the defendant's claim of innocence from the defendant's own lips. Similarly, first-person singular comments in the four ancient histories analyzed address the impulse for personal assurance that the narrator has the capability to narrate accurately the events chronicled.

Despite similarities in their employment of grammatical person, the narratives also exhibit differences in its application. The prefaces, which in ancient historiography developed to a degree into formal and conventional introductions and thus might be expected to make use of the same grammatical person, illustrate this diversity. Thucydides' prefaces employ third person singular for the most part, Polybius's is in first person plural, and Josephus uses first person singular in *War* and, in *Antiquities,* first person singular of the narrator individually and first person plural for the narrator and other Jews.

Nowhere are the grammatical differences among these writings more evident than in their adoption of first person plural to refer to the narrator individually. First person plural occurs rarely in Thucydides, and in the majority of those few instances it qualifies an assertion. Two hundred years later, Polybius displays a much greater penchant for first-person plural style. Not only does first person plural appear nearly seven hundred times more than in Thucydides, innovative enough in comparison to the earlier historian, but in addition Polybius introduces for the first time, as far as can be determined, event-level intermittent first-person plural narration. Indeed, there is reason to suspect that first person plural was Polybius's preferred grammatical construction for self-reference. His alone among the four histories explains its grammatical choices, justifying variation in grammatical person as a matter of narrative aesthetics. Josephus's two volumes, written approximately two hundred years after Polybius, also demonstrate diversity in the application of first person plural. In *War,* first person plural appears principally in formulaic comments concerning what the narrator reports in other sections of the narrative or the act of narrating. *Antiquities,* in addition to containing more of these conventional comments than *War,* applies first person plural in ways difficult to interpret but that, it is fair to say, add complexity and variety to the narrative's grammatical style.

Notwithstanding the differences in how and how often these four texts use first person plural of the narrator individually, they share certain effects of this grammatical style besides Polybius's specific claim of variety. Much like first person singular, first person plural creates a personal narrative tone that projects the involvement of the narrators in their stories and storytelling, that is, their closeness to and knowledge of events and, thus, their authority and competence to narrate the story.[42] Unlike first person singular, however,

---

42. Kurz, *Reading Luke-Acts,* 112–13.

first person plural moderates the emphasis on the narrators and, therefore, the responsibility for narrative claims by subsuming their individuality into the collective sense of first person plural. In addition, the "we" style conveys a sense of familiarity that draws readers into the stories.[43] Just like citizens or other groups that the royal and editorial "we" embrace, readers of these texts may feel an acquaintance with the "we" group and perhaps experience a shared sense of purpose. At some level, readers intuitively associate them-selves with the first-person plural company. The bond that readers develop with the first-person plural narrator can result in a compassionate and ap-preciative stance toward the narrator and, thus, acceptance of the narrator's perspective and a sympathetic reading of the narrative.

Review and Results: Significance for Acts

The way the four histories examined utilize grammatical-person con-structions is instructive for Acts. First, Thucydides, Polybius, and Josephus distance themselves as authors and actors from their roles as narrators by utilizing third-person narration for events that depict them as participants. This distinction is slippery and confusing, especially given that, with the exception of *Antiquities,* the narratives also explicitly identify the narrator with the named author, such as when Josephus opens *War* with "I, Jose-phus . . . propose to relate [in Greek] . . . what I originally composed in my native language" (*War* 1.3). In Acts, the distinction between the author and the narrator remains clearer because the author is unnamed. That is to say, Acts was written anonymously, a practice that in antiquity was not at all uncommon within or outside the biblical corpus.[44] Some have argued that the impetus behind anonymous authorship was a lack of interest among ancient authors and readers in the personality of the author.[45] The three historians studied, however, and the generally acknowledged desire on the part of ancient authors to protect their names against pseudonymous pre-tenders suggest that the reasons for anonymous publication of ancient texts

---

43. Tannehill, *Narrative Unity of Luke-Acts,* 2:247.

44. See, e.g., Joseph A. Fitzmyer, *The Gospel according to Luke,* 1:35–53; Kurt Aland, "The Problem of Anonymity and Pseudonymity in Christian Literature of the First Two Cen-turies," in *The Authorship and Integrity of the New Testament* (Theological Collections 4; London: SPCK, 1965), 1–13; repr. from *JTS* 2/12 (1961). In contrast, Martin Hengel (*Studies in the Gospel of Mark* [trans. John Bowden; Philadelphia: Fortress, 1985], 64–84; idem, *The Four Gospels and the One Gospel of Jesus Christ: An Investigation of the Collection and Origin of the Canonical Gospels* [trans. John Bowden; Harrisburg, Pa.: Trinity, 2000], 34–73) is repre-sentative of scholars who argue that the Gospels and Acts were not written anonymously.

45. E. M. Forster, *Anonymity: An Enquiry* (Hogarth Essays 12; London: Woolf, 1925; repr., Folcraft, Pa.: Folcraft, 1976), 15–16; Aland, "Problem of Anonymity," 5–11.

were complex.[46] Whatever the motivation, the effect of anonymity is to erase the actual (or "real") author from view and, in so doing, to minimize the identification of the actual author with the narrator character. To be sure, the prefaces to the Gospel of Luke and Acts allude to the narrator's role as the storywriter and thus do in fact associate the narrator with authorship. Nonetheless, because Acts was written anonymously, the author/narrator as narrative character is sharply distinguishable from the real author. On the other hand, the connection that Acts maintains between narrator and author, although minimal, means that the narrator character in Acts remains unnamed and, therefore, unidentifiable with any other character in the narrative. One consequence of the narrator's anonymity is that, in contrast to Thucydides, Polybius, and Josephus in *War*, the narrator of Acts never appears as a third-person actor in the narrative.

Another difference between Acts and the four texts analyzed is how infrequently Acts utilizes the first person (singular or plural) to refer to the narrator at the narrator level. The narrator rarely intrudes in the story to offer commentary, which allows the narrative to stand on its own merits. Only two instances each of first-person singular and plural narrator comments occur in Luke and Acts, both located in the prefaces (Luke 1:1–3 and Acts 1:1). The use of the first person in prefaces is not unusual, of course, as was discovered in the investigation of Polybius and Josephus. Similar as well to what was observed in the other ancient narratives, first-person comments in Luke and Acts are in texts supportive of the author/narrator's dependability.[47]

Although Acts barely uses first person plural in narrator-level commentary, it contains three intermittent event-level first-person plural passages of the kind encountered in Polybius. In the same way as Polybius, the "we" passages in Acts place the narrator character at the scene, an eyewitness to and participant in the events narrated. Again, the assertion that the "we" passages portray the narrator as an eyewitness to and participant in events is a narrative claim, not a historical one. That does not mean that the actual author or his source could not have been an eyewitness; however, the analysis of grammatical practice by ancient historians raises questions about the traditional argument that the first person plural establishes historical eyewitnessing. For one thing, the three ancient historians analyzed much prefer the third person when writing about their personal involvement in affairs. Even Polybius, who appears to favor first person plural and, in fact,

---

46. Terry L. Wilder, *Pseudonymity, the New Testament, and Deception: An Inquiry into Intention and Reception* (Lanham, Md.: University Press of America, 2004), 1–34. Pseudonymous authorship involves writing in someone else's name, whether real (forgery) or fictional (pen name).

47. Chapter 4 will consider in detail the use and effect of first-person grammatical style in the prefaces of the Third Gospel and Acts.

may have been responsible for introducing intermittent first-person plural style into narratives that present the author/narrator as a participant in events, only employs first person plural at the event level in two of the many passages in which he plays an active role. Further, in *Antiquities* Josephus utilizes first person plural as a reference to himself and the Jews who lived before him. Although the use of first person plural as a means of associating himself with his ethnic-religious forebears is not unusual grammatical practice, it assuredly is not meant to signal Josephus's historical presence among his Jewish ancestors. Finally, anonymous authorship largely dissociates the actual author of Acts from the narrator and thus from the events in which the narrator character participates. If the author wished to lift up his historical presence and participation in events, the grammatical guidance offered by these predecessors (Thucydides, Polybius, and Josephus) would seem to suggest that he identify himself by name, associate himself unmistakably with the narrator character, and report events in which he claims participation primarily in the third person.

Lastly, referring to the narrator as "we" in these ancient texts projects a sense of corroboration concerning the narrative eyewitness's version of the story: it is not just "my" word, but "our" word. The first person plural presents the narrator as the spokesperson for the group that shares the narrative experience in the "we" passages much as the royal "we" represents heads of state as spokespersons for their citizenry and the editorial "we" represents editorialists as spokespersons for the organizations under whose banner they opine, even though in each case first person plural indicates the speaker or writer individually. Chapter 4 will argue that, in similar fashion, Acts portrays the narrator as a trustworthy spokesperson so that readers are able to identify with him as part of the "we" group, empathize with his perspective, and give credence to his testimony.

3

Paul and Barnabas

COMPANIONS ON THE JOURNEY

I get by with a little help from my friends.

—John Lennon

Acts portrays Paul as a complex personality. In the course of the story, he is characterized as a strict Pharisaic Jew who in turn rabidly opposes the nascent Jesus movement and then becomes its most important and successful missionary and whose significant apostolic achievements are tempered by substantial failure and personal condemnation.[1] In his defense speech before Agrippa (26:1–23) after his arrest in Jerusalem, Paul claims that the activities that so upset the Jews were all undertaken in faithful response to his commission by the Lord as missionary to Jews and Gentiles (26:16–20). He has, he pleads to Agrippa and earlier before the Jewish leadership (23:1), "lived in obedience to his heavenly call."[2] Acts, however, does not represent the apostle simply as God's faithful servant wrongly persecuted and prosecuted for carrying out the tasks assigned to him. In his opening scene in the narrative, for instance, a youthful Saul not only consents to Stephen's stoning but minds the executioners' cloaks (7:58–8:1). Afterwards Paul harasses members of the Jesus movement in Jerusalem (8:3) and makes plans to extend his assault against them to Syria (9:1–2). On his way to Damascus to carry out the plan, however, he experiences a transforming encounter with Jesus Christ from which he emerges as champion of the movement he has been working diligently to eradicate (9:3–22).

The actions that Paul takes against the Jesus movement and his sudden

---

1. Paul is twice referred to as an apostle in Acts, both times jointly with Barnabas (14:4, 14). See appendix A for more details concerning the use of this term in Acts.

2. Tannehill, *Narrative Unity of Luke-Acts*, 2:285.

change of heart occur early in his performance in Acts and set the tone for the remainder of the narrative. Instead of leading to acceptance and trust on the part of movement members, his transformation is viewed with suspicion both by those who are part of the movement and by those who are not. Characters and groups associated with the Jesus movement in the narrative might be expected to embrace Paul after the Damascus road, but in fact they remain hesitant because, as Beverly Roberts Gaventa points out, "when Paul emerges as ardent proclaimer, the question concerning his identity does not disappear. He remains the enemy, although now the enemy who has been overthrown."[3] These misgivings are never far from the surface of the story, and Paul, hard though he may try, cannot overcome them entirely.

In other words, Acts presents Paul as a flawed messenger whose reversal understandably causes Jews and Gentiles within and outside the Jesus movement to mistrust him.[4] The story of the Damascus disciple Ananias (9:10–19) illustrates Paul's problem. Ananias questions the Lord Jesus' personal directive that he go to Paul and lay hands on him because he has heard of Saul's assault on the church in Jerusalem and his original purpose for traveling to Damascus (9:13–14). Only after Christ assures him that Paul is the "chosen instrument to carry my name among Gentiles as well as rulers and Israelites" (9:15) and that it is Paul who will suffer in the Lord's name (9:16) does Ananias carry out his instructions. Ananias's reaction is typical of the response to Paul throughout the narrative.

To be sure, Acts specifies several grounds for the antipathy toward Paul. Jews outside the movement express jealousy over the success of Paul's preaching of Jesus as the Christ (13:45; 17:1–5; 18:5–6) and the kingdom of God (19:8–9). In addition, a number of Jews attack Paul for advocating worship contrary to the law (18:12–15), including certain Judean Jesus movement members who oppose him over the issue of circumcision (15:1–2).[5] Gentiles attack Paul as well, however. In Philippi, for example, Gentiles

---

3. Beverly Roberts Gaventa, "The Overthrown Enemy: Luke's Portrait of Paul," in *Society of Biblical Literature 1985 Seminar Papers* (SBLSP 24; Atlanta: Scholars Press, 1985), 444.

4. Marie-Eloise Rosenblatt (*Paul the Accused: His Portrait in the Acts of the Apostles* [Zacchaeus Studies: New Testament; Collegeville, Minn.: Liturgical Press, 1995], 26, and her dissertation from which the monograph is drawn, "Under Interrogation: Paul as Witness in Juridical Contexts in Acts and the Implied Spirituality for Luke's Community" [Ph.D. diss., Graduate Theological Union, 1976]) also addresses the issue of ambivalence toward Paul in Acts owing to his contradictory stance concerning the Jesus movement.

5. A number of commentators have addressed possible historical reasons for Jewish opposition to Paul's gospel preaching. See, e.g., James D. G. Dunn, *The Acts of the Apostles* (Narrative Commentaries; Valley Forge, Pa.: Trinity, 1996), 183–84; I. Howard Marshall, *The Acts of the Apostles: An Introduction and Commentary* (TNTC; Grand Rapids: Eerdmans, 1980), 229–31; Philipp Vielhauer, "On the 'Paulinism' of Acts," in Keck and Martyn *Studies in Luke-Acts*, 40; Jacob Jervell, *Luke and the People of God: A New Look at Luke-Acts* (Minneapolis: Augsburg, 1972); idem, *The Theology of the Acts of the Apostles* (New Testament Theology;

have him arrested for interfering with their business (16:19), and Ephesian Gentiles incite a riot because he undermines the Artemis cult by preaching against idols (19:23–41).

More than simply opposition, Paul's portrayal in Acts is distinguished by what F. F. Bruce refers to as the overemphasis of hostility toward him.[6] Why, in other words, is the level of antagonism so intense that it provokes almost unbelievably violent reactions to his preaching, and why the lack of countervailing support for Paul among the groups that are depicted as generally sympathetic to him and his message? The key to understanding the potency of the credibility issue may be detected in Paul's two so-called defense speeches later in the narrative.[7] First, in his speech to the populace of Jerusalem (22:1–21), Paul reminds the audience of his role as a Jewish persecutor of the Jesus movement and how, after the apostle's Damascus road experience, Christ appeared while he was praying (in the Jerusalem temple, ironically) to send him to the Gentiles. Paul would not be able suc-cessfully to preach Christ in the synagogues of Jerusalem because of and/or despite—and the sense of the passage is suggestively ambiguous—being the approving cloak-boy at Stephen's stoning and the one responsible for the imprisonment of so many members of the Jesus movement. Later, at his trial before Agrippa and Festus (26:1–23), Paul offers another version of the story, again however delineating his part in the persecution of the Jesus movement prior to Damascus and the reversal in his position following his encounter with the Lord on the way to Damascus to ferret out movement members for deportation and prosecution.[8] As Gerhard Lohfink and, more recently, Gaventa have pointed out, Paul's speeches do not simply repeat the story; rather, in the retelling the account is intensified.[9] With each repetition, Saul's prosecutorial activities are "painted with increasingly darker colors," and his mission charge becomes "the object of sharper and more direct

Cambridge: Cambridge University Press, 1996), 88–90; and Haenchen, *Acts of the Apostles,* 115.

6. F. F. Bruce, *The Acts of the Apostles* (3rd ed.; Grand Rapids: Eerdmans, 1990), 54.

7. Ben Witherington III (*The Acts of the Apostles: A Socio-rhetorical Commentary* [Grand Rapids: Eerdmans, 1998], 684) is correct to point out that, technically speaking, there are no trial scenes in Acts before Paul's case is heard by the procurator Felix in Acts 24. As Witherington suggests, the episodes in which Paul is questioned and responds prior to that might better be called "pretrial hearings."

8. I agree with Gerhard Lohfink's (*The Conversion of St. Paul: Narrative and History in Acts* [Chicago: Franciscan Herald Press, 1976], 60) explanation of the different versions of Paul's experience in Acts 9; 22; and 26: "it is much more reasonable to ascribe the differences among the three accounts to the *creative literary activity and composition of the author* . . . [than] to the addition of specific historical data . . . [or] to different literary sources" (emphasis original).

9. Ibid., 92–95; Beverly Roberts Gaventa, *From Darkness to Light: Aspects of Conver-sion in the New Testament* (OBT; Philadelphia: Fortress, 1986), 71–73, 81–82.

focus."[10] The discontinuity in Saul's views and behavior and the mistrust of him that results from his transformation are not forgotten over the course of the narrative. These speeches, recited as they are at ever higher decibel levels, emphasize that the matter of Paul's conflicted background influences every facet of his portrayal. By drawing attention to both extremes, Paul's vehement opposition as well as his subsequent evangelical support of the Jesus movement, each speech in turn brings front and center the ongoing suspicion directed toward him. For Jews and Gentiles alike, whether part of the Jesus movement or opposed to it, the ghost of Paul's past lurks behind his every deed and word. None of these groups ever resolves completely the question of how much to trust Paul after his radical reversal.

The single named character who is supportive of Paul is Barnabas. Portrayed as Paul's advocate, mentor, colleague, and friend, Barnabas is for a time Paul's reliable partner and constant companion. After they are called and commissioned by the Holy Spirit, Barnabas accompanies Paul on his initial mission journey through Cyprus and Asia Minor (13:1–14:28). In addition, he defends Paul before the leadership of the Jesus movement in Jerusalem (9:27), recruits him from Tarsus to work in Antioch (11:25–26), delivers with him Antioch's famine relief collection for the church to the Jesus movement leaders in Jerusalem despite the danger to movement leaders posed by Herod (11:27–12:25), and serves with him in the delegation sent from Antioch to the Jerusalem council convened over the issue of mandatory circumcision for Jesus movement members (15:1–35).

Barnabas's character plays a particular role in the narrative as Paul's missionary partner and companion. Because of his trustworthiness, Barnabas legitimates the story of Paul's transformation from chief prosecutor to ardent proponent of the Jesus movement. In addition, he highlights and corroborates Paul's cooperation with God's plan and offers reassurance to characters and readers alike that Paul will successfully complete his mission tasks whatever the circumstances and despite difficulties he encounters as a result of his reversal of position. In other words, the narrative employs the character of Barnabas to address uncertainties about the consequences of Paul's background and reputation on his performance as the Lord's "chosen vessel." Jacob Jervell has in fact attributed such doubts about Paul to the original audience of Acts, arguing that "Luke is writing for readers who view Paul with suspicion."[11] In Acts 9 Barnabas explicitly acts in defense of Paul, but in most scenes his characterization as Paul's steadfast companion

---

10. Lohfink, *Conversion of St. Paul*, 93, 95.

11. Jacob Jervell, *Luke and the People of God*, 153–207. Jervell's reason for readers' suspicions about Paul centers on his faithfulness to Jewish customs; that is, they have heard "rumors of his apostasy from Moses" (197; see 21:21). In addition, Jervell argues that Luke uses the character of James "as legitimation for Paul's faithfulness to the law" (194).

creates the desired effect. Indeed, the narrative joins Barnabas and Paul by name no fewer than nineteen times, fourteen of which occur as compounds (Barnabas and Paul [or Saul] or the other way around).[12] This chapter examines these two characters and their relationship in Acts, detailing the ambivalence toward Paul that is a substantial part of his characterization and Barnabas's role as a reassuring presence for Paul and his mission.

Paul

Saul is initially presented in Acts as one of Judaism's most visible prosecutors and persecutors of the Jesus movement, an important leader of the opposition and a dangerous adversary to its members.[13] Indeed, in his first appearance young Saul is tending the garments of Stephen's executioners (7:58), a meek expression of his apparently wholehearted endorsement of the action taken against the deacon. Saul's reticence quickly gives way to active aggression against the Jerusalem church, however, and adherents of the Jesus movement are forced to flee the city or face the possibility of being unceremoniously hauled from their homes to prison (8:1–3). Saul's zealotry escalates as his activities become murderous, and, not satisfied with eliminating the church in Jerusalem, he seeks the high priest's permission to expand his jurisdiction beyond that city to Damascus (9:1–2).

The narrative surrounds Saul's introduction with the stories of two characters, Stephen and Philip, whose conduct stands in stark contrast to his. The narrative about Stephen precedes and leads to Paul's entrance (6:8–7:60). He is singled out among the seven men chosen to be deacons as "a man full of faith and the Holy Spirit" (6:5), described as "full of grace and power" (6:8), and compared to Moses (7:36), Jesus (2:22), and the apostles (2:43; 5:12) as someone who "performed great wonders and signs among the people" (6:8).[14] He boldly and creatively defends himself at trial before the Jerusalem Sanhedrin against charges that, by proclaiming that Jesus would destroy the temple and change the law, he profaned these hallowed Jewish institutions (6:11, 13–14; 7:1–53). Then, in the midst of being stoned, he offers with his dying breath prayers for the forgiveness of his opponents and executioners (7:60). In contrast, Saul silently and submissively holds the cloaks of those stoning Stephen. The difference between the two characters is ironically illustrated in the narrator's observation that, at the same time

---

12. Acts 11:30; 12:25; 13:1, 2, 7, 43, 46, 50; 14:12, 14; 15:2 (twice), 12, 22, 25, 35, 36, 37–38, 39–40.

13. It was not uncommon in the first century for Jews to have two names, one Hebrew and the other Roman. From his introduction in 7:58 until his apostolic commissioning in Antioch (13:1–3), Paul is referred to by his Hebrew name (Saul); thereafter he is exclusively called "Paul."

14. Gaventa, *Acts of the Apostles*, 117.

that Paul is harassing church members in Jerusalem, "devout men" bury Stephen and mourn for him (8:2–3).

Following Saul's brief debut, the narrative focus shifts to Philip, also one of the seven characterized as "full of the Spirit and wisdom" (6:3).[15] Sandwiched between accounts about Saul, Philip's story (8:4–40) sets his career as missionary and evangelist over against Saul's "campaign of violence."[16] Saul's persecution, in fact, is the provocation that motivates Philip's move to Samaria, as he is among those forced to leave Jerusalem because of Saul's attacks on the city's church (8:3–4). Ironically, Saul's attempt to eliminate the nascent Jesus movement is exactly the catalyst for its expansion. Still, the framing of the Philip narrative by accounts of Saul's vicious persecution (8:1–3; 9:1–2) hints at the danger Philip's ministry also faces because of Saul's crusade against the Jesus movement.[17] Unlike Saul, Philip persuades the Samaritans of the truth of his proclamation by the power of his preaching, exorcisms, and healings, not through the coercion of the sword. In addition, he is unwavering in his obedience to the Lord. When the Lord's messenger instructs him to walk a desert road in the middle of the day in the story of the Ethiopian eunuch, a time of day when no one would travel under ordinary circumstances, Philip immediately complies (8:26–40).[18]

Acts introduces Paul, therefore, as the antithesis of the Jesus movement's first martyr (Stephen) and first missionary (Philip). In contrast to the model characters on either side of Paul's first appearance, the narrative characterizes Saul as having such loathing for the fledgling offspring of Judaism that he quickly advances from disdainful bystander to dangerous opponent, actively pursuing extermination of the movement as well as swift and harsh punishment for its adherents. Saul's attitude is reversed, however, when he encounters Jesus on the road to Damascus (9:3–8). The

---

15. Introducing major characters into the narrative as bit players in brief opening appearances is not unusual in Acts. Stephen, Philip, Barnabas, and Paul all enter the story in this fashion (6:5; 7:58). A number of commentators have noted this narrative practice; see, e.g., Luke T. Johnson, *The Literary Function of Possessions in Luke-Acts* (SBLDS 39; Missoula, Mont.: Scholars Press, 1977), 24 n.1; Tannehill, *Narrative Unity of Luke-Acts*, 2:78, 99; Julius Wellhausen, *Kritische Analyse der Apostelgeschichte* (Berlin: Weidmann, 1914), 9, 14; Wilfrid L. Hannam, "The Man Who Saw the Grace of God: A Study of Barnabas," *Religion in Life* 5 (1936): 417–18, 419.

16. F. Scott Spencer, *The Portrait of Philip in Acts: A Study of Roles and Relations* (JSNTSup 67; Sheffield: JSOT Press, 1992), 246.

17. Ibid.

18. Literally, the Greek κατὰ μεσημβρίαν is a temporal phrase ("at midday"), but in some contexts it may have a geographically directional sense ("toward the south"). Some commentators argue that the latter ("southward") is the proper nuance here because folks did not travel at noon. That is precisely the reason, in my view, for taking it literally. See W. C. van Unnik, "Der Befehl an Philippus," *ZNW* 47 (1956): 181–91; Barrett, *Acts of the Apostles*, 1:422–33; Gaventa, *From Darkness to Light*, 101–2; Luke Timothy Johnson, *The Acts of the Apostles* (SP 5; Collegeville, Minn.: Liturgical Press, 1992), 154; Haenchen, *Acts of the Apostles*, 310.

experience transforms him from the Jesus movement's worst nightmare, an enemy with a badge, into one of its most unwavering advocates.[19] Unfortunately, Saul cannot rehabilitate his reputation as quickly. When he proceeds to the synagogues of Damascus after his encounter on the road, determined now to preach Jesus instead of incarcerating Christ's followers, disciples and synagogue audiences ask with understandable astonishment whether this is not the same individual who tried to annihilate the church in Jerusalem and traveled to Damascus expressly to arrest and extradite members of the Jesus movement (9:20–21). Indeed, as mentioned, Ananias even raises the issue of Saul's selection with the Lord himself! Further, Jews in Damascus fiercely reject their former champion and his new message, forging a plot to assassinate Paul that forces him to scurry back to Jerusalem under the cover of night (9:20–25).

Upon arriving in Jerusalem, Paul is again greeted with skepticism (9:26–30). The Jesus movement community there doubts his sincerity and requires assurances from Barnabas before allowing him into their midst. Jews who are not part of the movement react in a fashion reminiscent of Damascus. After first arguing with Saul, they concoct a scheme to kill him that, when discovered, leads to his prompt departure from the city.[20] It is fair to say that at this point in the narrative both the Jesus movement community and Jews not associated with the movement are distrustful of God's appointed messenger. Is it any wonder? He has persecuted one group and betrayed the other. Credibility problems haunt Paul for the remainder of the Acts narrative. At his next appearance in the story, for example, when Barnabas fetches him from Tarsus to assist with the church's work in Antioch (11:25–26), the narrator reminds readers that the gospel was originally preached in Antioch by those forced to emigrate from Jerusalem as a result of the persecution after Stephen's speech (11:19–21). The narrator does not need to add that Saul led that persecution.

The narrative presents the ambivalence toward Paul in other ways as well. After Jews successfully drive him out of Damascus and Jerusalem, the summary in 9:31 announces, "Then the church throughout Judea, Galilee, and Samaria was at peace and so was built up and . . . grew." Credit for the success of the gospel in the regions of Palestine, therefore, does not go to Paul. Indeed, his attempts at proclaiming Jesus cause division and disruption. Once his adversaries remove him from the scene, however, the church grows exponentially. Likewise, in Antioch Barnabas and those who fled Jerusalem to escape Saul's prosecutorial actions are responsible for the

---

19. See appendix A for observations on whether Paul's experience is properly considered "conversion."

20. The text refers to these Jews as "Hellenists." For clarification of this designation, see appendix A.

church's development (11:19–26, esp. 11:21, 24). Barnabas does not seek Saul's assistance until the community has expanded beyond their ability to manage its teaching needs (11:26; cf. 13:1).

Neither is Paul the apostle credited with opening the doors of the new movement to Gentiles. Immediately after his withdrawal to Tarsus in 9:30, the narrator tells the story of God directing Peter to bring the gospel to Gentiles in Cornelius's home at Caesarea and to redraw the community's boundaries to include these outsiders (10:1–48). Later, Paul receives significantly more criticism than Peter for accepting Gentiles into the movement without circumcision. Once Peter explains the circumstances, his detractors immediately cease their criticism, conceding that it was at God's initiative that uncircumcised Gentiles were admitted into the community (11:1–18). In contrast, Paul and Barnabas become embroiled in a bitter debate with circumcision proponents and are compelled to take the matter before the authorities in Jerusalem for adjudication (15:1–15). Based in no small measure on Peter's support at the hearing, James decides that circumcision will not be required of Gentiles. He and the council do impose certain purity regulations on them, however, something not demanded of Peter in his work among Gentiles.

Paul's reception on his return visit to Jerusalem further demonstrates the shallowness of support for him in Acts (21:15–23:30). Non–Jesus movement Jews are not the first group said to have concerns about him. Rather, James and the elders inform Paul of thousands of Jewish members of the Jesus movement in Jerusalem who, judging from the leadership's suggestion that the apostle attempt to convince them otherwise, are prepared to believe rumors that he does not observe Jewish customs and instructs others not to observe them as well (21:20–24). Members of the Jesus movement are apparently willing to accept without question the word of other Jews against one of their own, someone recognized as a leader in the movement, according to Tertullus, who at Paul's trial before Felix calls him one of the sect's ringleaders (24:5). Non–Jesus movement Jews in Jerusalem are not neutral toward Paul either. They murderously attack him over accusations made by certain Diaspora Jews while he is in the midst of a week-long purification ritual undertaken to demonstrate his loyalty to Jewish customs (21:26–31). When that attempt fails and the Jerusalem Sanhedrin is unable to reach consensus against him (22:30–23:10), the nonmovement Jewish majority in Jerusalem recruits assassins from within its ranks to complete the job (23:12–15).

Paul fares no better when he begins to minister to Gentiles. For example, he and Barnabas at first experience considerable success among the Gentiles of Pisidian Antioch (13:46–49). For their part, the Gentiles are overjoyed at the prospect of becoming the focus of the apostles' mission, and many in Antioch and the surrounding region are converted. Nonetheless, Jewish opposition is able to turn the city's Gentile leaders against Paul and Barnabas, forcing them to abandon their efforts there. Subsequently, Jews in Iconium instill sufficient doubt about the missionaries in the minds of Iconium's Gentile population to divide them over the issue and to persuade those antagonistic to the apostles to join Jews in their attempt to stone them (14:1–6). Fleeing to Lystra, Paul and Barnabas are hailed as gods after Paul heals a disabled man and, despite their strenuous protestations, have difficulty dissuading the Lystrans from offering sacrifices to them. In spite of this, Jews who are not residents of the city still are able to obtain permission from the citizens of Lystra to execute Paul (14:6–19). Lastly, the Gentiles of Philippi, persuaded by certain slaveholders that Paul is encouraging the adoption of illegal Jewish customs, beat and incarcerate him (16:19–24). It epitomizes the response to Paul in Acts that he is beaten and imprisoned by Gentiles in Philippi as a Jew advocating that Gentiles adhere to Jewish customs (16:19–24), then beaten and imprisoned by Jews in Jerusalem for advocating that Diaspora Jews not follow the identical regulations (21:27–32).

Beyond the resistance that Paul encounters from all sides, in Acts he is never able to garner sufficient backing among his supporters to withstand opposing forces. In Damascus, all his disciples can do to keep him out of the clutches of Jews offended by him is to engineer a harrowing midnight escape (9:23–25). The Jerusalem church does little better in standing up to his attackers and so ships him off to Tarsus to protect him (9:30). The pattern repeats itself time and again. He is forced out of Pisidian Antioch, Iconium, and Lystra without so much as a word being uttered on his behalf from any among the increasing numbers who accept the gospel. No one offers assistance or resistance when he is beaten and imprisoned in Philippi or when, after apologizing for their treatment of him, officials request that he leave town (16:19–40). The Jesus movement community in Thessalonica must conceal him until darkness can provide the cover necessary for his safe removal to Beroea (17:1–10), where his supporters can only elude the uproar caused by Jews who follow him from Thessalonica by sending him to Athens (17:13–15). The churches in Corinth and Ephesus respond to opposition against Paul with silence (18:5–17), and not one of the thousands of the "Jerusalem believers" (21:20) nor any of their leaders lifts a finger to assist him when he encounters trouble. Rescue in this instance arrives from two unlikely sources: the timely intervention of the Roman commander in Jerusalem (21:31–32); and the willingness of Paul's nephew to report the plot against Paul's life to the commander (23:16–22). The question arises: Where are Paul's defenders? Where are his advocates? One might understand how James and Peter could fall victim to Herod's wrath without defenders stepping forward (12:1–5)—he is, after all, the ruler—but Paul's opponents are usually not the politically powerful. Paul's supporters are unwilling or unable to take up his cause against marginal groups, specifically Jews living in regions with Gentile majorities, sometimes Jews who are not even local residents, and "working-class" Gentiles.

Barnabas

Barnabas is the one named character in the narrative who does defend Paul with words as well as actions. "Named" is an important qualifier because, as the next chapter will argue, the anonymous narrator character replaces Barnabas in this role. The function of these characters is to legitimate Paul's transformation and call, to highlight his cooperation with God's plan, and to reassure characters and readers that his mission will be successful in the face of obstacles that he confronts. The ability of these characters to fulfill this role successfully is dependent on their reliability, and Barnabas's trustworthiness is established at his introduction into the narrative in Acts 4:36–37.

The brevity of Barnabas's initial appearance is another example of the technique used to introduce Paul, Stephen, and Philip, but his introduction still discloses significant and vital character traits.[21] First, he has ties both to Jews and Gentiles, groups equally resistant to Paul. On one hand, his description as a Levite gives him unimpeachable Jewish credentials.[22] By the first century C.E. Levites represented a minor class of clerics within Judaism, composed in theory of males from the tribe of Levi who were not direct descendants of Aaron (priests) or Zadok (high priests). They assisted the priests in their temple duties, performing such tasks as helping worshipers with their sacrificial animals, carrying firewood, guarding the temple gate, providing singing and instrumental music, and staffing the temple police force.[23] On the other hand, Barnabas is also said to be of Cyprian nationality, a region native to Gentiles that Acts paints as something of a hotbed of activity for the Jesus movement. Besides Barnabas, the first missionaries to Antioch (11:20) and the disciple Mnason, who provides lodging for Paul in or on his way to Jerusalem (21:16), also hail from the eastern Mediterranean island. In addition, the narrative singles Cyprus out several times for mention as mission territory; for example, it is noted as one of the places evangelized by Jesus movement members expelled from Jerusalem (11:19), as the first stop on Barnabas and Saul's mission journey (13:4–12), and as

---

21. See n. 15.

22. Wayne Meeks and Robert Wilken, *Jews and Christians in Antioch in the First Four Centuries of the Common Era* (SBLSBS 13; Missoula, Mont.: Scholars Press, 1978), 14.

23. Joachim Jeremias, *Jerusalem in the Time of Jesus: An Investigation into Economic and Social Conditions during the New Testament Period* (trans. F. H. and C. H. Cave; Philadelphia: Fortress, 1969), 207–21; E. P. Sanders, *Judaism: Practice and Belief, 63 BCE to 66 CE* (London: SCM, 1992), 77–101.

Barnabas's initial destination with John Mark after separating from Paul (15:39). With roots in both the Jewish and Gentile communities, Barnabas has no axe to grind for or against either group. For that reason, he is able to become the ideal diplomat in Acts, representing at various times Saul before the apostles, the Jerusalem Jesus movement community at Antioch, the Antioch church at Jerusalem, and, of course, the Jesus movement to Jews and Gentiles in Cyprus and Asia Minor.

Barnabas belongs to Jerusalem's burgeoning Jesus movement community, which, by the time readers meet him, has expanded from a handful (1:13–14) to over five thousand members (4:4; see also 1:15; 2:41). He enjoys a close personal relationship with the Jerusalem apostles, the leaders of the church. They are so familiar, in fact, that the apostles nickname him "Barnabas" (his name is actually Joseph). The appellation is one of admiration. The Greek translation offered for the name "Barnabas," "son of encouragement" or "son of consolation,"[24] while inaccurate, nonetheless is an apt description of Joseph's personal qualities as a member of the Jesus movement community and his vocational attributes as a missionary.[25] Barnabas's character is further manifested in the matter of his donation (4:37). He exemplifies the ideal community member, one who delivers the entire proceeds from the sale of property to the apostles. Questions have been raised concerning the plausibility of Barnabas's character possessing property, since a number of biblical texts report that Levites were prohibited from owning land (Num 18:20–21; Deut 10:9; 12:12; 14:29; Josh 14:3–4). Several commentators have proposed, however, that historically the ban was a "dead letter" early on: the law existed but was never fully implemented or enforced.[26] Indeed, Josh 21:1–41 records cities and lands that were dis-

---

24. The word παράκλησις can mean encouragement, consolation, or appeal. Many commentators prefer "encouragement," in large measure because it seems to coincide with Barnabas's call for the Antiochenes to remain resolutely faithful (11:23). There is no need to resolve the ambiguity, however, since Barnabas's activities in Acts encompass the range of available meanings for the term. See Barrett, *Acts of the Apostles*, 1:258–59; Bruce, *Acts of the Apostles*, 160; Kirsopp Lake and Henry J. Cadbury, eds., *English Translation and Commentary* (vol. 4 of *The Beginnings of Christianity, Part 1: The Acts of the Apostles*; London: Macmillan, 1933), 49.

25. The etymology of "Barnabas" widely regarded as the most plausible is that proposed by Adolf Deismann (*Bible Studies: Contributions Chiefly from Papyri and Inscriptions to the History of the Language, the Literature, and the Religion of Hellenistic Judaism and Primitive Christianity* [Edinburgh: T&T Clark, 1901], 187–88, 307–10), namely, that it originated as Bar-Nebo (ברנבו, "son of Nebo," the Babylonian god), attested in Palmyrene inscriptions, and that it was later grecized; see also Henry J Cadbury, "Some Semitic Personal Names in Luke-Acts," in *Amicitiae Corolla* (ed. H. G. Wood; London: University of London Press, 1933), 47–48.

26. I. Howard Marshall, *Acts of the Apostles*, 110; William S. LaSor, *Great Personalities of the New Testament: Their Lives and Times* (Westwood, N.J.: Revell, 1961), 119.

tributed to the Levite tribe as part of the Jewish settlement in Canaan.[27] Whether the regulation was originally enforced or not, by the time Acts was written in the first century C.E., the law had apparently been relaxed. Josephus, himself a priest, admits to owning property (*Life* 422), and it is likely that other wealthy Levites did as well.[28]

Some scholars argue that the naming of Barnabas by the apostles and his delivery to them of proceeds from the sale of his land, specifically that he placed the money "at the feet of the apostles" (4:37), signify their authority and control over him more than his trustworthiness and the apostles' regard for him.[29] To the degree that the act of naming in the Bible has any bearing on the one named, however, more often than not it conveys not dominion and control but recognition on the part of the one giving the name of the qualities possessed by the named that have already been or will be displayed in the narrative.[30] The renaming of Peter by Jesus in Luke 6:14, often cited as confirmation of the domination theory, is a good example. If the naming of Peter is a sign of Jesus' power over him, why are the other apostles—who are also listed in Luke 6:14–16—not treated similarly? Are they under Jesus' authority to any lesser degree? Not at all. Rather, the naming of Peter reflects the depth of Jesus' feeling for him as well as his singular qualities and special role in Luke's story. Likewise, the naming of the Barnabas character in Acts 4:36 indicates his deep bond with the apostles and his unique personal qualities, and it foreshadows his activities in the upcoming story.

The argument that the act of laying something at someone's feet, here Barnabas's possessions at the apostles' feet, is an acknowledgement of authority is similarly problematic. Ananias and Sapphira are also said to have deposited proceeds "at the apostles' feet" (5:2), but that story concerns the couple's *refusal* to submit to the community's authority. Indeed, there is considerable doubt that the death penalty they receive as a consequence of their actions is at Peter's initiative and thus in any sense representative of apostolic authority over them. C. K. Barrett, for example, argues that "Peter is not actually said to have caused, or even to have willed, the two deaths. . . . [I]n fact he foretells [Sapphira's] death, but foretelling is not willing, and with Ananias he did not go even so far."[31] Moreover, whatever control might be symbolized by the phrase "at the feet" would apply to

---

27. Johnson, *Acts of the Apostles*, 87.

28. Jeremias, *Jerusalem in the Time of Jesus*, 105; Sanders, *Judaism*, 77; Johnson, *Acts of the Apostles*, 87.

29. See, e.g., Johnson, *Acts of the Apostles*, 87, 91, 174, 209; idem, *Literary Function of Possessions*, 204.

30. George Ramsey, "Is Name-Giving an Act of Domination in Genesis 2:23 and Elsewhere?" *CBQ* 50 (1988): 30–35; Phyllis Trible, *God and the Rhetoric of Sexuality* (OBT; Philadelphia: Fortress, 1978), esp. 99–100.

31. Barrett, *Acts of the Apostles*, 1:262; see also Johnson, *Acts of the Apostles*, 92.

that which is actually at the feet, not to the one who places it there. Luke T. Johnson, who argues for domination, concedes as much in his statement that "the consistent reality symbolized by *being at the feet of another* is submission; conversely, *to have another at one's feet* symbolizes authority, dominion."[32] When Stephen's executioners place their garments "at the feet" of Saul in 7:58, for instance, there is no hint of him having power over them. If anything, when they delegate to young Saul the task of safeguarding their belongings while they attend to Stephen, he is under their authority. On the other hand, Paul acknowledges Gamaliel's authority as his teacher when he speaks of his education "at the feet of Gamaliel" (22:3). When the narrative refers to possessions being placed at the feet of the apostles in 4:35 and 37, therefore, it is signaling that responsibility of the apostles for the welfare of the community involves concretely their control of the collection and distribution of funds for the church's benefit. Their sovereignty is exercised over the assets that Barnabas and other church members voluntarily relinquish to them, not over the members themselves.

Just as Paul's image is sharpened by the Stephen and Philip narratives that surround his entrance into Acts, the narrative context of Barnabas's introduction deepens the picture of his honesty, cooperation, and obedience. The account of Ananias and Sapphira withholding part of the proceeds from their property sale and then lying to Peter about it (5:1–11) immediately follows Barnabas's initial appearance. His character is presented as the antithesis of this uncooperative and deceitful couple, that is, as a community member who is completely without guile. It is inconceivable that Barnabas would hold back proceeds or lie to the apostles, and, just as Peter knows of the couple's conspiracy of fraud and deceit without ever asking (his questioning of Sapphira in 5:8 is simply to confirm her collusion in the affair), it is unnecessary for the apostles to audit Barnabas's contribution. The contrast between the couple and Barnabas is underscored in dramatic fashion when Ananias and Sapphira pay the ultimate price for their misdeed.

The narrative demonstrates the Jerusalem church's esteem for Barnabas in the account of his appointment as its emissary to the Jesus movement community at Antioch (11:22). Barnabas's selection for this task mirrors the Jerusalem community's delegation of Peter to minister in Samaria (8:14–25), a comparison that confirms Barnabas's standing within the Jerusalem community (the significant difference between the two delegates is that Barnabas is not responsible for the reception of the Holy Spirit by the Antiochenes; cf. 8:14–17; 11:22–24).[33] There is no discussion about whom to send to Antioch. Neither does anyone question Barnabas's handling of the situation

---

32. Johnson, *Literary Function of Possessions,* 201 (emphases added).

33. Lake and Cadbury, *English Translation and Commentary,* 129; Kirsopp Lake, "The Twelve and the Apostles," in *Additional Notes to the Commentary* (ed. Kirsopp Lake and

upon his arrival there because he is "a good man" who, like the exemplary Stephen, is "full of the Holy Spirit and faith" (11:24; cf. 6:5).[34] In fact, Barnabas is the only character in the Lukan corpus besides Joseph of Arimathea in Luke 23:50–51 who is described as "good" (ἀγαθός).[35] Barnabas's activities in Antioch and the acceptance of his leadership by its Jesus movement community confirm his estimable character and testify that the admiration of his intimates in Jerusalem is well-founded. He demonstrates exceptional insight when he arrives by recognizing and approving as God's work the efforts of the original missionaries (11:23). Shortly thereafter he assumes the principal leadership role in the Antioch church and major responsibility for the gospel's success among the city's population (11:23–26). His ascendancy at Antioch is confirmed by his nomination (with Saul) to deliver famine relief to the Jerusalem community (11:27–30) and by the primacy his name receives on the list of the city's prophets and teachers in 13:1. What is more, leadership of the Jesus movement community in Antioch would not be an insignificant matter, given the city's standing. As Wayne A. Meeks and Robert L. Wilken explain, Antioch was "one of the three or four most important cities in the Roman Empire . . . [a key] administrative and commercial center" in Palestine, close to Jerusalem, a convenient stopover for travelers between Palestine and Asia Minor, and "one of the principal centers of Christianity."[36]

To summarize, Barnabas's character embodies the model community member described in Acts (2:44–45; 4:32–35). He is entirely responsible and absolutely reliable. Unwavering in his commitment to the community and the welfare of Jesus movement members, he willingly acquiesces to the expectations of the movement's leadership by gifting the entirety of his resources without hesitation or equivocation and, in return, is respected—indeed beloved—by them. As James D. G. Dunn has noted, "The warmth of the testimony on Barnabas' behalf . . . is unusual even in Acts and surely indicates a man of rare quality, a community builder, able to promote and sustain warm and constructive personal relations."[37]

Barnabas as Paul's Companion

In the Acts narrative, Barnabas's unassailable character and credibility are enlisted in support of Paul from the inception of Paul's apostleship. In fact, only Barnabas's intervention enables Saul's ministry to gain any mo-

---

Henry J. Cadbury; vol. 5 of *The Beginnings of Christianity, Part 1: The Acts of the Apostles*; London: Macmillan, 1933), 54, 58.

34. See Tannehill, *Narrative Unity of Luke-Acts*, 2:147 n. 3.

35. Barrett, *Acts of the Apostles*, 1:553; see also Johnson, *Acts of the Apostles*, 204.

36. Meeks and Wilken, *Jews and Christians in Antioch*, 1.

37. Dunn, *Acts of the Apostles*, 60.

mentum at all. When Saul's past threatens his application for admittance to Jerusalem's Jesus movement community, Barnabas uses his influence to gain a hearing for Saul before the apostles (9:26–27). Accompanying him to the inquiry and acting as his advocate, Barnabas presents the credentials of the former prosecutor to the movement's leaders and convinces them to accept him. The efficacy of Barnabas's reliability is on full display in this narrative. His report of Saul's Damascus road experience and subsequent bold proclamation of Jesus as the Christ in the synagogues of Damascus in the face of dangerous opposition corresponds exactly with the narrative's earlier account that Saul abandoned his original program of persecution after encountering Jesus and escaped the murderous wrath of the Jews in Damascus only through the ingenuity of Jesus movement members who had become his disciples (9:19b–25). Significantly, Barnabas is able to corroborate the story of Saul's transforming experience and subsequent gospel activity to the apostles' satisfaction, even though Barnabas was not himself present for any of the events he describes. The results speak to Barnabas's clout with the apostles and the wider community. Not only is Saul enrolled in the Jerusalem church; he is allowed to preach (9:28).

Later Barnabas restarts Paul's career by retrieving him from Tarsus—where Paul had disappeared from the narrative after fleeing the assassination attempt in Jerusalem (9:29–30; 11:25)—to assist in Antioch because of the spectacular growth of its Jesus movement community (11:19–26). From that point forward, the narrative portrays Barnabas and Paul as inseparable until their quarrel over John Mark prior to the second missionary journey (15:36–40). Once Paul returns with Barnabas to Antioch, his stature within the movement begins to increase, as illustrated by the fact that he is trusted to accompany Barnabas in the delivery of the relief collection to Jerusalem (11:29–30).

After Paul and Barnabas return to Antioch from Jerusalem, the Holy Spirit calls them for the initial missionary enterprise in Cyprus and Asia Minor (13:1–4). This may seem a natural extension of their previous work and association, but in fact the task that follows is distinct from what has preceded. First, the Spirit's intervention marks the initial instance of explicit divine missionary instructions in Paul's ministry. Second, from this point forward Paul's work is distinguished by its missionary quality; that is, journeying to foreign locations and peoples to preach the gospel. Third, Paul assumes the prominent missionary role, and Barnabas evolves into his partner in ministry, constant companion, and witness. The narrative indicates this new stage by referring to Paul from this point forward as "Paul" instead of "Saul." The change in Paul's ministry and role becomes evident in the story of their experience at Cyprus, the first station on their mission journey (13:5–12). The narrative chronicles that Paul performs his first miracle (the temporary blinding of Bar-Jesus in 13:11) and gains his first named con-

vert (the proconsul, Sergius Paulus, in 13:12) on the island. It makes clear
that Barnabas is present through references to him by name and the use of
third-person plural grammatical style (which in this passage includes John
as well; 13:5); however, Barnabas plays no active narrative role in the events
that transpire there. At their next stopover, Antioch of Pisidia, the narrative
records that both Paul and Barnabas attend synagogue on the Sabbath but
that, when invited to speak, Paul is the one who responds with a lengthy
discourse (13:13–41). At Lystra, Paul again preaches, although the narrative
does not report what he says, and heals a man who from birth had been
unable to walk (14:8–11). Paul is the one who is stoned and left for dead
outside that city and who miraculously recovers to continue his journey
with Barnabas (14:19–20).

The mission narrative, therefore, begins with an account of God send-
Although he no longer exercises the leadership role, Barnabas is still
portrayed as an active partner in the mission. After Paul's synagogue speech
at Pisidian Antioch, Barnabas also talks to Jews and proselytes who follow
them from the synagogue service (13:43), and, although the Jews specifically
dispute what Paul says and vilify him personally, both Paul and Barnabas
boldly confront their adversaries (13:45–47). In Iconium, the narrative de-
picts Paul and Barnabas as co-workers in the successful evangelization of
Jews and Gentiles through preaching and miracles (14:1–3), and both risk
stoning from the opposition (14:5–7). At Lystra, the crowds who witness
Paul's healing of the disabled man consider Paul and Barnabas both to be
gods, and the two of them work together to disabuse the group of that mis-
taken notion (14:11–18). Lastly, when the two missionaries revisit each city
on their return trip to Antioch, both are responsible for appointing elders
in the communities and for appealing to the new disciples in each locale to
remain faithful despite adversity (14:21–26).

The mission narrative, therefore, begins with an account of God sending Paul and Barnabas to preach the gospel in Cyprus and Asia Minor, a
calling to which they respond affirmatively. Nonetheless, once they embark
on their mission, it immediately becomes evident that Paul's work is the
focus of the narrative. Paul is the principal missionary, the primary preacher
and miracle worker. Acts 13:13 explicitly references his leadership position
when it mentions him as the center of the group.[38] Barnabas plays an important role in the mission, however, a role that is subtly represented by
the order of their names.[39] Before the missionary journey, when Barnabas's

---

38. Barrett, *Acts of the Apostles*, 1:626.
39. Variation in the order of the names of Paul and Barnabas is more complex than the
argument that the reversal of order from Barnabas and Paul (Saul) to Paul and Barnabas signals
the moment at which Paul assumes leadership; see, e.g., F. F. Bruce, *Acts of the Apostles*, 338;
Lake and Cadbury, *English Translation and Commentary*, 175. Neither is it the case, however,
that there is no explanation for the differences in the sequence; see, e.g., Richard Bauckham,
"Barnabas in Galatians," *JSNT* 2 (1979): 62.

and Paul's (or Saul's) names are mentioned together, Barnabas's name is listed first (11:30; 12:25; 13:1, 2). This order makes sense, since in Antioch Barnabas is the recognized leader of the Jesus movement. Indeed, the letter that the Jerusalem leaders send with Barnabas and Paul to the church at Antioch following the Jerusalem council acknowledges Barnabas's seniority in that city by naming him first (15:25). Once they leave Antioch for Cyprus and Asia Minor, however, the order of their names alternates based on the focus of the narrative. When Paul's activities are the center of attention, Barnabas's name appears first, lifting up his presence with Paul, but as an observer and witness not an actor in the scene (13:7; 14:12). When the narrative concerns the joint endeavors of the missionaries, Paul's name is listed first, indicating his leadership role in the mission journey and tasks (13:43, 46, 50).[40] Consistent with this scheme but also an indication of the shift that has occurred in their narrative roles since departing from Antioch, Paul's name continues to lead as he and Barnabas resume their ministry together in that city (15:2, 22, 35).[41]

Barnabas's role, then, has become secondary to but, because of the undercurrent in the narrative fueled by ambivalence toward Paul's character, significant for Paul's portrayal. As Paul's partner and companion and as someone with impeccable credentials, the character of Barnabas allays the anxiety of other characters and of readers about Paul's background and reputation and their effect on his work. In addition, his presence highlights Paul's cooperation with the plan of God and provides assurance that the constant opposition to Paul—even fierce hostility, such as being stoned and left for dead—will not interfere with the completion of his mission duties. Paul and Barnabas terminate their partnership before the start of the second missionary journey in Acts 15, however, and after the two missionaries separate, another character, the narrator, replaces Barnabas as Paul's companion. Chapter 4 will probe the narrator character's assumption of the role previously played by Barnabas.

---

40. An exception occurs in 14:14, where Barnabas's name is listed first even though both he and Paul are actors in the scene. One reason for the order might be that this narrative concerns consequences of Paul's miracle in 14:8–10.

41. Again, the listing of Barnabas's name first in 15:12 appears to be an exception, but he may be given priority because they are speaking as delegates from the church in Antioch.

4

The "We" Character

*[W]hat is really interesting is not the schema of convention but
what is done in each individual application of the schema to give
it a sudden tilt of innovation or even to refashion it radically for
the imaginative purposes at hand.*

—Robert Alter

Barnabas and Paul's partnership dissolves when they quarrel over John
Mark's involvement in the new mission journey (15:36–39). As Barnabas
sails off to Cyprus with Mark in 15:39, he sails out of the Acts narrative.
Shortly thereafter narration shifts from third to first plural grammatical person in several event-level passages as the narrator character steps in front
of the camera to replace Barnabas as the reliable presence in Paul's missionary activities. The "we" narrator's role parallels that of Barnabas in several
ways. First, the credentials of the "we" character are established at his introduction into the narrative. Second, divine demands upon Paul precede and
signal the narrator's appearance as Paul's companion. Third, the narrator
escapes the various punishments inflicted on the apostle while they are together. Fourth, the narrator summons his own presence at pivotal points in
the story to highlight and corroborate Paul's cooperation with God's plan
and to provide assurance that the apostle will overcome all the challenges
encountered to complete his mission tasks.

In Acts as in the ancient texts analyzed in chapter 2, the effect of first-
person plural grammatical style at the event level is to cast the narrator
character as an eyewitness and, in so doing, to emphasize his narrative authority and his version of the story. Again, this is a narrative claim, not a
historical one, a distinction sharpened by the distance that the anonymous
authorship of Acts establishes between the narrator and the actual author.
On the other hand, first person plural qualifies the narrator's involvement by
characterizing him as part of a broader eyewitness group, explicitly (when
there are additional discernible referents) or implicitly (when the pronoun

refers to the narrator character individually). This lessens the focus on the narrator's personal word by simultaneously projecting a sense of corroboration for his account. In addition, first person plural draws readers into the story by conveying a sense of familiarity and shared purpose. Readers experience a connection to the "we" group, perhaps even feel part of it, which encourages a sympathetic disposition toward the "we" narrator and thus acceptance of his perspective and story.

Introduction of the Narrator Character

Just as the introduction of Barnabas's character establishes his trustworthiness, the case for the narrator character's credibility is made at his initial appearance in the preface to the Third Gospel and reinforced in the Acts preface.[1] The analysis of ancient historical literature in chapter 2 determined that ancient narratives may employ the first person in prefaces and elsewhere to advance the personal involvement of author/narrators in events or in the research and critical assessment of sources. Use of narrators' own voices projects personal confidence in their knowledge of the stories, and that sense of narrative authority increases narrators' believability. At the same time, defense of their work boosts the personal credibility of narrators. The effect of the first person (singular and plural) in the Gospel and Acts prefaces, therefore, is to strengthen the narrator's assurance to Theophilus that he has investigated carefully from the beginning all the things fulfilled among them just as these matters were handed down by eyewitnesses and preachers and, therefore, that the narrative to follow will provide certainty concerning information his dedicatee has previously received (Luke 1:1–4). The Gospel preface boasts that the systematically presented account to follow is dependable because the narrator's inquiry has been diligent, so his information—whether obtained through research or personal association—is thorough and accurate. Loveday C. A. Alexander has demonstrated that in general the purpose of ancient prefaces was "to arouse readers' expectations and to give them certain clues, implicit or explicit, as to what is to come."[2] As she argues, however, Luke's prefaces are too vague about the content of the two volumes to stimulate readers in that regard.[3] The expectations raised by the prefaces in Luke and Acts focus on the reliability of the storyteller more than on the content of the story. The narrator's assurances create an atmosphere of trust in him and, because of his reliability, in the account he presents.

As in Thucydides, Polybius, and Josephus, there is a question concerning the referents of first person plural in the preface of Luke's Gospel. Alexan-

---

1. For explanation of the use of masculine pronouns of the narrator, see introduction, n. 2.
2. Alexander, *Preface to Luke's Gospel*, 200.
3. Ibid., 113, 201.

der and others distinguish the referents of "us" in Luke 1:1 ("the events that have come to fulfillment among us") and 1:2 ("handed down to us") because, in their view, the "phraseology of verses 1 and 2 clearly implies two groups of people, those among whom the events were 'accomplished' and those to whom the tradition was handed down."[4] These commentators judge that in Luke 1:1 the pronoun includes the narrator with all believers past and present (similar to Josephus), while in the next verse it refers either to the narrator and those who wrote before him or to the narrator and his generation of believers.[5] Other scholars, however, associate both instances of "us" with a single group but differ as to the group's identity. Cadbury, for example, argues that both first-person plural occurrences refer to Luke and his predecessors (the "many [who] endeavored to compile a narrative" in Luke 1:1) and differentiate between events to which they were eyewitnesses (1:1) and events they learned of secondhand (1:2).[6] Richard Dillon and Luke Timothy Johnson also argue for a single referent to "us" but regard the referent in both cases to be Luke's generation.[7] Still another assessment is that the referents of the first-person plural pronouns in the preface include only the author/narrator (traditionally named "Luke") and the dedicatee, Theophilus.[8] The analysis of first-person plural grammatical practice in Thucydides, Polybius, and Josephus has demonstrated that any of these proposals is possible. Indeed, it would not be unusual for the narrator to employ the first person plural to associate himself with different groups and to refer to himself individually in the same sentence. The context of the Gospel preface provides little guidance as to the makeup of its first-plural group. What is clear is that the utilization of first person singular and plural in the preface underscores the narrator's knowledge and, consequently, reliability: he is one of those among whom the events have been fulfilled, he is among those to whom the tradition has been handed down, and he has fully investigated the matters at hand.

My understanding of grammatical style in the Gospel preface assumes the applicability of the preface to both volumes of Luke's work, the Third Gospel and Acts, a premise that has come under increasing scrutiny.[9] Some

---

4. Ibid., 112.

5. Ibid.; Fitzmyer, *Gospel according to Luke*, 1:296.

6. Cadbury, "Knowledge Claimed in Luke's Preface," 411–17.

7. Richard Dillon, "Reviewing Luke's Project from his Prologue," *CBQ* 43 (1981): 214, 217; Luke Timothy Johnson, *The Gospel of Luke* (SP 3; Collegeville, Minn.: Liturgical Press, 1991), 27.

8. Paul Minear, "Dear Theo: The Kerygmatic Intention and Claim of the Book of Acts," *Int* 27 (1973): 134.

9. See, e.g., Parsons and Pervo, *Rethinking the Unity of Luke-Acts*, 45–83, esp. 60–65; Alexander, *Preface to Luke's Gospel*, 145–46; Haenchen, "'We' in Acts and the Itinerary," 95–99.

commentators who dispute Cadbury's thesis that Luke-Acts represents "a single continuous work" in two volumes, with Acts as "an integral part of the author's original plan and purpose," argue that the two books have separate narrators as well.[10] Mikeal Parsons and Richard Pervo, for example, scholars who question Cadbury's unity thesis, argue that the "we" group in the Gospel preface is distinct from the "we" in the first-person plural passages in Acts and, therefore, that the narrators of the two volumes are different as well.[11] But narrative unity as Cadbury proposed is not required for the narrator characters to be identical. Even if Acts were conceived after the completion of the Gospel, the opening verse clearly links it to the first volume—a sequel, if you will—and identifies the narrator as the same character: "In the first book, O Theophilus, I wrote about everything that Jesus began to do and teach" (Acts 1:1). In addition, Acts 1:1 opens the second volume as the Gospel preface had the first by declaring to Theophilus and other readers the reliability of the narrator and his narrative, again utilizing first-person grammatical style in this effort. The narrator of the two books is the same, therefore, and consequently so too must be the narrator referent of the first-person plural style in the "we" passages later in Acts.

First Appearance of the "We" Character (Acts 16:10–17)

Following the Gospel preface, first-person plural grammatical style does not reemerge until after Barnabas's final scene in Acts 15:39. As the two missionaries separate, the narrative portrays both as implementing Paul's suggestion in 15:36 that they revisit the places to which they had previously traveled together. Barnabas sets out along the original route with John Mark, while Paul takes Silas and heads the other direction, overland through Syria and Cilicia (15:39–41).[12] Just as the Holy Spirit commanded Paul and

---

10. For Cadbury's position, see *Making of Luke-Acts*, 8–9; idem, "Commentary on the Preface of Luke," 491; W. C. van Unnik, "Luke-Acts, A Storm Center in Contemporary Scholarship," in Keck and Martyn, *Studies in Luke-Acts*, 18.

11. Parsons and Pervo, *Rethinking the Unity of Luke-Acts*, 66. They are building on the argument of William Kurz ("Narrative Approaches to Luke-Acts," *Bib* 68 [1987]: 210; idem, *Reading Luke-Acts*, 42–44, 73–124) that the "we" groups do not correspond and that the first person is used differently in Acts than in the Gospel.

12. Outside of Antioch, the narrative makes only the barest allusion to Paul and Barnabas working together in Syria or Cilicia. Granted, the Syrian port of Seleucia is the first city mentioned on their missionary journey, but they quickly sail for Cyprus (13:4), and no other Syrian cities are numbered among the locales they visit. Likewise, the only time the narrative speaks of the two missionaries being in Cilicia is when Barnabas goes to Tarsus to bring Saul back to Antioch (11:25–26). On the other hand, the letter sent with Barnabas and Paul outlining the Jerusalem council's decision regarding regulations applicable to Gentiles in their churches is addressed "to the brothers and sisters from the Gentiles in Antioch and Syria and Cilicia" (15:23), hinting that these regions are to be numbered among the places in which they had previously ministered.

Barnabas to carry the mission to Asia Minor (15:2, 4), divine instructions that Paul receives to carry his mission activities to different locations precede each appearance of the "we" character. Before the first "we" passage, Paul receives a vision that he and the narrator conclude is from God, summoning him to Macedonia to proclaim the gospel there (16:9–10). Later, he resolves in the Spirit to go through Macedonia and Achaia to Jerusalem (19:21). Finally, the Lord instructs Paul that he must witness to the gospel in Rome (23:11). Each time, as Paul carries out his mission instructions the first person plural narrator character travels with him as Barnabas had, and, like Barnabas, the "we" character's presence highlights Paul's response, corroborates the account as only an eyewitness report can, and draws readers into the story as a vicarious part of the witnessing group.

It soon becomes apparent that God means for Paul's second mission to extend beyond the territories originally visited. First, the Spirit prevents Paul and his entourage from preaching in Asia or from entering into Bithynia, confining their operations to a corridor bordered on one side by Galatia, Bithynia, and the coastline of the Sea of Marmara and on the other side by Phrygia and Mysia (16:6–8).[13] Then, after the group arrives in Troas, Paul receives a vision during the night in which a Macedonian appeals for his assistance (16:9). At that moment the narrative shifts to first-person plural grammatical style as the "we" character confirms that the vision represents God's call for Paul (and the narrator) to proclaim the gospel in Macedonia (16:10). The text does not explain how the narrator character learns of the vision, leading an early manuscript witness to expand the text of 16:10 to provide an explanation: "When [Paul] awoke, he described the vision to us in detail, and we apprehended that the Lord had called us to preach the gospel to those in Macedonia."[14] The narrative continues in first-person plural style, with the narrator character describing their decision to sail for Philippi, the "foremost city of the district of Macedonia" (16:12), by the most direct route possible, namely, through the Macedonian port city of Neapolis by way of the northern Aegean island of Samothrace.[15] Paul and the "we" character arrive at their destination, a distance of some 160 miles,

---

13. The Spirit is identified as the Holy Spirit in 16:6 and the Spirit of Jesus in 16:7, but, as Haenchen (*Acts of the Apostles*, 484) argues, both references are to "the same divine power." Although this represents the singular occurrence in the New Testament of the expression "Spirit of Jesus," Gaventa (*Acts of the Apostles*, 234) points out that Paul's letters contain similar language, e.g., "Spirit of Jesus Christ" (Phil 1:19) and "Spirit of Christ" (Rom 8:9).

14. Frederick H. Scrivener, ed., *Bezae Codex Cantabrigiensis* (1864; repr., Pittsburgh: Pickwick, 1978), 386; see also Bruce M. Metzger, *A Textual Commentary on the Greek New Testament* (London: United Bible Societies, 1971), 443–44.

15. There is an alternative Greek reading of Acts 16:12 that some scholars prefer: "a city of the first district of Macedonia." For a clarification of Philippi's status in the first century C.E., see appendix A.

in two days (16:11–12). Although with favorable winds and barring any delay, covering the 150 mile distance from Troas to Neapolis that quickly would be possible, the speed with which the two missionaries reach Philippi indicates the dispatch with which they implement their divine instructions.[16] The arrival of Paul and his entourage at Philippi marks the beginning of the important mission to Greece that eventually includes not only a number of cities in Macedonia (Amphipolis, Apollonia, Thessalonica, and Beroea in addition to Neapolis and Philippi; 17:1–14), but also Athens, Corinth, and Cenchreae in Achaia (17:15–18:18).

The narrative reports the group's stay in Philippi through the eyes of the "we" character, recounting that during the time there the missionaries have an opportunity to speak with some women gathered for prayer, among them Lydia, a businesswoman and immigrant from the city of Thyatira in Asia, the province of Asia Minor in which, ironically, Paul was forbidden to speak (16:6, 12–15). Although the narrative says that "*we* began to speak to the assembled women" (16:13), Lydia is convinced by what *Paul* says and is baptized together with her entire household (16:14–15). Like Barnabas, the "we" character is not simply an observer but an integral part of Paul's missionary endeavors. Nonetheless, his missionary role is secondary to Paul's; his primary narrative function is as witness to Paul's work. The "we" character next tells how they are accosted by a slave girl with the gift of divination who follows them around shouting, "These people who are proclaiming a way of salvation to you are slaves of the Most High God" (16:17; note again that both Paul and the "we" character are included in her description). When Paul tires of the distraction and exorcises the slave's divining spirit, her masters, who have profited from her prophesying, become incensed over the ruinous effect the apostle's action will have on business and haul Paul and Silas before the authorities, who have them beaten with rods and jailed (16:18–24).

The opposition in Philippi is also similar to the pattern in the journey of Paul and Barnabas: the missionaries encounter resistance because of the effect of their preaching, which eventually leads to punishment for Paul. Although Barnabas is driven out of several places along with Paul (13:50; 14:5–6), when Paul is stoned at Lystra by the Jews who had come there from Antioch and Iconium, Barnabas is not harmed (14:19–20). Likewise, when Paul is beaten and jailed in Philippi, the "we" character retreats offstage as the narrative reverts to third-person style (16:18–40). Paul's narrative witnesses are not subjected to the incarcerations or beatings that the apostle

---

16. S. V. McCasland, "Travel and Communication in the NT," *IDB* 4:693; Edwin Yamauchi, "Troas," *ABD* 6:666.

endures. Paul, after all, is the one whom the Lord set apart to suffer for the sake of the gospel (9:16).[17]

The narrator's presence created through the first-person plural grammatical style strengthens the narrative claims in several ways. First, it reinforces the assertion that the expansion of Paul's mission from Asia Minor to Greece is mandated by God in a vision to the apostle. As Ernst Haenchen explains, "The fact that this decision is brought about by a vision given by God to Paul receives, so to speak, its documentation by means of 'we.'"[18] Second, it testifies that Paul obeys his divine instructions without question or hesitation, sailing to Macedonia immediately and tackling its most prominent city without reservation. Finally, it provides assurance that Paul's successes in Philippi and the adverse reaction of the slave girl's owners to Paul's exorcism are part of God's plan, consistent with what Jesus reveals to Ananias about Paul in Acts 9:15–16, that he will carry Christ's name to the Gentiles, but not without considerable personal suffering.

Second Appearance of the "We" Character (Acts 20:5–21:18)

The "we" character reemerges during Paul's succeeding journey from Antioch (18:23–21:16). The appearance of the "we" narrator is again preceded by a vision. Proceeding west through the Galatian and Phrygian regions of Asia Minor, Paul settles in Ephesus, the capital of Asia, the Roman province he was prevented from entering on his previous campaign (18:23; 19:1). After an interval of nearly three years in Ephesus—the narrative of Paul's ministry there reports that he lectured for three months in the synagogue followed by two years in the hall of Tyrannus (19:8–9)—Paul is said to have "resolved through the Spirit" to travel to Jerusalem as soon as he has visited Macedonia and Achaia (19:21). A number of Acts scholars interpret 19:21 as an idiom referring to Paul's mental activity rather than to the Holy Spirit; that is, Paul "made up his mind" or "resolved in his mind."[19] Reading the phrase idiomatically is problematic, however, considering the use of the Greek word for "spirit" (πνεῦμα) elsewhere in Acts and Luke.[20] Most occurrences of the term refer to the divine Spirit (Holy Spirit, God's Spirit, Spirit of the Lord, Spirit of Jesus, or simply Spirit). Sometimes it is used of other

---

17. Kurz, "Narrative Approaches to Luke-Acts," 219. Silas is Paul's disciple but is not in Acts portrayed as a witness in the mold of Barnabas and the "we" character and may, therefore, be subjected to the afflictions visited upon Paul.

18. Haenchen, " 'We' in Acts and the Itinerary," 85.

19. E.g., Barrett, Acts of the Apostles, 2:919; Fitzmyer, Acts of the Apostles, 652; see also BAGD, s.v. τίθημι II.1.c.; Louw and Nida 1.30.76; NAB; NEB; NIV; NJB).

20. Robert P. Menzies, The Development of Early Christian Pneumatology with Special Reference to Luke-Acts (JSNTSup 54; Sheffield: Sheffield Academic Press, 1991), 224 n. 2; 227 n. 2; G. W. H. Lampe "The Holy Spirit in the Writings of St. Luke," in Studies in the Gospels: Essays in Memory of R. H. Lightfoot (ed. D. E. Nineham; Oxford: Blackwell, 1955), 196.

nonphysical beings (unclean, evil, divining, or bodiless spirits). Occasionally it has to do with the life-sustaining force within humans or human personality, and, admittedly, there are a few instances where its meaning is unclear (the spirit of Elijah in Luke 1:17; Mary's spirit in Luke 1:47). Only in Acts 17:16, however, which tells of Paul's mounting anger over the idols in Athens ("his spirit was provoked"), does the word indicate someone's state of mind. Indeed, the author of the Third Gospel and Acts usually refers to the heart (καρδία) as the location of psychic processes (Luke 1:66; 21:14; Acts 5:4). In addition, the use of "must" (δεῖ) in 19:21, a term often applied to the divine will, suggests that Paul's decision is in accord with God's plan.[21] The narrative subsequently confirms that the Holy Spirit is meant in 19:21 when, in Paul's speech to the elders of the Ephesian church, he declares that, "having been bound by the Spirit, I go to Jerusalem" (20:22).

Grammatical person shifts to first person plural in 20:5 as the narrator comes forward to provide eyewitness testimony about Paul's journey to Jerusalem. Delay, detour, and distraction characterize the return to Jerusalem. These problems begin before Paul leaves Ephesus, thus before the "we" narrator's presence, when the apostle's departure for Greece is postponed by a near riot over the silversmith Demetrius's accusation that Paul's mission might diminish support for the popular Artemis cult and negatively impact certain guilds financially dependent on her worshipers (19:22–40). Once that disturbance subsides, Paul travels through Macedonia and Greece for three months (20:1–3). Instead of sailing directly for Syria as planned, Paul decides to backtrack through Macedonia to avoid a plot against him (20:3). It is at this point that the narration moves into first person plural, with the "we" character noting that Paul sends emissaries ahead to Troas from Greece while Paul, the "we" character, and others in the entourage leave from Philippi (20:3–6).[22] A number of Acts commentators argue that the reemergence of the "we" style in Philippi, the location at which it previously ceased, is evidence that first person plural represents a historical

---

21. Haenchen, *Acts of the Apostles*, 568; Charles H. Cosgrove, "The Divine Δεῖ in Luke-Acts: Investigations into the Lukan Understanding of God's Providence," *NovT* 26 (1984): 168–90; Squires, *Plan of God in Luke-Acts*, 174–75.

22. Acts 20:4–5 is a notoriously difficult passage to unravel, one that grammatically permits a number of interpretations. To date, no consensus exists on which of the named characters travel with Paul and which sail ahead to Troas. Haenchen (*Acts of the Apostles*, 581–82; "'We' in Acts and the Itinerary," 89) discusses several of the possibilities: (1) Paul and his seven named companions went ahead to Troas and awaited the narrator and unnamed others; (2) the seven went on to Troas while Paul and the narrator visited the congregation in Philippi; (3) the Asians, Tychicus and Trophimus, being familiar with shipping in Asia Minor, were sent ahead to Troas, and all the others accompanied Paul to Philippi. Haenchen prefers the third option. I agree with his conclusion but would carry his insight to its logical conclusion, namely, that the Macedonians traveled with Paul to Philippi, and the Asians, including Gaius and Timothy, who were from Derbe and Lystra respectively, went ahead to Troas.

eyewitness. Their claim is that the "we" character's reappearance in the city where he last appeared in the narrative demonstrates that the author or his source indeed accompanied Paul to Philippi but remained behind when the apostle departed for other parts of Greece in 16:40.[23] One difficulty with this argument is that it fails to account for the disappearance of "we" from the narrative in the midst of Paul's activities in Philippi (16:18–40). In addition, it does not explain the "we" character's retreat later in the narrative in the middle of Paul's stay in Jerusalem (21:19) or the fact that he next appears at Caesarea as Paul is about to depart for Rome (27:1). This historical interpretation overlooks the fact that the utilization of geographical locations to create narrative links, particularly to characters whose appearances have been interrupted by other scenes, is a literary technique employed several times in Acts.[24] For example, Saul is sent off to Tarsus (9:30), and his following appearance in the narrative begins with Barnabas searching for him there (11:25). Similarly, Philip completes his mission work in Caesarea (8:40) and, in his next scene, hosts Paul at his house in that city (21:8). Likewise, the "we" character exits from the narrative in Philippi (16:17) only to reemerge in the same locale (20:5).

Evidence of delay continues to mount, as the "we" character narrates how time consuming it is just getting as far as Troas (20:6). First, Paul and his group do not leave Philippi until after the seven days of Unleavened Bread. Then it takes five days to reach Troas, the trip that they made (sailing in the other direction) in as few as two days (16:11–12). If the additional time is meant to reflect unfavorable wind conditions, as some scholars suggest, the narrative gives no hint of it.[25] Finally, they linger in Troas for seven days without explanation. When at last depart from Troas, Paul once more slows their travel and delays their arrival in Jerusalem by deciding to walk the twenty miles to Assos (20:13). A few days later he bypasses Ephesus to save time but then remains in Miletus until the Ephesian elders can traverse the thirty miles from the capital to Miletus to hear his final address to them (20:15–38). The time involved for the elders to travel from Ephesus to Miletus would depend on their mode of transportation, a detail not supplied in the narrative. Nonetheless, it would undoubtedly have been quicker for Paul to stop in Ephesus to see them than for him to sail sixty miles from Chios to Samos, stay overnight, travel to Miletus (20:15), send messengers to Ephesus to summon the elders, and wait for them to walk or sail from Ephesus to Miletus to meet with him (20:17). After Paul's speech in Miletus

---

23. E.g., Barrett, *Acts of the Apostles*, 2:949; Haenchen, *Acts of the Apostles*, 581–82; idem, " 'We' in Acts and the Itinerary," 89; Bruce, *Acts of the Apostles*, 424.

24. Tannehill, *Narrative Unity of Luke-Acts*, 2:124, who does not mention the Philippi passages (16:17; 20:5).

25. Barrett, *Acts of the Apostles*, 2:950; Bruce, *Acts of the Apostles*, 425.

to the Ephesian elders, the pace toward Jerusalem quickens as his group sets a straight course for Syria, even bypassing Cyprus, the site of Paul's initial missionary efforts (21:1–3), so as not to postpone further their arrival in Jerusalem. On reaching Syria, however, they visit with the disciples in Tyre for seven days, spend a day with the believers in Ptolemais, and visit Philip and his family in Caesarea for several days before finally reaching their destination (21:3–14).

The sheer number of stopovers mentioned during Paul's journey underscores the deliberate pace of the narrative and the lack of narrative urgency for Paul to reach his ultimate destination. The distances between various ports argue against the proposition that each represents a day's journey; for example, Mitylene is half the distance from Assos as Chios is from Mitylene, yet each of these legs takes one day by ship. Other Acts commentators have proposed that the naming of cities in this section of Acts has narrative significance. A. D. Nock suggests that the detail of stops might have the "literary value" of providing readers a momentary respite from the tension of the story.[26] Hans Conzelmann maintains that the "addition of unimportant stopping places along the way can be explained on purely literary grounds," as a frame to hold reports of events that occurred in various places.[27] The insights of these scholars attest that the itinerary of ports serves a narrative function, but the dramatic force of enumerating the stopping places along the way, especially in the context of the other narrative events reported, is to accentuate the delay of Paul's arrival in Jerusalem.

Why does Paul not carry out the divine directive immediately, as he did in Acts 16? In two passages the "we" narrator character who is traveling with him hints at the reason: grave problems await Paul in Jerusalem. First, as already noted, a scheme against Paul while he is in Greece is serious enough to force him to alter his travel plans (20:3). Second, in the Eutychus incident at Troas, what begins as a festive occasion turns successively into moments of tedium, then distress, and finally relief (etched with a touch of humor; 20:7–12). The "we" narrator soon provides confirmation of the severe challenges that await Paul in Jerusalem. Without offering specifics, the narrator discloses in Paul's farewell speech to the Ephesian elders the Spirit's revelation to Paul that he should anticipate chains and afflictions in Jerusalem (20:22–23). Further, Paul informs the elders that he will never again return to any of the places he has visited during his mission work (20:25, 37–38). The warnings become more pronounced as Jerusalem gets

---

26. A. D. Nock, "The Book of Acts," in *Arthur Darby Nock: Essays on Religion and the Ancient World* (ed. Zeph Stewart; 2 vols.; Oxford: Clarendon, 1972), 2:824; see also Dupont, *Sources of Acts*, 139.

27. Hans Conzelmann, *Acts of the Apostles* (trans. James Limburg, A. Thomas Kraabel, and Donald H. Juel; Hermeneia; Philadelphia: Fortress, 1987), xl.

closer. First, the disciples at Tyre warn Paul "through the Spirit" not to go on (21:4). Then, while Paul's entourage is visiting Philip in Caesarea, the prophet Agabus alerts them in no uncertain terms as to what Paul's welcome in Jerusalem will be. Binding his own hands and feet with Paul's belt, Agabus claims to have learned from the Spirit that the Jews in Jerusalem will do likewise to the belt's owner and hand him over to the Gentiles (21:11). Upon hearing this, the "we" character and the residents of Caesarea urge Paul not to proceed (21:12).

At the same time, the "we" narrator confirms Paul's determination to obey his divine instructions. In his Miletus speech, after acknowledging the dangers that await him in Jerusalem, Paul proclaims that completing the course as received from Jesus Christ to testify to the gospel, including in Jerusalem (19:21; 23:11), is more important to him than his own safety (20:24). Later in Caesarea, when the "we" character and others lobby him to avoid Jerusalem, Paul persists. "What are you doing, crying and breaking my heart?" he asks, adding emphatically, "For I am ready not only to be imprisoned but also to die in Jerusalem for the name of the Lord Jesus" (21:13). The voice of the "we" character fortifies the narrative's claim that Paul is committed to carry out the demands of the vision in 19:11 and to reach his required destination regardless of the consequences. Indeed, the "we" narrator reports that Paul refuses to listen even to the narrator's own counsel in the matter! In the end, the response of the "we" character and others in Caesarea to Paul's determination is, appropriately, surrender to God's plan: "Let the Lord's will be done," they respond, and they prepare to depart for Jerusalem (21:14–15). After an initial hospitable welcome from the Jesus movement community in Jerusalem, James and other Jerusalem leaders advise Paul that his reputation among Jewish members of the community is suspect (21:16–21). As the indignities that are to befall Paul begin to unfold, the "we" character retreats from the narrative once again.

Paul's circumstances have changed on this journey. Unlike his immediate response to the first vision in 16:9–10, delay, detour, and distraction characterize the return to Jerusalem. The use of first-person plural grammatical style conveys the "we" narrator character's presence and involvement in the events narrated and engages readers in the story on a personal level. On one hand, we—readers and the collective narrative "we"—have a sense of urgency for Paul to respond to the Spirit's instructions. On the other hand, "we" are hesitant and anxious for Paul's safety. The "we" character confirms that, despite the delays, Paul follows the Spirit's directive. Indeed, the "we" character serves to bolster the narrative's claim that Paul's determination to obey the divine command is unabated by knowledge of what awaits him in Jerusalem.

Paul (and the Narrator?) in Jerusalem and Caesarea
(Acts 21:19–26:32)

Paul's troubles in Jerusalem continue for over two years, and for the five chapters that Acts spends delineating them, the "we" character remains offstage (21:19–26:32). Paul's difficulties begin when the leaders of the Jerusalem church coerce him into participating in a week-long purification ritual at the temple with four others, whose expenses he agrees to pay, all in an attempt to counter rumors that his teaching opposes observance of the law by Jews (21:19–26). Unfortunately, the effort at swaying public opinion does not succeed. Many of the city's residents, suspecting Paul of going so far as to desecrate the temple itself, seize him, drag him from the temple, and attempt to beat him to death (21:27–31). The mob would have accomplished its objective, except that the commander of the Roman garrison stationed in Jerusalem intervenes to save Paul. The tribune, however, adds to the apostle's escalating woes by arresting and chaining him before so much as ascertaining the facts (21:32–36). According to H. W. Tajra, historically this reaction is atypical of Roman authorities, who normally took someone into custody only on the basis of accusations made in writing, not oral denunciations by rioters.[28] On the other hand, in Roman provinces during that period, victims were oftentimes held responsible for provoking commotion that was itself a violation of the law.[29]

To add insult to injury, the tribune mistakes Paul for a certain Egyptian insurrectionist accused of leading four thousand *sicarii* in revolt (21:37–39).[30] Moreover, permission for the apostle to speak to the crowd leads to a hardening of the mob's resolve to see him dead (21:40–22:23). The tribune then decides to scourge Paul in the conduct of his investigation into the reasons for the hostility toward the apostle. This brutal form of interrogation, as Brian Rapske notes, often "result[ed] in crippling or even death before the truth had been arrived at."[31] More violence erupts after Paul's claim of Roman citizenship compels the tribune to jettison the idea of scourging. The commander determines instead to force the Jerusalem Sanhedrin to con-

---

28. H. J. Tajra, *The Trial of St. Paul: A Juridical Exegesis of the Second Half of the Acts of the Apostles* (WUNT 35; Tübingen: Mohr Siebeck, 1989), 69; but cf. Brian Rapske, *The Book of Acts and Paul in Roman Custody* (vol. 3 of *The Book of Acts in Its First Century Setting*; ed. Bruce W. Winter; Grand Rapids: Eerdmans, 1994), 136.

29. Henry J. Cadbury, "Roman Law and the Trial of Paul," in Lake and Cadbury, *Additional Notes to the Commentary*, 299–300; Bruce, *Acts of the Apostles*, 451.

30. This may be the same character mentioned by Josephus in *War* 2.261–263 and *Ant.* 20.169–172. For the relationship between Acts and the writings of Josephus, see Steve Mason, *Josephus and the New Testament* (Peabody, Mass.: Hendrickson, 1992), 185–225; Henry J. Cadbury, "Subsidiary Points," in Foakes Jackson and Lake, *Prolegomena II, Criticism*, 355–58; Bruce, *Acts of the Apostles*, 43–44.

31. Rapske, *Book of Acts and Paul*, 139.

sider the case in order that he might learn through its deliberations what he wants to know (22:24–23:10). Subsequently, a plot to assassinate Paul by conspirators serious enough about their undertaking to vow a fast until they succeed convinces the commander that the only way to protect his prisoner is to deliver him to the governor in Caesarea (23:12–33).

The change of venue, however, does not alter Paul's fortunes. Felix brings him to trial but never renders a verdict (23:34–24:22). Instead, he holds the apostle in custody for the remaining two years of his governorship under what might be labeled "minimum security" conditions, hoping to extort money from him (24:23–26). Felix's anticipation of financial gain never materializes, but upon leaving office he continues Paul's imprisonment as a favor to the Jews (24:27). His replacement as governor, Festus, also tries Paul but withholds his verdict despite the inability of Paul's Jewish accusers to prove their charges while he attempts to persuade Paul to submit to a retrial in Jerusalem in order to curry favor with the Jews (25:6–9). Jewish leaders had petitioned Festus to transfer Paul to Jerusalem when the new governor first arrived in the province, intending to ambush Paul on his way there (25:1–3). Although the narrative gives no reason to suspect Festus of being part of the plot—originally he did not acquiesce to their request—the narrative suggests that he is now endeavoring, perhaps unwittingly, to give the Jewish leaders an opportunity to carry out their plan against Paul.

Paul will have none of it, however, and petitions the governor for permission to appeal his case to Caesar in Rome (25:10–12). It is unclear whether Paul's appeal is based on his claim of Roman citizenship, as some scholars argue. In earlier passages Paul invokes his citizenship rights to protest or moderate the treatment he receives. In Philippi, he demands and receives an apology from the magistrates for flogging and imprisoning him despite his Roman citizenship (16:37–39), and, as mentioned, the Roman tribune in Jerusalem rescinds the order to scourge Paul once he is informed of the apostle's citizenship status (22:25–29). In the present account, however, Roman citizenship is not explicitly asserted as the legal grounds for Paul's appeal, nor is the absoluteness of such a privilege apparent.[32] In the previous incidents, Paul was dealing with local officials, not the provincial governor, who had much broader authority. In addition, Festus consults his council before acceding to Paul's request (25:12) and later tells Agrippa that he made the decision to send Paul to Caesar (25:25), both of which weigh against the view that the governor was obliged to grant the appeal.[33] Before dispatching

---

32. Cadbury, "Roman Law," in Lake and Cadbury, *Additional Notes to the Commentary*, 317.

33. So also Rapske, *Book of Acts and Paul*, 186–89, but against this conclusion, see Cadbury, "Roman Law," 297–338; A. N. Sherwin-White, *Roman Society and Roman Law in the New Testament* (Oxford: Oxford University Press, 1963; repr., Grand Rapids: Baker, 1978), 48–70; Tajra, *Trial of St. Paul*, 135–71.

Paul to Rome, Festus subjects the accused to one more hearing, this time before the Jewish king Agrippa and his sister Bernice (25:13–26:32). At the conclusion of the final hearing, during which Paul gives a lengthy speech that is as much a gospel proclamation as a defense of his work (as Agrippa's protest that Paul is attempting "to make me a Christian" [26:28 RSV] indicates), those who hear Paul concede that he has committed no serious wrongdoing, and Agrippa confesses to Festus that the apostle would have been eligible for release if not for his appeal to Rome.[34]

By the time Paul departs Palestine, he has defended his innocence five times since his arrest in Jerusalem: to the people (21:29–22:21); to the Jerusalem Sanhedrin (23:1–8); to Felix (24:1–21); to Festus (25:6–12; 25:17–21, 24–25); and to Agrippa and Bernice (25:23–26:39). He has been warned, bribed, threatened, wrongly accused, nearly beaten to death, arrested, harshly interrogated, mistakenly identified, and the target of two assassination plots, and he has languished in prison for over two years. This sequence of events unfolds in third-person narration, and, as the prior examination of the writings of ancient historians revealed, one rhetorical effect of third-person grammatical style is to project a sense of objectivity concerning narrative claims. In the case of Thucydides, Polybius, and Josephus, the impression of impartiality was heightened by narrating their personal involvement in the events in the third person as well. In this section of Acts, the narrator is not explicitly characterized as present during the incidents recorded, but the inference of his proximity is unmistakable in the narrative context, since first-person plural passages surround these chapters: the narrator arrives in Jerusalem with Paul (21:15–18) and sails with him when he departs for Rome (27:1–2).

Final Appearance of the "We" Character (Acts 27:1–28:16)

In the midst of his problems, Paul receives another vision, a christophany telling him that he "must" (δεῖ) witness to the Lord in Rome as he had in Jerusalem (23:11; cf. 19:21), the so-called "divine δεῖ" signaling that it is part of God's plan for him to do so.[35] The directive offers a measure of reassurance in the current turmoil that Paul's fate is in God's hands and that his work will not come to a tragic end in Jerusalem or Caesarea. The command is not altogether unexpected, either, because Rome has been the summit on

---

34. Gaventa, *Acts of the Apostles*, 338–48. For an extended treatment of Paul's utilization of custody settings to proclaim the gospel, see Matthew L. Skinner, *Locating Paul: Places of Custody as Narrative Settings in Acts 21–28* (SBLAcBib 13; Atlanta: Society of Biblical Literature, 2003). For a discussion of the translation problems associated with Acts 26:28, see Barrett, *Acts of the Apostles*, 2:1169–71.

35. Cosgrove, "The Divine Δεῖ in Luke-Acts," 168–90; Squires, *Plan of God in Luke-Acts*, 174–75; Haenchen, *Acts of the Apostles*, 568. •

the geographical horizon of the Third Gospel and Acts for some time (Luke 24:47; Acts 1:8; 19:21; 25:12). As Paul sets sail for the capital, his "we" partner reemerges one last time to accompany him and to witness to the extreme dangers that confront the apostle during his final journey in Acts (27:1–2). The narrative style of Paul's voyage to Rome in Acts 27–28 has, in the words of F. F. Bruce, "much in common" with other ancient narratives of Mediterranean crossings, historical or fictional, which from Homer forward "regularly contained" storms and shipwrecks.[36] One effect characteristic of such stories is to intensify the sense of adventure and action of the narrative, a dramatic quality that is further enhanced in the Acts narrative through the inclusion of significant nautical details.[37]

The initial leg of the journey is uneventful. The "we" narrator recounts that, after boarding an Adramyttium ship bound for the ports of Asia, the travelers sail first up the Mediterranean coastline to Sidon (27:1–3).[38] The wind begins to shift both meteorologically and figuratively, however, as soon as they set sail from Sidon. From Phoenicia, they are forced to chart a course along the southern coast of Cyprus to shield the ship from unfavorable winds (27:4). The wind becomes ever more uncooperative after they transfer at the Lycian port city of Myra (located on the southern coast of Asia Minor) to an Alexandrian ship bound for Italy, causing them to reroute their voyage southward toward the Mediterranean island of Crete (27:6–8). Owing to the delays and detours occasioned by the adverse and worsening wind conditions, the ship makes the harbor of Fair Havens on the southern coast of Crete too late in the season to continue on safely, a matter that Paul brings to the attention of the centurion responsible for the prisoners onboard (27:9–10). Paul's warning of the perils that await them if they embark at that time of the year goes unheeded by the ship's owner and captain, who argue that the Fair Havens harbor is unsuitable for wintering and who, together with the centurion, decide to try for the preferable Cretan port of Phoenix (27:11–12).

Not surprisingly, an intense storm strikes soon after they set sail for Phoenix, and for fourteen straight days typhoon-strength winds buffet the ship and its occupants (27:14–20). In their attempt to ride out the storm, the sailors quit struggling to sail against the wind and allow it to carry the ship in whatever direction it blows, becoming proactive only in an effort to guide the vessel away from the shallow gulfs known as the Syrtis off the coast of

---

36. Bruce, *Acts of the Apostles,* 508.

37. Pervo, *Profit with Delight,* 12–57; Cadbury, *Making of Luke-Acts,* 235; Dibelius, *Studies in the Acts,* 204; Conzelmann, *Acts of the Apostles,* 221; Praeder, "Narrative Voyage," 5, 227–45; idem, "Acts 27:1–28:16: Sea Voyages in Ancient Literature and the Theology of Luke-Acts," *CBQ* 46 (1984): 683–706; Robbins, "By Land and by Sea," 232.

38. Adramyttium was a Mysian city in the province of Asia, i.e., in northwest Asia Minor; see John Wineland, "Adramyttium," *ABD* 1:80.

Libya in northern Africa. As the storm continues unabated, they set about casting cargo and equipment overboard to keep the ship afloat. After two weeks in the middle of the northeaster, all passengers and crew except Paul abandon hope of surviving the storm.

After admonishing those who overruled him back at Fair Havens, Paul tries to restore hope to those onboard by disclosing that an angel of God had assured him in a vision that only the ship would be lost in the storm, not their lives, and that they would come ashore on an island somewhere (27:21–26). Needless to say, events unfold exactly as Paul predicts. The sailors sense land nearing and begin to test the depth of the water at different intervals to avoid the shallows (27:27–29). When the water level drops to fifteen fathoms, they anchor and wait for morning to avoid steering the ship into rocks in the darkness and sinking (27:29). During the night, however, the sailors attempt to abandon the ship in the lifeboat, and Paul enlists the soldiers to prevent their escape by cutting the skiff loose (27:30–32). Neither of these moves is a particularly good omen for what the morning will bring, but Paul again offers hope by reminding them that not one life will be lost and then encouraging them to eat something (27:33–34). In an act with eucharistic overtones, he begins to eat, and the other 275 people onboard follow his lead (27:35–37).[39] Buoyed by Paul's words and their own full stomachs, the ship's company tosses the remainder of the grain supplies overboard to lighten the ship, a risky maneuver at best (27:38). In the morning, while trying to reach the beach of Malta, an island sixty miles south of the coast of Sicily that in the daylight they discover is close by, they manage to run the ship onto a reef or a sandbar, and it breaks up and sinks (27:39–41; 28:1). While the ship is foundering, the soldiers decide to execute all prisoners onboard to prevent any of them from escaping by swimming away unnoticed during the commotion (27:42). The centurion, who is concerned for Paul's safety, comes to the prisoners' rescue, vetoing the plan of the guards and substituting one of his own. In his desire to spare Paul, the centurion saves the lives of everyone on the ship (27:43–44).

On the island, Paul again becomes responsible for the lives of the survi-

---

39. The relationship of this meal to the eucharistic Last Supper narrative is debated by Luke-Acts commentators. Tannehill (*Narrative Unity of Luke-Acts*, 2:334–35) argues that the meal on the ship echoes other significant meal accounts in Luke-Acts, including the feeding of the multitude (Luke 9:16), the Emmaus supper (Luke 24:30), and various meals in Acts (2:42, 46; 20:7, 11). In his judgment, "Paul's meal, then, is as sacramental as any other meal in Luke-Acts." Others minimize the eucharistic overtones in the present passage; e.g., Conzelmann, *Acts of the Apostles*, 220; Haenchen, *Acts of the Apostles*, 707; Bruce, *Acts of the Apostles*, 525. Praeder steers a middle ground, arguing that historically the meal "could not have been a eucharistic meal" and that narratively it cannot represent "a celebration of the Christian community" ("Acts 27:1–28:16," 699). Nevertheless, "the meal on the ship has been styled to suggest a Christian meal of some sort."

vors. After first welcoming the strangers, the natives turn against Paul when he is bitten by a poisonous snake, a sign in their minds that he must be a murderer (28:1–4; ironically, this judgment recalls Paul's actions toward the Jesus movement before meeting the Lord on the way to Damascus in 8:1–3 and 9:1–2). The islanders' momentary suspicion turns to adulation when Paul is unharmed by the snakebite (28:5–6), and the remainder of the stay on Malta goes well. The shipwrecked travelers are treated with warm hospitality by the ruler, Publius, and showered by the locals with gifts and generous quantities of supplies when they prepare to leave for Rome. For his part, Paul cures a number of the island's inhabitants, including Publius's father (28:7–11). The group's pleasant visit on the island anticipates the remainder of their journey to Rome, which goes as smoothly as it had begun in 27:1–3. The calm beginning and ending of the voyage account serve as a frame or *inclusio* that focuses attention on the series of tumultuous events that have transpired within its borders.

Boarding another Alexandrian ship, this one ironically carrying the figures of the Greek gods considered protectors of mariners (the so-called Twin Brothers Castor and Polydeuces), Paul and his traveling companions, including the "we" character, sail from Malta to Syracuse, Rhegium, and their final port, Puteoli, without incident (28:11–13). Members of the Jesus movement in Italy greet them cordially. Indeed, the narrative tone of Paul's arrival is almost triumphal, comparable to receptions recorded in Hellenistic literature for visiting dignitaries.[40] The Jesus movement community at Puteoli invites them to visit for a week before continuing on to Rome, while those from the Jesus movement at Rome walk thirty or forty miles to the towns of Forum of Appius and Three Taverns to greet Paul and his entourage along their route (28:14–15).

The celebration of Paul's arrival is in sharp contrast to all that he has endured and stands as an exclamation point to the narrative declaration that he has successfully overcome every obstacle placed in his path to "witness to [the Lord] also in Rome" (23:11). The "we" character is present for all that has occurred, and his personal account enables readers to share in the experiences, while, at the same time, his presence lends credibility to some otherwise incredible events. The "we" character's story is a litany of adventures that jeopardize Paul's chances of making it to the capital safely: (1) unfavorable winds that slow the ship's progress and push it off its intended course; (2) a gale, packing typhoon-strength winds, that holds the ship in its grip for two weeks and tosses it wherever it wishes, costing cargo and equipment and causing crew and passengers alike to despair; (3) an attempted mutiny by the crew; (4) shipwreck; (5) the threat of execution by the soldiers; (6) a poisonous snakebite; and (7) hostile islanders. Accord-

---

40. Bruce, *Acts of the Apostles*, 536; Barrett, *Acts of the Apostles*, 2:1232.

ing to the narrator's eyewitness testimony, without Paul all the passengers, soldiers, and crew onboard would surely have perished. The "we" character attributes their safe passage to Paul's nautical expertise and calm demeanor, his prophetic and healing abilities, and his pastoral skills. In addition, as Paul protects the ship's company from the elements and their own mistakes, divine and human assistance safeguard Paul. The "we" narrator shares in the crises and thus is able to provide firsthand testimony that "nothing can stop God's intention that [Paul] should reach Rome."[41]

Once in Rome, Paul is placed under house arrest (28:16). Although his circumstances are significantly less difficult than in Philippi, Jerusalem, or Caesarea, his mobility is limited, and he is restricted to hosting visitors at his home.[42] In addition, the crowds that had cheered Paul's arrival moments earlier in the narrative vanish without a trace, abandoning him to face the Jewish community in Rome alone, with predictably mixed results (28:17–24). Although lacking the severity of previous scenes of Paul's imprisonment, the situation is sufficient cause for the "we" character to retreat from the narrative for the last time.

Summary

As in Thucydides, Polybius, and Josephus, first-person plural grammatical style in Acts projects the narrator's involvement in the story and, therefore, his competence and knowledge of certain events. In these ancient historical works and in Acts, this claim has more to do with narrative characterization than with the facts of history. With Acts, however, the distinction between narrative and historical eyewitnessing is acute because the anonymity of the author nearly effaces him entirely from the production and telling of the story.[43]

The "we" character is the narrative replacement for Barnabas as Paul's mission companion and the reliable presence and credible witness to the apostle's cooperation with God's plan in urgent circumstances. Indeed, the role of the "we" character parallels that of Barnabas in significant ways. He

---

41. Barrett, *Acts of the Apostles*, 2:1180.

42. Paul's confinement to his residence is confirmed in several ways. First, the use of the middle form of the verb συγκαλέω ("summon") suggests that Paul invites the Jewish leaders to visit him (28:17; Barrett, *Acts of the Apostles*, 2:1236). Second, εἰς τὴν ξενίαν in 28:23 can mean "unto his hospitality" or "to his lodging." Either meaning, however, indicates that Paul is host, as Barrett (*Acts of the Apostles*, 2:1243) argues: "[I]f the Jews came to Paul's lodging he was their host . . . and if he entertained them at all it must have been at his lodging"; see also, Bruce, *Acts of the Apostles*, 540; Henry J. Cadbury, "Lexical Notes on Luke-Acts: III. Luke's Interest in Lodging," *JBL* 45 (1926): 319–21. Third, the narrative states that Paul received all those who *came to him* during the following two years (28:30).

43. For further discussion of anonymous authorship and its effects, see the section entitled "Review and Results: Significance for Acts" in chapter 2.

is introduced into the narrative in the Gospel preface as a trustworthy and reliable character, and he becomes an active participant in Paul's missionary activities, secondary to Paul certainly but important nonetheless. Acts 16:10, for example, reports that "God had called *us* to proclaim the gospel" to the Macedonians, and the slave with the gift of divination announces that "*these people* who proclaim to you the way of salvation are servants of the most high God" (16:17). Furthermore, just as the call of Paul and Barnabas by the Holy Spirit represents the divine command for their journey and mission work together (13:2, 4), so also each appearance of the "we" character with Paul is a response to divine instructions (16:9–10; 19:21; 23:11). Finally, the "we" narrator succeeds Barnabas as the character with impeccable credentials who corroborates Paul's own testimony that, although he maliciously opposed the Jesus movement at first, after the Damascus road experience his actions are fully in accord with the divine instructions that the Lord advised would be forthcoming (9:6, 15–16).

To be sure, the narrative circumstances and emphases of each appearance of the "we" character are different. His first appearance is noteworthy for the immediate response of the missionaries to what they consider God's summons for them to preach in Macedonia, although the original purpose of the journey had been simply to revisit the churches that Paul and Barnabas had previously established (15:36). In contrast, the second instance of first-person plural narration is marked by delay, distraction, and detour as Paul doggedly works his way to Jerusalem despite the challenges encountered along the way and despite the disasters that await him in the city. The focus of the third "we" passage on the dangerous adventures of Paul and the "we" companion during their sea voyage to Rome to appeal Paul's case to the emperor demonstrates how Paul and God assure the safe arrival of all passengers onboard. In these diverse narrative situations, the "we" character individually, collectively, and with readers personally testifies to Paul's chosenness and to his full cooperation with the divine instructions he receives.

Conclusion

Who Are "We" in Acts?

ASKING THE QUESTION DIFFERENTLY

In the past, scholars undertaking literary analyses of Acts often retreated to more traditional ground when confronted with the dilemma of the "we" passages. One early study on the Acts narrator, for example, abandons almost two hundred pages devoted to the book's literary character when the discussion turns to the "we" passages:

> the effect of "eyewitness" narration at the points in the narrative at which they occur is negated by the relative insignificance of the plot events at those points of the narrative. . . . This fact may indicate the need for fresh impetus to be given to the source consideration for these breaks in the narration posture. When literary criticism fails to provide adequate explanation for aporias such as the "we" material, the student of Acts is forced to consider afresh such traditional avenues of historical investigation.[1]

The introductory review of the explanations previously proposed for first person plural in Acts suggests why this is so. The most influential proposals have been those arguing that "we" style indicates the presence of a historical eyewitness, either the author or one or more sources. Scholars in the author-as-eyewitness and source-as-eyewitness camps have maintained forcefully and consistently that the use of the first person bespeaks a historical eyewitness to the events narrated, and a glance at recent Acts commentaries confirms that this view continues to dominate interpretation of the "we" passages. In his magisterial two-volume commentary on Acts, for example, C. K. Barrett, while acknowledging the factual problems contained in the Acts narrative when compared to Paul's letters, continues to frame the "we"

---

1. Allen J. Walworth, "The Narrator of Acts" (Ph.D. diss., Southern Baptist Theological Seminary, 1984), 176–77; see also Kurz, "Narrative Approaches to Luke-Acts," 218–19.

passage argument as a choice between the author or a source as eyewitness to the events narrated:

> In a number of passages the narrative is set in the first person plural, which *prima facie* suggests that the story is being told by one who was present. . . . [But] the author, though he greatly admired Paul, did not fully understand him and at some points misunderstood him. . . . That Acts as a whole was written by one of Paul's immediate circle is [therefore] very difficult to believe; that the author, whoever he may have been, was able to draw on one or two sources derived from that circle—the We-passages and perhaps some others—is probable.[2]

Acts in general and the "we" passages in particular, however, have proven to be stubbornly resistant to traditional historical-critical investigation, including historical-critical literary analysis (source, form, and redaction criticism). Author-as-eyewitness solutions have not been able to explain satisfactorily gaps in the author/narrator's eyewitness testimony nor to overcome what Barrett calls "the errors found in the Acts account of Paul . . . [which] differences and problems . . . are more than sufficient to cast doubt on the identification of our author with a Pauline traveling companion."[3] In addition, proponents of this theory have not adequately addressed the question raised by the anonymous authorship of Acts: Why would the author conceal his identity throughout the two volumes only to reveal his presence during the last part of Acts in such an incomprehensible way as the intermittent employment of first person plural grammatical style? On the other hand, source-as-eyewitness proposals have yet to offer an acceptable explanation for the author's decision to introduce (or retain) first-person plural style in passages that, by this grammatical choice, suggest the presence of the author/narrator but in reality describe events at which he was not present and, in fact, refer to someone else.

The intractable problems facing historical solutions as well as the emergence and development of literary approaches in biblical studies have led to a reevaluation of the narrative possibilities of the first person plural style. Robbins and Plümacher, although failing to provide sufficient parallels from ancient sources to sustain their proposals, nevertheless have helpfully advanced the issue by demonstrating that grammatical conventions in ancient literature are more complex than historical solutions recognize, opening up the possibility that the first person plural could be used of a nonhistorical reference. Narrative critics such as Tannehill, Kurz, and Gaventa have considered the effect on readers of first-person plural style in Acts. Indeed, even

---

2. Barrett, *Acts of the Apostles*, 2:xxv–xxix; see also Fitzmyer, *Acts of the Apostles*, 98–103. Gaventa's commentary is an exception; see *Acts of the Apostles*, 58–59, 230, 278, 350–51, 353.

3. Barrett, *Acts of the Apostles*, 2:xliv.

Haenchen, Dibelius, and Cadbury, scholars advocating historical solutions, recognized the contribution of the literary character of the "we" passages to the narrative and thus the importance of grasping the narrative impact of the "we" style for an adequate understanding of the story unfolding in Acts.

This study has attempted to build on these narrative and literary insights. In focusing on the narrative character and function of the "we" passages, it has not directly addressed the question of whether events reported in the "we" sections are historical and, if so, the possibility that the author or his source/s may have been present at them, although it has challenged the claim that first-person style is, in and of itself, sufficient evidence of either historicity or historical eyewitnessing. The principal task of the study has been to identify and elaborate the narrative role of the first person plural style in Acts within the boundaries of acceptable ancient grammatical practices and, in so doing, to establish narrative literary strategy as a viable and fruitful approach in the interpretation of the "we" passages.

To that end, the study has analyzed the use of grammatical person in the writings of several prominent ancient historians, an analysis that reveals remarkable freedom and variety among these authors in grammatical practice. Thucydides, Polybius, and Josephus all overwhelmingly prefer the third person for event-level narratives in which the author is an actor. Third-person references to the author as a participant in the narrative project a sense of objectivity in the storytelling by separating the storyteller (narrator) from the events he is narrating, that is, by characterizing the narrator as an "objective observer" of the events being described. In narrator-level commentary, however, the histories utilize the first person (singular and plural) in addition to the third person to refer to the narrator. Thucydides favors third-person style for the author/narrator, although on rare occasions he employs the first person. Polybius and Josephus, however, usually refer to the author/narrator in the first person at the narrator level.

If third person is the grammatical style of objectivity, first person singular is the style of personal integrity and trustworthiness. The passages in which it is employed in the writings of these historians often voice the narrator's defense of his qualifications to report the events contained in the narrative, identifying either his personal involvement or his thorough research and critical assessment of them. First person plural is used in a variety of contexts in these histories, particularly in Polybius and Josephus. Similar to first person singular, first person plural creates a sense of the narrator's closeness to and, therefore, knowledge of and competence to report events. On the other hand, first plural grammatical person subsumes the narrator within the collective "we." When first person plural refers to the narrator individually, it is not unlike the royal and editorial "we" that implicates as well those on whose behalf the governmental or editorial authority speaks or writes.

This effect moderates the narrator's responsibility for narrative claims and, at the same time, conveys a familiarity between narrator and reader that draws readers into the story, bonds them to the first-person plural company that includes the narrator, and encourages them to evaluate positively the narrator's perspective and to accept the narrator's version of events. Indeed, even when the narrative identifies the first-person plural referents, readers experience a more personal relationship with the group and, therefore, a more sympathetic view of the narrator's perspective than is the case with third-person narration. Not only is this so at the narrator level, but it is also the case in Polybius's event-level first-person plural narrative sections, despite his explicit argument that he uses first person plural to improve the aesthetics of his narrative, that is, as a more tasteful alternative to overusing his name or to referring constantly to himself in first person singular ("I/me"), a grammatical style that he considers even more obnoxious. In addition, narrating events at which the narrator is present and in which the narrator participates (that is, event-level narratives) in first person plural instead of the third person injects a deeper sense of personal involvement by the author/narrator in the events, with the other characters who are part of the scene, and with readers who are themselves drawn into the narrative on a more personal level by "we" style.

The first-person narrator character in Acts reflects the ancient grammatical practice and effects noted in the histories of Thucydides, Polybius, and Josephus. The first-person singular and plural passages in the Acts narrative defend and project the narrator's personal knowledge as eyewitness or researcher and, therefore, his credentials for telling the story accurately so that, as Luke 1:4 claims, Theophilus and by extension all readers can be assured of the truth of the information. The "we" character's primary role is to replace Barnabas as Paul's companion and witness in urgent times, to defend Paul's credibility in the story in ways that the apostle himself cannot, and to provide reassurance that Paul carries out God's directives as charged in spite of obstacles constructed by human characters or by nature. Paul is unable to provide this witness on his own merits because the narrative portrays his reversal of position with respect to the Jesus movement as creating a credibility problem for him among Jews and Gentiles inside and outside the movement. As the narrative unfolds, reaction to God's appointed messenger ranges from ambivalence to malevolence, and it becomes clear early on that he will never completely overcome the difficulty. The narrative provides two characters with impeccable credentials, Barnabas and the "we" narrator, to bridge Paul's credibility gap in the story and for readers.

In order to play such a role, Barnabas is introduced and portrayed as a highly trustworthy and trusted character. Likewise, the narrator character's reliability is established at his introduction in the preface of Luke's Gospel, so that, when he becomes an active participant in Paul's missionary work after

Barnabas and Paul separate, he too is able to corroborate Paul's obedience to divine instructions and thus the apostle's cooperation with God's plan. The narrator's role is dramatically played out in the three "we" passages of Acts: first, as a major influence in the decision to respond immediately to the divine call to expand Paul's mission activity beyond the familiar and reasonably successful region of Asia Minor to uncharted territories in Macedonia and Greece; second, as an observer—and on one occasion advocate—of events that seem determined to slow or to stop Paul's arrival at Jerusalem and the difficult fate that awaits him there; and third, as part of the ship's company who embark on the dangerous voyage to deliver Paul to the emperor for final disposition of his case, a verdict that the experiences at sea attest is unnecessary (as Agrippa and Festus agree in 26:31–32) by demonstrating that Paul has been "acquitted by a tribunal no less formidable than the divinely controlled ocean itself."[4]

The literary character of first-person plural grammatical style in Acts, therefore, is integral to the narrative. First person plural is not simply a historical marker indicating the presence at that point in the story of the actual author of Acts or source/s that have been incorporated into the narrative, but plays an important role in the story that the narrator tells. Too often in the past the narrative significance of the "we" passages—that is, the narrator as narrative character—has been underappreciated. Indeed, subordinating the narrative possibilities of first-person plural style to its historical possibilities has contributed to the confusion over the "we" passages that has troubled Acts scholarship for the past two centuries. Attending to the literary character of first-person plural narration in Acts in the context of ancient grammatical practice has the potential to move "we" passage scholarship forward. No longer need narrative analysis yield to historical solutions, despairing of any literary substance to first-person plural grammatical style in Acts. Instead of surrendering the "we" passages to the category of "insoluble riddle," readers can appreciate them as vital to the Acts drama of divine-human collaboration in shaping the emergence and expansion of the early church.

---

4. Gary B. Miles and Garry Trompf, "Luke and Antiphon: The Theology of Acts 27–28 in Light of Pagan Beliefs about Divine Retribution, Pollution, and Shipwreck," *HTR* 69 (1976): 267.

Appendix A

Frequently Asked Questions

Is Paul Considered an "Apostle" in Acts?

Paul is twice referred to as an apostle in Acts, both times jointly with Barnabas (14:4, 14). In the Third Gospel and Acts taken together, therefore, the term designates both the office of the Twelve and those commissioned by God for God's work. Although Paul is not one of the Twelve, the assertion by F. F. Bruce that the application of the term to Paul in Acts is different from the "special sense in which he uses the designation of himself in his letters" is flawed.[1] "Apostle" in Acts 14 associates, although it does not identify, Paul's commissioning with that of the Twelve as a result of having been called directly and equally by God (9:5–6, 15–16; 13:2–3; 22:10–15; 26:16–18). This understanding is precisely the view Paul expresses in his letters (Rom 1:1–6; Gal 1:1, 12, 15–19; 1 Cor 15:3–11).[2]

Is Paul's Experience on the Way to Damascus Properly Called "Conversion"?

It is problematic to speak of Paul's experience in Acts 9 (see also 22:6–11; 26:12–18) as "conversion" in any religious sense because both before and afterwards he is a professing Pharisaic Jew (see, e.g., 21:39; 22:3). Gaventa, agreeing that Paul's change "has little to do with theological concepts or

---

1. Bruce, *Acts of the Apostles*, 319.

2. For additional information, see Barrett, *Acts of the Apostles*, 1:671–72; Andrew C. Clark, "The Role of the Apostles," in *Witness to the Gospel: The Theology of Acts* (ed. I. Howard Marshall and David Peterson; Grand Rapids: Eerdmans, 1978), 169–90; Kirsopp Lake, "The Twelve and the Apostles," in Lake and Cadbury, *Additional Notes to the Commentary*, 37–59; Edwin S. Nelson, "Paul's First Missionary Journey as Paradigm: A Literary-Critical Assessment of Acts 13–14" (Ph.D. diss., Boston University, 1982), 111–13; Walter Schmithals, *The Office of Apostle in the Early Church* (London: SPCK, 1971), 63, 74–79; Stephen G. Wilson, *The Gentiles and the Gentile Mission in Luke-Acts* (SNTSMS 23; Cambridge: Cambridge University Press, 1973), 112–20.

religious affiliation," nonetheless considers it "not inaccurate to characterize Acts 9:1–31 as a conversion narrative. Saul does not hear a proclamation of the gospel and respond to it (cf. 2:37–39, 8:32–37). What is converted is Saul's identity. Acts 9 describes the reversal of the church's most vehement and aggressive enemy."[3] Gaventa classifies Paul's experience as "pendulum conversion," one of the categories of conversion she proposes based on the work of William James, A. D. Nock, and Richard Travisano. This type of conversion consists in "the rejection of past convictions and affiliations for an affirmed present and future."[4] But Paul does not abandon his past convictions and affiliations in Acts. Indeed, when accused of advocating that Diaspora Jews forsake Torah regulations, he agrees to undergo a week-long ritual of purification in the temple to demonstrate that the accusations are false (21:20–26). Consequently, understanding Paul's Damascus road experience as a conversion should be resisted; however, it is suited to another of Gaventa's classifications, namely, "transformation . . . (that is,) a radical change of perspective in which some newly gained cognition brings about a changed way of understanding."[5]

Who Are the "Hellenists" in Acts?

"Hellenist," a word not found in literature written before Acts, seems to be a term of linguistic rather than ethnic or doctrinal distinction, that is, a reference to Greek speakers belonging to any number of ethnic or religious groups. For that reason, the decision regarding the ethnic makeup or religious affiliation of Hellenists can be made only on the basis of context. The circumstances of 6:1, where the term "Hellenist" first appears in Acts, make clear that the reference is to Greek-speaking Jesus movement members. On the other hand, Acts notes as early as the Pentecost story that many foreign-speaking Jews reside in Jerusalem (2:5–11), some of whom might not be sympathetic to the Jesus movement and its messengers (2:12–13). Indeed, just such groups oppose and execute Stephen (6:9). Readers may not assume, therefore, that the Hellenists who oppose Paul in Acts 9:29 are Greek-speaking members of the Jerusalem Jesus movement community. In that context, the Hellenists who want Paul dead can only be Jews, a conclusion confirmed by the contrast of "Hellenist" with "brothers and sisters" (οἱ ἀδελφοί; 9:30), a term that is used of various groups in discourse material

---

3. Gaventa, "Overthrown Enemy," 444.

4. Gaventa, *From Darkness to Light*, 148; see also 8–14.

5. Ibid., 10; see also A. D. Nock, *Conversion: The Old and the New in Religion from Alexander the Great to Augustine of Hippo* (Oxford: Oxford University Press, 1933), 1–16; Krister Stendahl, *Paul among Jews and Gentiles and Other Essays* (Philadelphia: Fortress, 1976), 7–23.

in Acts (believers, Jews, siblings) but always refers to the Jesus movement in nondiscourse narration.[6]

What Was the Status of Philippi in the First Century C.E.?

The question arises because the Greek reading overwhelmingly attested in ancient textual witnesses to Acts 16:12 refers to Philippi as the "foremost city of the district of Macedonia" (πρώτη μερίδος τῆς Μακεδονίας πόλις). Philippi was not the capital of Macedonia, however, nor its most populous city (Thessalonica held both honors). It was not even the capital of its own district (Amphipolis was). Indeed, it was not the first Macedonian city on Paul's journey (Neapolis had that distinction).[7] Being at a loss as to what "first city of the district of Macedonia" might signify, a number of textual critics have concluded that the original text of Acts suffered corruption that was adopted by subsequent witnesses, and they set about reconstructing a more plausible reading. For example, the majority of United Bible Society editorial committee members abandoned the weighty testimony of Greek manuscript witnesses for a conjecture paralleled in three late Vulgate manuscripts because of their inability to reconcile the text with Philippi's historical status.[8]

Other scholars accept the widely attested Greek text but soften the textual claim by translating πρώτη πόλις as "a leading city."[9] This move is unnecessary, however, since what is considered "foremost" is measured differently depending on what criteria are taken into consideration and the judgment of the evaluator. For example, Americans would differ as to which U.S. city they consider the most prominent. Some might say New York, others Washington, D.C., still others Los Angeles, Chicago, Philadelphia, or Chicago. W. M. Ramsay came to a similar determination over a hundred years ago, concluding that the author of Acts "was specially interested in Philippi, and had the true Greek pride in his own city."[10]

---

6. For additional information, see Craig Hill, *Hellenists and Hebrews: Reappraising Division within the Earliest Church* (Minneapolis: Fortress, 1992), esp. 1–24; Martin Hengel, *Between Jesus and Paul: Studies in the Earliest History of Christianity* (trans. John Bowden; London: SCM, 1983), 1–29; idem, *Acts and the History of Earliest Christianity* (trans. John Bowden; Philadelphia: Fortress, 1980), 71–80; Johnson, *Acts of the Apostles*, 105; Witherington, *Acts of the Apostles*, 240–47.

7. Metzger, *Textual Commentary*, 445.

8. Ibid.

9. Lake and Cadbury, *English Translation and Commentary*, 188.

10. W. M. Ramsay, *St. Paul the Traveller and the Roman Citizen* (New York: Putnam, 1896), 206. See also, Cadbury, *Making of Luke-Acts*, 245; Conzelmann, *Acts of the Apostles*, 139; Bruce, *Acts of the Apostles*, 357 (who objects that Luke "expressed himself misleadingly, if Ramsay is right.")

What Is "Plan of God" Theology in Acts?

The plan of God is a prominent and distinctively Lukan theme.[11] As Gaventa explains, in the Third Gospel and Acts the phrase "plan of God" (βουλὴ τοῦ θεοῦ) "refers to God as the one whose intention and oversight governs the events that unfold, encompassing both the events of Jesus' own life [in the Gospel] and the way in which the witness moves throughout the cities of the Mediterranean world [in Acts]."[12] The Third Gospel and Acts emphasize that God's plan governs the unfolding of history and that that plan concerns the salvation of humankind. The plan of God, in other words, has to do with salvation history. Only in Luke among the Synoptic Gospels is Jesus called the "savior" (Luke 2:11; Acts 5:31; 13:23) through whose coming and activity God's salvific plan is achieved (Luke 1:69, 71; 19:9; Acts 4:12; 13:26, 47; 16:17). In addition to Jesus' activity, the Gospel and Acts demonstrate the centrality of God's plan in the narrative through allusions to the necessity of foreordained events and their subsequent realization for the fulfillment of God's plan (referred to as the "divine δεῖ").

The two events that Luke's narrative presents as at the core of the plan of God are Jesus' crucifixion and the mission to Gentiles. For example, throughout the reflection on Jesus' execution in Luke 24, his crucifixion is lifted up as necessary and in accord with Scripture (Luke 24:6–7, 25–27, 44–46). Later in Acts, Peter claims that Jesus' fate was "by God's definitive plan and foreknowledge" (Acts 2:23; see also 4:28). As for the Gentile mission, Luke 24:47 argues that Scripture prophesied not only Christ's crucifixion but also that the gospel had to be preached to all nations, and Acts consistently maintains that the mission to Gentiles is part of God's plan (e.g., Acts 9:15; 10:1–11:18; 22:21; 23:11; 26:16–18).

God's apparent control of history has caused some scholars to argue that the Third Gospel and Acts portray humanity as lacking freedom of

---

11. Squires, *Plan of God in Luke-Acts*, 1–3. Squires's work represents the most thorough study of the plan of God motif in Luke and Acts and has, therefore, been used extensively to shape the present discussion. See also Fitzmyer, *Gospel according to Luke*, 1:18–27; Cosgrove, "The Divine Δεῖ in Luke-Acts," 168–90; Minear, "Dear Theo," 131–50; Hans Conzelmann, *The Theology of St. Luke* (trans. Geoffrey Buswell; New York: Harper & Row, 1961), 149–69; Nils A. Dahl, "The Purpose of Luke-Acts," in *Jesus in the Memory of the Early Church: Essays* (Minneapolis: Augsburg, 1976), 87–98; David Peterson, "Luke's Theological Enterprise: Integration and Intent," in Marshall and Peterson, *Witness to the Gospel*, 521–44; idem, "The Motif of Fulfillment and the Purpose of Luke Acts," in *The Book of Acts in Its Ancient Literary Setting* (ed. Bruce W. Winter and Andrew D. Clarke; vol. 1 of *The Book of Acts in Its First Century Setting*; ed. Bruce W. Winter; Grand Rapids: Eerdmans, 1993), 83–104; Paul Schubert, "The Place of the Areopagus Speech in the Composition of Acts," in *Transitions in Biblical Scholarship* (ed. J. Rylaarsdam; Chicago: University of Chicago Press, 1968), 235–61; idem, "The Structure and Significance of Luke 24," in *Neutestamentlich Studien für Rudolf Bultmann* (ed. Walther Estester; Berlin: Töpelmann, 1954), 165–86.

12. Gaventa, *Acts of the Apostles*, 31.

choice. Ernst Haenchen, for example, argues that God's preeminent role in historical events in Acts reduces human response to "very nearly the twitching of human puppets."[13] God's plan, however, never operates at the expense of human freedom in Luke's two volumes. Rather, divine providence and human freedom are cooperative motifs. Indeed, it is in the exercise of human freedom that God's plan comes to fruition, whether human activity assists or opposes that plan. The philosophical problems and implications of this do not trouble Luke very much—they are left for others to ponder.

---

13. Haenchen, *Acts of the Apostles*, 362.

Appendix B

Greek Text and English Translations of Selected Passages from Thucydides, Polybius, and Josephus

Thucydides in the Third Person[1]

1.1.1 Θουκυδίδης Ἀθηναῖος ξυνέγραψε τὸν πόλεμον τῶν Πελοποννησίων καὶ Ἀθηναίων, ὡς ἐπολέμησαν πρὸς ἀλλήλους, ἀρξάμενος εὐθὺς καθισταμένου καὶ ἐλπίσας μέγαν τε ἔσεσθαι καὶ ἀξιολογώτατον τῶν προγεγενημένων, τεκμαιρόμενος ὅτι ἀκμάζοντές τε ῃ]σαν ἐς αὐτὸν ἀμφότεροι παρασκευῇ τῇ πάσῃ καὶ τὸ ἄλλο Ἑλληνικὸν ὁρῶν ξυνιστάμενον πρὸς ἑκατέρους, τὸ μὲν εὐθύς, τὸ δὲ καὶ διανοούμενον.

Thucydides, an Athenian, wrote the history of the war between the Peloponnesians and the Athenians while they were at war with one another, beginning immediately as it was breaking out and expecting it would be great and more noteworthy than any that had come before, taking as an indication the fact that both were at the peak of preparedness for war in every way and observing the rest of the Hellenic people allying themselves with one side or the other, some at once, others intending to do so.

5.26.1 Γέγραφε δὲ καὶ ταῦτα ὁ αὐτὸς Θουκυδίδης Ἀθηναῖος ἑξῆς, ὡς ἕκαστα ἐγένετο, κατὰ θέρη καὶ χειμῶνας, μέχρι οὗ τήν τε ἀρχὴν κατέπαυσαν τῶν Ἀθηναίων Λακεδαιμόνιοι καὶ οἱ ξύμμαχοι, καὶ τὰ μακρὰ τείχη καὶ τὸν Πειραιᾶ κατέλαβον.

The same Thucydides, an Athenian, has written down these events in the order that each occurred, by summers and winters, up to the time when the Lacedaemonians and their allies put an end to the domination of the Athenians and seized the Long Walls and Piraeus.

4.104.4 οἱ δὲ ἐναντίοι τοῖς προδιδοῦσι, κρατοῦντες τῷ πλήθει ὥστε μὴ αὐτίκα τὰς πύλας ἀνοίγεσθαι, πέμπουσι μετὰ Εὐκλέους τοῦ στρατηγοῦ, ὃς ἐκ τῶν Ἀθηνῶν

---

1. The Greek critical edition used is that of H. S. Jones and J. E. Powell, eds., *Thucydides Historiae* (2 vols.; Oxford: Clarendon, 1942). As noted in chapter 2, I have translated the passages literally—without, I hope, losing the sense of the original—in order to convey adequately the use of grammatical person.

παρῆν αὐτοῖς φύλαξ τοῦ χωρίου, ἐπὶ τὸν ἕτερον στρατηγὸν τῶν ἐπὶ Θράκης, Θουκυδίδην τὸν Ὀλόρου, ὃς τάδε ξυνέγραψεν, ὄντα περὶ Θάσον (ἔστι δὲ ἡ νῆσος Παρίων ἀποικία, ἀπέχουσα τῆς Ἀμφιπόλεως ἡμίσεος ἡμέρας μάλιστα πλοῦν), κελεύοντες σφίσι βοηθεῖν. **4.104.5** καὶ ὁ μὲν ἀκούσας κατὰ τάχος ἑπτὰ ναυσὶν αἳ ἔτυχον παροῦσαι ἔπλει, καὶ ἐβούλετο φθάσαι μάλιστα μὲν οὖν τὴν Ἀμφίπολιν, πρίν τι ἐνδοῦναι, εἰ δὲ μή, τὴν Ἠϊόνα προκαταλαβών. **4.105.1** Ἐν τούτῳ δὲ ὁ Βρασίδας δεδιὼς καὶ τὴν ἀπὸ τῆς Θάσου τῶν νεῶν βοήθειαν καὶ πυνθανόμενος τὸν Θουκυδίδην κτῆσίν τε ἔχειν τῶν χρυσείων μετάλλων ἐργασίας ἐν τῇ περὶ ταῦτα Θράκῃ καὶ ἀπ' αὐτοῦ δύνασθαι ἐν τοῖς πρώτοις τῶν ἠπειρωτῶν, ἠπείγετο προκατασχεῖν, εἰ δύναιτο, τὴν πόλιν, μὴ ἀφικνουμένου αὐτοῦ τὸ πλῆθος τῶν Ἀμφιπολιτῶν, ἐλπίσαν ἐκ θαλάσσης ξυμμαχικὸν καὶ ἀπὸ τῆς Θράκης ἀγείραντα αὐτὸν περιποιήσειν σφᾶς, **4.105.2** οὐκέτι προσχωροίη . . . **4.406.3.3** καὶ οἱ μὲν τὴν πόλιν τοιούτῳ τρόπῳ παρέδοσαν, ὁ δὲ Θουκυδίδης καὶ αἱ νῆες ταύτῃ τῇ ἡμέρᾳ ὀψὲ κατέπλεον ἐς τὴν Ἠϊόνα. . . . **4.407.1** Μετὰ δὲ τοῦτο ὁ μὲν τὰ ἐν τῇ Ἠϊόνι καθίστατο, ὅπως καὶ τὸ αὐτίκα, ἢν ἐπίῃ ὁ Βρασίδας, καὶ τὸ ἔπειτα ἀσφαλῶς ἕξει, δεξάμενος τοὺς ἐθελήσαντας ἐπιχωρῆσαι ἄνωθεν κατὰ τὰς σπονδάς.

4.104.4 The opponents of the betrayers, prevailing in number so that, for the moment, the gates were not opened, together with the general, Eucles, who had come to them from Athens as the protector of the district, sent to the other commander of the areas in Thrace, Thucydides, son of Olorus—he wrote the history of these [events]—who was near Thasos (it is the island colony of Paria, a voyage of about a half-day from Amphipolis) urging him to come to their assistance. **4.104.5** And he, when he heard, set sail in haste with seven ships that happened to be at hand. He actually wished most of all to reach Amphipolis before it yielded, but if not to take possession of Eion before [the enemy]. **4.105.1–2** In the meantime, Brasidas, fearing the assistance of the ships from Thasos, and learning that Thucydides controlled the working of the gold mines in that part of Thrace and because of it had influence over the most prominent of the inhabitants on the mainland, was hastening to gain possession of the city beforehand if he could, lest when he [Thucydides] arrived, the population of Amphipolis should no longer surrender, hoping that he, having gathered allied forces out of the sea and from Thrace, would rescue them. . . . **4.406.3.3** They handed over the city in this way, and late on the same day Thucydides and the ships sailed into Eion. . . . **4.407.1** After this he set things up in Eion so that both for the present— should Brasidas attack it—and thereafter it would be secure, welcoming those who wished to join him from above in accordance with the truce.[2]

---

2. The name "Thucydides" also appears briefly in 1.117.2 and 8.92.8, but it is unclear whether either of these is a reference to the historian.

First Person Singular in Thucydides

5.26.4 αἰεὶ γὰρ ἔγωγε μέμνημαι, καὶ ἀρχομένου τοῦ πολέμου καὶ μέχρι οὗ ἐτελεύτησε, προφερόμενον ὑπὸ πολλῶν ὅτι τρὶς ἐννέα ἔτη δέοι γενέσθαι αὐτόν. **5.26.5** ἐπεβίων δὲ διὰ παντὸς αὐτοῦ αἰσθανόμενός τε τῇ ἡλικίᾳ καὶ προσέχων τὴν γνώμην, ὅπως ἀκριβές τι εἴσομαι· καὶ ξυνέβη μοι φεύγειν τὴν ἐμαυτοῦ ἔτη εἴκοσι μετὰ τὴν ἐς Ἀμφίπολιν στρατηγίαν, καὶ γενομένῳ παρ' ἀμφοτέροις τοῖς πράγμασι, καὶ οὐχ ἧσσον τοῖς Πελοποννησίων διὰ τὴν φυγήν, καθ' ἡσυχίαν τι αὐτῶν μᾶλλον αἰσθέσθαι. **5.26.6** τὴν οὖν μετὰ τὰ δέκα ἔτη διαφοράν τε καὶ ξύγχυσιν τῶν σπονδῶν καὶ τὰ ἔπειτα ὡς ἐπολεμήθη ἐξηγήσομαι.

5.26.4 For indeed I remember, from the beginning of the war until it came to an end, it being ever proposed by many that it was fated to last three times nine years. **5.26.5** And I lived through all of it being, in adulthood, fully capable of understanding and devoting attention to it so that I would know it accurately. And it happened that I fled my own country for twenty years after the command in Amphipolis and being present at the affairs of both sides—and just as much at those of the Peloponnesians on account of the banishment—learned better their events because of the respite. **5.26.6** The disagreement, then, after ten years, and the violation of the truce and events thereafter when hostilities broke out, I shall relate in full.

2.48 λεγέτω μὲν οὖν περὶ αὐτοῦ ὡς ἕκαστος γιγνώσκει καὶ ἰατρὸς καὶ ἰδιώτης, ἀφ' ὅτου εἰκὸς ἦν γενέσθαι αὐτό, καὶ τὰς αἰτίας ἅστινας νομίζει τοσαύτης μεταβολῆς ἱκανὰς εἶναι δύναμιν ἐς τὸ μεταστῆσαι σχεῖν· ἐγὼ δὲ οἷόν τε ἐγίγνετο λέξω, καὶ ἀφ' ὧν ἄν τις σκοπῶν, εἴ ποτε καὶ αὖθις ἐπιπέσοι, μάλιστ' ἂν ἔχοι τι προειδὼς μὴ ἀγνοεῖν, ταῦτα δηλώσω αὐτός τε νοσήσας καὶ αὐτὸς ἰδὼν ἄλλους πάσχοντας.

Then let both physician and lay person speak about [the plague] as each decides: from what was it likely to have been produced and what causes he considers are sufficient to be able to introduce so significant a change. But I shall tell how it occurred, and from this whoever investigates, having knowledge beforehand, should certainly be able to recognize it if it should ever attack again. I shall describe this, as I myself was sick and personally saw others suffering.

1.1.3 τὰ γὰρ πρὸ αὐτῶν καὶ τὰ ἔτι παλαίτερα σαφῶς μὲν εὑρεῖν διὰ χρόνου πλῆθος ἀδύνατα ἦν, ἐκ δὲ τεκμηρίων ὧν ἐπὶ μακρότατον σκοποῦντί μοι πιστεῦσαι ξυμβαίνει οὐ μεγάλα νομίζω γενέσθαι οὔτε κατὰ τοὺς πολέμους οὔτε ἐς τὰ ἄλλα.

For it was impossible to recover clearly the events before these and affairs even more ancient because of the extent of time, but from the evidence that, after having examined it in the greatest depth, it turns out that I can trust, I do not consider them to have been important either in terms of wars or in other ways.

1.22.1 Καὶ ὅσα μὲν λόγῳ εἶπον ἕκαστοι ἢ μέλλοντες πολεμήσειν ἢ ἐν αὐτῷ ἤδη ὄντες, χαλεπὸν τὴν ἀκρίβειαν αὐτὴν τῶν λεχθέντων διαμνημονεῦσαι ἦν ἐμοί τε ὧν αὐτὸς ἤκουσα καὶ τοῖς ἄλλοθέν ποθεν ἐμοὶ ἀπαγέλλουσιν· ὡς δ' ἂν ἐδόκουν ἐμοὶ ἕκαστοι περὶ τῶν αἰεὶ παρόντων τὰ δέοντα μάλιστ᾽ εἰπεῖν, ἐχομένῳ ὅτι ἐγγύτατα τῆς ξυμπάσης γνώμης τῶν ἀληθῶς λεχθέντων, **1.22.2** οὕτως εἴρηται. τὰ δ᾽ ἔργα τῶν πραχθέντων ἐν τῷ πολέμῳ οὐκ ἐκ τοῦ παρατυχόντος πυνθανόμενος ἠξίωσα γράφειν, οὐδ᾽ ὡς ἐμοὶ ἐδόκει, ἀλλ᾽ οἷς τε αὐτὸς παρῆν καὶ παρὰ τῶν ἄλλων ὅσον δυνατὸν ἀκριβείᾳ περὶ ἑκάστου ἐπεξελθών.

1.22.1 And as for speeches individuals made, either as they were about to go to war or were already in it, it was difficult to remember distinctly the very precision of the things they said—both for me the speeches I myself heard and for those who reported [speeches] to me from elsewhere. Therefore, it has been reported what each of them seemed to me most likely to have said concerning the circumstances at the time, holding as closely as possible to the general purport of what they actually said. **1.22.2** I thought it fitting to write the facts of what took place in the war not by inquiring from someone who happened to be present nor as seemed plausible to me, but about those at which I myself was present and those from others by investigating as fully as possible the accuracy of each.

First Person Plural in Thucydides

1.13.4 ναυμαχία τε παλαιτάτη ὧν ἴσμεν γίγνεται Κορινθίων πρὸς Κερκυραίους·
The earliest sea battle of the ones we know was of the Corinthians against the Corcyraeans.

1.18.1 ἡ γὰρ Λακεδαίμων μετὰ τὴν κτίσιν τῶν νῦν ἐνοικούντων αὐτὴν Δωριῶν ἐπὶ πλεῖστον ὧν ἴσμεν χρόνον στασιάσασα ὅμως ἐκ παλαιτάτου καὶ ηὐνομήθη καὶ αἰεὶ ἀτυράννευτος ἦν·
For Lacedaemon after settlement by the Dorians who inhabit it now, even though it was in rebellion for the greatest length of time of any area we know, nevertheless was from the earliest date orderly and always free of tyrants.

7.87.5 ξυνέβη τε ἔργον τοῦτο [Ἑλληνικὸν] τῶν κατὰ τὸν πόλεμον τόνδε μέγιστον γενέσθαι, δοκεῖν δ᾽ ἔμοιγε καὶ ὧν ἀκοῇ Ἑλληνικῶν ἴσμεν, καὶ τοῖς τε κρατήσασι λαμπρότατον καὶ τοῖς διαφθαρεῖσι δυστυχέστατον·
This (Hellenic) battle turned out to be the most memorable of any in the war, and indeed it seems to me also of those Hellenic battles we know by report, both the most magnificent to those who conquered and the most unfortunate to those who were destroyed.

8.41.2 καὶ ἐς Κῶν τὴν Μεροπίδα ἐν τῷ παράπλῳ ἀποβὰς τήν τε πόλιν ἀτείχιστον οὖσαν καὶ ὑπὸ σεισμοῦ, ὃς αὐτοῖς ἔτυχε μέγιστός γε δὴ ὧν μεμνήμεθα γενόμενος, ξυμπεπτωκυῖαν ἐκπορθεῖ, τῶν ἀνθρώπων ἐς τὰ ὄρη πεφευγότων, καὶ τὴν χώραν καταδρομαῖς λείαν ἐποιεῖτο, πλὴν τῶν ἐλευθέρων· τούτους δὲ ἀφίει.
After landing at Cos (a.k.a. Meropis) during the coasting voyage, he pillaged the city, which was unfortified and had collapsed under an earthquake that had befallen them—indeed of those we remember, it was the worst—the

people having fled into the mountains. And through raids, he made booty of the country except for free people; these he released.
2.102.6 τὰ μὲν περὶ Ἀλκμέωνα τοιαῦτα λεγόμενα παρελάβομεν.
With respect to the things concerning Alcmaeon, such are the reports we have received.

Polybius in the Third Person[3]

24.6.3 ταῦτα δὲ βουλευσάμενοι προεχειρίσαντο πρεσβευτὰς Λυκόρταν καὶ Πολύβιον καὶ σὺν τούτοις Ἄρατον, υἱὸν Ἀράτου τοῦ Σικυωνίου, τοὺς ἅμα μὲν εὐχαριστήσοντας τῷ βασιλεῖ περί τε τῶν ὅπλων ὧν πρότερον ἀπέστειλε καὶ τοῦ νομίσματος, ἅμα δὲ παραληψομένους τὰ πλοῖα καὶ πρόνοιαν ποιησομένους περὶ τῆς ἀποκομιδῆς αὐτῶν. **24.6.4** κατέστησαν δὲ τὸν μὲν Λυκόρταν διὰ τὸ κατὰ τὸν καιρόν, καθ᾽ ὃν ἐποιεῖτο τὴν ἀνανέωσιν τῆς συμμαχίας ὁ Πτολεμαῖος, στρατηγοῦντα τότε συνεργῆσαι φιλοτίμως αὐτῷ, **24.6.5** τὸν δὲ Πολύβιον, νεώτερον ὄντα τῆς κατὰ τοὺς νόμους ἡλικίας, διὰ τὸ τήν τε συμμαχίαν αὐτοῦ τὸν πατέρα πρεσβεύσαντα πρὸς Πτολεμαῖον ἀνανεώσασθαι καὶ τὴν δωρεὰν τῶν ὅπλων καὶ τοῦ νομίσματος ἀγαγεῖν τοῖς Ἀχαιοῖς, **24.6.6** παραπλησίως δὲ καὶ τὸν Ἄρατον διὰ τὰς προγονικὰς συστάσεις πρὸς τὴν βασιλείαν.
24.6.3 Having determined this, they selected as envoys Lycortas, Polybius, and with them Aratus, the son of Aratus of Sicyon, who were to thank the king for the arms and money that he previously sent and at the same time were to receive the ships and make preparations for their return. **24.6.4** They appointed Lycortas because at the time Ptolemy made the renewal of the alliance, holding the office of strategus, he eagerly cooperated with him, **24.6.5** and Polybius—although younger than the legal age—because his father, as envoy to Ptolemy, had renewed the alliance and brought back to the Achaeans the gift of arms and money. **24.6.6** Likewise, [they appointed] Aratus because of his parents' friendship with the king.
28.7.8 πολλῆς δ᾽ οὔσης ἀπορίας ὁ Πολύβιος ἀναστὰς ἐποιήσατο μὲν καὶ πλείονας λόγους, μάλιστα δὲ προσέδραμε πρὸς τὴν τῶν πολλῶν γνώμην, ὑποδείξας τὸ γεγονὸς ἐξ ἀρχῆς ψήφισμα τῶν Ἀχαιῶν ὑπὲρ τῶν τιμῶν, ἐν ᾧ γεγραμμένον ἦν ὅτι δεῖ τὰς ἀπρεπεῖς ἀρθῆναι τιμὰς καὶ τὰς παρανόμους, **28.7.9** οὐ μὰ Δί᾽ ἁπάσας. τοὺς δὲ περὶ Σωσιγένη καὶ Διοπείθη, δικαστὰς [Ροδίους] ὑπάρχοντας κατ᾽ ἐκεῖνον τὸν καιρὸν καὶ διαφερομένους ἔκ τινων ἰδίων πρὸς τὸν Εὐμένη, λαβομένους ἔφη τῆς ἀφορμῆς ταύτης πάσας ἀνατετροφέναι τὰς τιμὰς τοῦ βασιλέως· **28.7.10** καὶ τοῦτο πεποιηκέναι παρὰ τὸ τῶν Ἀχαιῶν δόγμα καὶ παρὰ τὴν δοθεῖσαν αὐτοῖς ἐξουσίαν, καὶ τὸ μέγιστον, **28.7.11** παρὰ τὸ δίκαιον καὶ τὸ καλῶς ἔχον. οὐ γὰρ ω̈ς ἠδικημένους τι τοὺς Ἀχαιοὺς βουλεύσασθαι τὰς τιμὰς αἴρειν τὰς Εὐμένους, ἀλλὰ μείζους αὐτοῦ ζητοῦντος τῶν εὐεργεσιῶν, τούτῳ προσκόψαντας ψηφίσασθαι τὸ

---

3. The critical edition used is that of T. Büttner-Wobst, ed., *Polybii Historiae* (4 vols.; 1889–1905; repr., Stuttgart: Teubner, 1962–1967).

πλεονάζον παρελεῖν. **28.7.**12 διόπερ ἔφη δεῖν, καθάπερ οἱ δικασταὶ τὴν ἰδίαν ἔχθραν ἐπίπροσθεν ποιήσαντες τοῦ τῶν Ἀχαιῶν εὐσχήμονος ἀνέτρεψαν πάσας τὰς τιμάς, οὕτω τοὺς Ἀχαιοὺς κυριώτατον ἡγησαμένους τὸ σφίσι καθῆκον καὶ πρέπον διορθώσασθαι τὴν τῶν δικαστῶν ἁμαρτίαν καὶ καθόλου τὴν πρὸς τὸν Εὐμένη γεγενημένην ἀλογίαν, **28.7.**13 ἄλλως τε καὶ μέλλοντας μὴ μόνον ἐπ' αὐτὸν τὸν βασιλέα τὴν χάριν ἀπερείδεσθαι ταύτην, ἔτι δὲ μᾶλλον εἰς τὸν ἀδελφὸν Ἄτταλον.

28.7.8 While there was much perplexity, Polybius stood and made a longer speech, and emphatically joined sides with the judgment of the majority, indicating what the original decree of the Achaeans was concerning the honors, in which was written that it was necessary for unseemly and unlawful—not, by Zeus, all—honors to be revoked. **28.7.**9 "But," he said, "those around Sosigenes and Diopeithes (who at that time were judges—Rhodian!—and differed with Eumenes in certain private matters) used this pretext to overturn all the honors of the king. **28.7.**10 And they did this contrary to the decision of the Achaeans and exceeding the authority given them and, what is most important, against what was just and good." **28.7.**11 For not because they had been wronged in some way did the Achaeans determine to take away the honors of Eumenes, but, because he was seeking more than his good services warranted, they took offense at this and voted to withdraw what was excessive. **28.7.**12 "Therefore," he said, "just as the judges, placing their personal enmity before the honor of the Achaeans, overturned all the honors, so also the Achaeans, considering to be most legitimate what is appropriate and fitting for them, must correct the error of the judges and the general lack of respect accorded Eumenes, **28.7.**13 especially since they will be directing this favor not only toward the king himself, but even more unto his brother Attalus."

First Person Singular in Polybius

3.4.13 ὑπὲρ ἧς διὰ τὸ μέγεθος τῶν ἐν αὐτῇ πράξεων καὶ τὸ παράδοξον τῶν συμβαινόντων, τὸ δὲ μέγιστον, διὰ τὸ τῶν πλείστων μὴ μόνον αὐτόπτης, ἀλλ' ὧν μὲν συνεργὸς ὢν δὲ καὶ χειριστὴς γεγονέναι, προήχθην οἷον ἀρχὴν ποιησάμενος ἄλλην γράφειν.

Concerning [the period after Rome's worldwide ascendance], because of the significance of the events in it and the incredibleness of the things that took place, but most of all because I have been not only an eyewitness to most of them but of some a participant and of others even an administrator, I was persuaded to write as if making another beginning.

36.1.3 ἐγὼ δὲ διότι μὲν οὐκ ἀποδοκιμάζω τοῦτο τὸ μέρος, ἐν πλείοσι τόποις τῆς ἱστορίας δῆλον πεποίημαι, πολλάκις ἀπηγγελκὼς δημηγορίας καὶ συντάξεις ἀνδρῶν πολιτικῶν· **36.1.**4 ὅτι δ' οὐκ ἐκ παντὸς τρόπου τοῦτο προαιροῦμαι πράττειν, νῦν ἔσται συμφανές· οὔτε γὰρ ὑπόθεσιν ἐπιφανεστέραν ταύτης εὑρεῖν ῥᾴδιον οὔθ' ὕλην πλείω καὶ παράθεσιν. **36.1.5** καὶ μὴν οὐδὲ προχειρότερον ἕτερον ἐμοὶ τῆς τοιαύτης παρασκευῆς. **36.1.6** ἀλλ' οὔτε τοῖς πολιτικοῖς ἀνδράσιν οἶμαι πρέπειν πρὸς πᾶν τὸ προτεθὲν διαβούλιον εὑρησιλογεῖν καὶ διεξοδικοῖς χρῆσθαι λόγοις, ἀλλ' ἀεὶ τοῖς ἁρμόζουσι πρὸς τὸν ὑποκείμενον καιρόν, **36.1.7** οὔτε τοῖς ἱστοριογράφοις ἐμμελετᾶν τοῖς ἀκούουσιν οὐδ' ἐναποδείκνυσθαι τὴν αὐτῶν δύναμιν, ἀλλὰ [τὰ] κατ' ἀλήθειαν ῥηθέντα [καθ'] ὅσον οἷόν τε πολυπραγμονήσαντας διασαφεῖν, καὶ τούτων τὰ καιριώτατα καὶ πραγματικώτατα.

36.1.3 That I do not reject this part I have made clear in many places in the history by reporting often the speeches and compositions of politicians, **36.1.4** but that I do not prefer the practice in every situation will now be evident. For it is not easy to find a more conspicuous occasion than this one nor a more significant matter or instance. **36.1.5** And indeed nothing is easier for me than such a practice. **36.1.6** But I do not think it seemly for politicians to invent ingenious pretexts and employ detailed speeches for every debate put forward, but always those that suit the occasion at hand, **36.1.7** nor for historians to practice on their readers or make a show of their ability but, after inquiring closely into all such matters, to make clear what was actually said, and of these the things most timely and most related to the subject.

29.21.8 ἐγὼ δὲ κατὰ τὴν γραφὴν ἐπιστὰς τοῖς καιροῖς καθ' οὓς συνέβη καταλυθῆναι τὴν Μακεδόνων βασιλείαν, οὐκ ἔκρινον ἀνεπιστάτως παραδραμεῖν, ἄτε γεγονὼς αὐτόπτης τῆς πράξεως, ἀλλ' αὐτός τε τὸν πρέποντα λόγον ἐπιφθέγξασθαι καὶ Δημητρίου μνησθῆναι· **29.21.9** δοκεῖ γάρ μοι θειοτέραν ἢ κατ' ἄνθρωπον τὴν ἀπόφασιν ποιήσασθαι· σχεδὸν γὰρ ἑκατὸν καὶ πεντήκοντα πρότερον ἔτεσι τἀληθὲς ἀπεφήνατο περὶ τῶν ἔπειτα συμβησομένων.

29.21.8 And I, when I turned my attention in the writing to the time when the Macedonian monarchy was deposed, did not choose injudiciously to pass over it, inasmuch as I had been an eyewitness to the event, but to utter myself a fitting word and to recall those of Demetrius. **29.21.9** For it seems to me that the prediction he made was more divine than human, for he made known the truth perhaps a 150 years earlier about the things that would happen afterwards.

First Person Plural in Polybius

1.1.1 Εἰ μὲν τοῖς πρὸ ἡμῶν ἀναγράφουσι τὰς πράξεις παραλελεῖφθαι συνέβαινε τὸν ὑπὲρ αὐτῆς τῆς ἱστορίας ἔπαινον, ἴσως ἀναγκαῖον ἦν τὸ προτρέπεσθαι πάντας πρὸς τὴν αἵρεσιν καὶ παραδοχὴν τῶν τοιούτων ὑπομνημάτων διὰ τὸ μηδεμίαν ἑτοιμοτέραν εἶναι τοῖς ἀνθρώποις διόρθωσιν τῆς τῶν προγεγενημένων πράξεων ἐπιστήμης.

If it had been characteristic of those who recorded events before us to neglect the praise of history itself, perhaps it would have been necessary to urge everyone toward the study and acceptance of treatises such as this, because there is no more certain corrective for human beings than the knowledge of events that have occurred previously.

1.1.4 αὐτὸ γὰρ τὸ παράδοξον τῶν πράξεων, ὑπὲρ ὧν προρήμεθα γράφειν, ἱκανόν ἐστι προκαλέσασθαι καὶ παρορμῆσαι πάντα καὶ νέον καὶ πρεσβύτερον πρὸς τὴν ἔντευξιν τῆς πραγματείας.

For the very unexpectedness of the events about which we have chosen to write is sufficient to challenge and stimulate all, both young and old, to the study of the treatise.

36.11.1 Ὅτι προσπεσόντων εἰς τὴν Πελοπόννησον γραμμάτων τοῖς Ἀχαιοῖς παρὰ τοῦ Μανιλίου διότι καλῶς ποιήσουσι Πολύβιον τὸν Μεγαλοπολίτην ἐκπέμψαντες μετὰ σπουδῆς εἰς Λιλύβαιον, ὡς χρείας οὔσης αὐτοῦ δημοσίων ἕνεκεν πραγμάτων, ἔδοξε τοῖς Ἀχαιοῖς ἐκπέμπειν ἀκολούθως τοῖς ὑπὸ τοῦ ὑπάτου γεγραμμένοις. 36.11.2 ἡμεῖς δὲ νομίζοντες ἑαυτοῖς καθήκειν κατὰ πολλοὺς τρόπους τὸ πειθαρχεῖν Ῥωμαίοις, πάντα τἆλλα πάρεργα [θέμενοι] θερείας ἀρχομένης ἐξεπλεύσαμεν. 36.11.3 ἀφικόμενοι δ᾽ εἰς Κέρκυραν καὶ καταλαβόντες αὐτοῦ γράμματα παρὰ τῶν ὑπάτων προσπεπτωκότα τοῖς Κερκυραίοις, ἐν οἷς διεσάφουν ὅτι τοὺς μὲν ὁμήρους ἤδη παραδεδώκασιν αὐτοῖς οἱ Καρχηδόνιοι, πάντως ἕτοιμοι δ᾽ εἰσὶν αὐτοῖς πειθαρχεῖν, 36.11.4 νομίσαντες διαλελύσθαι τὸν πόλεμον καὶ μηκέτι χρείαν ἡμῶν εἶναι μηδεμίαν, αὖθις ἀπεπλεύσαμεν εἰς τὴν Πελοπόννησον.[4]

36.11.1 When instructions arrived in the Peloponnese for the Achaeans from Manilius that they would do well to send Polybius the Megalopolitan with haste to Lilybaeum as there was need of him for affairs of state, the Achaeans resolved to send him in accordance with the petition of the consul. 36.11.2 We, thinking it our duty for many reasons to obey the Romans, putting aside all other matters, set sail when summer began. 36.11.3 Arriving in Corcyra and finding there a letter from the consuls that had been sent to the Corcyraeans in which they made quite clear that the Carthaginians had already handed over the hostages to them and were prepared in every way to obey them, 36.11.4 thinking that the war had been brought to end and there was no further any need of us, we sailed back again to the Peloponnese.

39.8.1 ταῦτα μὲν οὖν ἡμεῖς καταπράξαντες ἐκ τῆς Ῥώμης ἐπανήλθομεν, ὡσανεὶ κεφάλαιά τινα τῶν προπεπολιτευμένων κατειργασμένοι, χάριν ἀξίαν τῆς πρὸς Ῥωμαίους εὐνοίας. 39.8.2 διὸ καὶ πᾶσι τοῖς θεοῖς εὐχὰς ποιούμεθα τὸ λοιπὸν μέρος τῆς ζωῆς ἐν τούτοις καὶ ἐπὶ τούτων διαμεῖναι, θεωροῦντες τὴν τύχην ὡς ἔστιν ἀγαθὴ φθονῆσαι τοῖς ἀνθρώποις καὶ μάλιστα κατὰ τοῦτο τὸ μέρος ἰσχύει καθ᾽ ὅ τις ἂν δοκῇ μάλιστα μακαρίζεσθαι καὶ κατορθοῦν ἐν τῷ βίῳ. 39.8.3 Καὶ ταῦτα μὲν οὕτω γενέσθαι συνέπεσεν· ἡμεῖς δὲ παραγεγονότες ἐπὶ τὸ τέρμα τῆς

---

4. This represents the first known use of occasional first-person style in a third-person narrative, as Thornton notes: "haben wir in Polybius das erste Beispiel dafür, wie die durchgängige Er-Form durch die Ich-Erzählung durchbrochen wird. Leider wissen wir zu wenig über die genauen Hintergründe dieses formalen Umbruchs Bescheid, vor allem deshalb nicht, weil uns aus dem 3. Jahrhundert v.Chr. so außerordentlich wenig erhalten geblieben ist" (*Der Zeuge des Zeugen*, 182).

ὅλης πραγματείας βουλόμεθα, προσαναμνήσαντες τῆς ἀρχῆς καὶ τῆς προεκθέσεως ἧς ἐποιησάμεθα καταβαλόμενοι τὴν ἱστορίαν, συγκεφαλαιώσασθαι τὴν ὅλην ὑπόθεσιν, οἰκειώσαντες τὴν ἀρχὴν τῷ τέλει καὶ καθόλου καὶ κατὰ μέρος. **39.8.1** After accomplishing these things, then, we returned from Rome, having been successful, as it were, with respect to certain principal aims of the previous political activities, a favor worthy of the goodwill toward the Romans. **39.8.2** Therefore, we offer prayers to all the gods that the remaining part of life continues in these ways and on these paths, observing that fate, as much as it is good, is envious of humankind and is forceful especially against this instance, viz., insofar as anyone seems especially to have been blessed and to succeed in life. **39.8.3** And it turned out that these things happened in this way. And we, as we come to the end of the whole treatise, wish—after recalling the beginning and the introduction that we composed when we committed the history to writing—to sum up the entire subject, reconciling the beginning to the end both overall and in particulars.

Multiple-Person Passages in Polybius

36.1.1 Ἴσως δέ τινες ἐπιζητοῦσι πῶς ἡμεῖς οὐκ ἐν ἀγωνίσματι κεχρήμεθα προφερόμενοι τοὺς κατὰ μέρος λόγους, τοιαύτης ὑποθέσεως ἐπειλημμένοι καὶ τηλικαύτης πράξεως· **36.1.2** ὅπερ οἱ πλεῖστοι ποιοῦσι τῶν συγγραφέων, εἰς ἀμφότερα τὰ μέρη διατιθέμενοι τοὺς ἐνόντας λόγους.[5]

36.1.1 Perhaps some are asking further how it is possible that we, having undertaken such a subject and such an event, have not made use of passionate oratory by presenting particular speeches— **36.1.2** precisely what most of those who write do as they recite the speeches possible on both sides.

38.21.1 καὶ ἐπιστρέψας ἐξ αὐτῆς καὶ λαβόμενός μου τῆς δεξιᾶς "ὦ Πολύβιε," ἔφη "καλὸν μέν, ἀλλ᾽ οὐκ οἶδ᾽ ὅπως ἐγὼ δέδια καὶ προορῶμαι μή ποτέ τις ἄλλος τοῦτο τὸ παράγγελμα δώσει περὶ τῆς ἡμετέρας πατρίδος·"

And turning from her and taking my hand, he said, "Polybius, it is good, but—I know not how—I fear and foresee that at some time someone else will give this order with regard to our country."

31.23.1 Τῆς δὲ κατὰ τὴν διήγησιν ἐφόδου καὶ τῶν καιρῶν ἐφεστακότων ἡμᾶς ἐπὶ τὴν οἰκίαν ταύτην, βούλομαι τὸ κατὰ τὴν προτέραν βύβλον ἐν ἐπαγγελίᾳ καταλειφθὲν συνεκπληρῶσαι τῶν φιληκόων ἕνεκα. **31.23.2** προϋπεσχόμην γὰρ διηγήσασθαι διὰ τί καὶ πῶς ἐπὶ τοσοῦτο προέκοψε καὶ θᾶττον ἢ καθῆκεν ἐξέλαμψεν ἡ τοῦ Σκιπίωνος ἐν τῇ Ῥώμῃ δόξα, **31.23.3** σὺν δὲ τούτῳ πῶς ἐπὶ τοσοῦτον αὐξηθῆναι συνέβη τῷ Πολυβίῳ τὴν πρὸς τὸν προειρημένον φιλίαν καὶ συνήθειαν ὥστε μὴ μόνον ἕως τῆς Ἰταλίας καὶ τῆς Ἑλλάδος ἐπιδιατείνειν τὴν περὶ αὐτῶν φήμην, ἀλλὰ καὶ τοῖς πορρωτέρω γνώριμον γενέσθαι τὴν αἵρεσιν καὶ συμπεριφορὰν αὐτῶν. **31.23.4** διότι μὲν οὖν ἡ καταρχὴ τῆς συστάσεως ἐγενήθη τοῖς προειρημένοις

---

5. Grammatical person shifts to first person singular for 36.1.3–7 (see p. 104).

ἔκ τινος χρήσεως βυβλίων καὶ τῆς περὶ τούτων λαλιᾶς δεδηλώκαμεν· 31.23.5
προβαινούσης δὲ τῆς συνηθείας καὶ τῶν ἀνακεκλημένων ἐκπεμπομένων ἐπὶ τὰς
πόλεις, διέσπευσαν ὅ τε Φάβιος καὶ ὁ Σκιπίων οἱ τοῦ Λευκίου νεανίσκοι πρὸς τὸν
στρατηγὸν μεῖναι τὸν Πολύβιον ἐν τῇ Ῥώμῃ.

31.23.1 Since the plan and the state of affairs in the narrative have called
our attention to this family, I wish to fulfill for the sake of those who would
enjoy hearing what was left as a promise in the previous book. **31.23.2** For
I promised before to describe in detail why and how the fame of Scipio in
Rome advanced so much and burst forth more quickly than was his due,
31.23.3 and with this how it happened that Polybius grew in friendship and
intimacy with the aforementioned person to such an extent that, not only
did the report about them extend as far as Italy and Greece, but their conduct and companionship also became well-known in more distant regions.
31.23.4 We have, therefore, indicated in what has been said previously that
the beginning of the friendship between the aforementioned men came out
of a certain loan of books and the conversation about them. **31.23.5** But as
intimacy increased, and when those who had been summoned were sent out
to the cities, Fabius and Scipio, the sons of Lucius, strongly recommended to
the praetor that Polybius remain in Rome.

Polybius's Explanation of His Use of Person

36.12.1 Οὐ χρὴ δὲ θαυμάζειν ἐὰν ποτὲ μὲν τῷ κυρίῳ σημαίνωμεν αὑτοὺς ὀνόματι,
ποτὲ δὲ ταῖς κοιναῖς ἐμφάσεσιν, οἷον οὕτως "ἐμοῦ δὲ ταῦτ᾽ εἰπόντος" καὶ πάλιν
"ἡμῶν δὲ συγκαταθεμένων." **36.12.2** ἐπὶ πολὺ γὰρ ἐμπεπλεγμένων ἡμῶν εἰς τὰς
μετὰ ταῦτα μελλούσας ἱστορεῖσθαι πράξεις, ἀναγκαῖόν ἐστι μεταλαμβάνειν τὰς
περὶ αὑτῶν σημασίας, ἵνα μήτε τοὔνομα συνεχῶς προφερόμενοι προσκόπτωμεν
ταυτολογοῦντες μήτε πάλιν "ἐμοῦ" καὶ "δι᾽ ἐμέ" παρ᾽ ἕκαστον λέγοντες λάθωμεν
εἰς φορτικὴν διάθεσιν ἐμπίπτοντες, **36.12.3** ἀλλὰ συγχρώμενοι πᾶσι τούτοις καὶ
μεταλαμβάνοντες ἀεὶ τὸ τῷ καιρῷ πρέπον ἐφ᾽ ὅσον οἷόν τε διαφεύγωμεν τὸ λίαν
ἐπαχθὲς τῆς περὶ αὑτῶν λαλιᾶς, **36.12.4** ἐπειδὴ φύσει μὲν ἀπρόσδεκτός ἐστιν
ὁ τοιοῦτος λόγος, ἀναγκαῖος δ᾽ ὑπάρχει πολλάκις, ὅταν μὴ δυνατὸν ἄλλως ἢ
δηλῶσαι τὸ προκείμενον. **36.12.5** γέγονε δέ τι πρὸς τοῦτο τὸ μέρος ἡμῖν οἷον
ἐκ ταὐτομάτου συνέργημα τὸ μηδένα μέχρι γε τῶν καθ᾽ ἡμᾶς καιρῶν ταὐτὸν ἡμῖν
ὄνομα κεκληρονομηκέναι κυρίως, ὅσον γε καὶ ἡμᾶς εἰδέναι.

36.12.1 One need not be surprised if we refer to ourselves sometimes by
proper name and other times by common expressions such as "when I said
this" and again "when we assented." **36.12.2** For since we have been much
involved in the events to be recorded hereafter, it is necessary to alter the
designations for ourselves so that we might not offend by repeating what
is said in continuously mentioning the name nor, again, that we should fall
into a boorish rhetorical style without being aware by constantly interjecting "of me" or "on account of me." **36.12.3** But by making use of all these

and substituting always what is fitting at the time, we should avoid as much as possible the exceeding offensiveness of speaking about ourselves, 36.12.4 since by nature such expression is unacceptable but is often necessary when what is being represented cannot be signified in a different way. 36.12.5 It has been some support to us for this matter, by accident as it were, that no one up to our time has inherited a proper name identical to ours, at least as far as we know.

Josephus in the Third Person in *War*[6]

2.568 τῆς δὲ Γοφνιτικῆς καὶ Ἀκραβεττηνῆς ὁ Ἀνανίου Ἰωάννης ἡγεμὼν ἀποδείκνυται καὶ τῆς Γαλιλαίας ἑκατέρας Ἰώσηπος Ματθίου· προώρ-ιστο δὲ τῇ τούτου στρατηγίᾳ καὶ Γάμαλα τῶν ταύτ πόλεων ὀχυρωτάτη.

John, son of Ananias, was appointed commander of Gophna and Acrabetta, and Josephus, son of Matthias, of each of the two Galilees; Gamala, the most secure of the cities in this region, had been added to this command.

3.142 δ' ὁ Ἰώσηπος . . . φθάνει παρελθὼν εἰς τὴν Ἰωταπάταν ἐκ τῆς Τιβεριάδος καὶ πεπτωκότα τοῖς Ἰουδαίοις ἐγείρει τὰ φρονήματα. 3.143 Οὐεσπασιανῷ δέ τις εὐαγγελίζεται τὴν μετάβασιν τοῦ ἀνδρὸς αὐτόμολος καὶ κατήπειγεν ἐπὶ τὴν πόλιν ὡς μετ' ἐκείνης αἱρήσοντα πᾶσαν Ἰουδαίαν, εἰ λάβοι τὸν Ἰώσηπον ὑποχείριον. 3.144 ὁ δ' ἁρπάσας ὥσπερ μέγιστον εὐτύχημα τὴν ἀγγελίαν, καὶ προνοίᾳ θεοῦ τὸν συνετώτατον εἶναι δοκοῦντα τῶν πολεμίων οἰόμενος εἰς εἱρκτὴν αὐθαίρετον παρελθεῖν, εὐθέως μὲν σὺν χιλίοις ἱππεῦσιν πέμπει Πλάκιδον καὶ δεκαδάρχην Αἰβούτιον . . . περικατασχεῖν κελεύσας τὴν πόλιν, ὡς μὴ λάθοι διαδρὰς ὁ Ἰώσηπος.

3.142 Josephus . . . passing unnoticed, arrived in Jotapata from Tiberias and lifted the spirits—which had fallen—of the Jews. 3.143 A deserter brought the good news of the move of the man to Vespasian and was urging him on to the city because after its capture, all Judea, if he could get Josephus in hand. 3.144 Grasping the report as a great piece of good luck and thinking it by the providence of God that the one thought to be the most intelligent of the enemy had voluntarily entered into prison, he immediately sent Placidus and the decurion, Aebutius, with a thousand cavalry troops . . . to shut the city in so that Josephus, if he ran, would not escape.

First Person Singular in *War*

1.3 προυθέμην ἐγὼ τοῖς κατὰ τὴν Ῥωμαίων ἡγεμονίαν Ἑλλάδι γλώσσῃ μεταβαλὼν ἃ τοῖς ἄνω βαρβάροις τῇ πατρίῳ συντάξας ἀνέπεμψα πρότερον ἀφηγήσασθαι Ἰώσηπος Ματθίου παῖς ἐξ Ἱεροσολύμων ἱερεύς, αὐτός τε Ῥωμαίους πολεμήσας τὰ πρῶτα καὶ τοῖς ὕστερον παρατυχὼν ἐξ ἀνάγκης·

---

6. The critical edition used is that of B. Niese, ed., *Flavii Iosephi Opera* (7 vols.; Berlin: Weidmann, 1885–1895).

I, Josephus (a priest from Jerusalem, son of Matthias), having myself fought the Romans at the beginning, and present at events afterwards out of compulsion, propose to relate to those under Roman rule, after translating into the Greek language, what I originally composed in my native language and sent to the barbarians inland.

First Person Plural in *War*

2.114 Ἄξιον δὲ μνήμης ἡγησάμην καὶ τὸ τῆς γυναικὸς αὐτοῦ Γλαφύρας ὄναρ, ἥπερ ἦν θυγάτηρ μὲν Ἀρχελάου τοῦ Καππαδόκων βασιλέως, γυνὴ δὲ Ἀλεξάνδρου γεγονυῖα τὸ πρῶτον, ὃς ἦν ἀδελφὸς Ἀρχελάου περὶ οὗ διέξιμεν, υἱὸς δὲ Ἡρώδου τοῦ βασιλέως, ὑφ' οὗ καὶ ἀνῃρέθη, καθάπερ δεδηλώκαμεν.

I regard the dream of his wife, Glaphyra, worthy of mention. She was the daughter of Archelaus, the king of Cappadocia, having first been the wife of Alexander, who was the brother of Archelaus concerning whom we are reporting, and son of Herod the king, by whom he was also killed, just as we have set forth.

7.135 λίθοι τε διαφανεῖς, οἱ μὲν χρυσοῖς ἐμπεπλεγμένοι στεφάνοις, οἱ δὲ κατ' ἄλλας ποιήσεις, τοσοῦτοι παρηνέχθησαν, ὥστε μαθεῖν ὅτι μάτην εἶναί τι τούτων σπάνιον ὑπειλήφαμεν.

So many transparent stones—some embedded in gold crowns, some in other creations—were carried past, so as to learn it to be folly that we have supposed any of them rare.[7]

Multiple-Person Passages in *War*

1.9 Οὐ μὴν ἐγὼ τοῖς ἐπαίρουσι τὰ Ῥωμαίων ἀντιφιλονεικῶν αὔξειν τὰ τῶν ὁμοφύλων διέγνων, ἀλλὰ τὰ μὲν ἔργα μετ' ἀκριβείας ἀμφοτέρων διέξιμι, τοὺς δ' ἐπὶ τοῖς πράγμασι λόγους ἀνατίθημι τῇ διαθέσει καὶ τοῖς ἐμαυτοῦ πάθεσι διδοὺς ἐπολοφύρεσθαι ταῖς τῆς πατρίδος συμφοραῖς. . . . **1.11** εἰ δή τις ὅσα πρὸς τοὺς τυράννους ἢ τὸ ληστρικὸν αὐτῶν κατηγορικῶς λέγοιμεν ἢ τοῖς δυστυχήμασι τῆς πατρίδος ἐπιστένοντες συκοφαντοίη, διδότω παρὰ τὸν τῆς ἱστορίας νόμον συγγνώμην τῷ πάθει· . . . **1.12b** εἰ δέ τις οἴκτου σκληρότερος εἴη δικαστής, τὰ μὲν πράγματα τῇ ἱστορίᾳ προσκρινέτω, τὰς δ' ὀλοφύρσεις τῷ γράφοντι.

1.9 In truth, striving against those who magnify the deeds of the Romans, I decided not to exaggerate the deeds of my race, but am relating the actions of both sides with accuracy. On the other hand, while giving the accounts about the events, I am imparting my own feelings as well as my emotions to lament over the misfortunes of my homeland. . . . **1.11** Indeed, should anyone criticize that we might say such things categorically against the tyrants

---

7. The referents of additional first-person plural comments encompass more than the narrator: sometimes readers in general (1.1; 6.267; 6.425), occasionally other Jews (1.6; 1.16; 5.137; 5.140) and in one instance Titus and/or the Roman soldiers with the narrator (6.216).

or their piracy or lament over our homeland's misfortunes, let him make allowance for emotion contrary to the law of history.... **1.12b** Should anyone be a harsher judge of compassion, let him adjudge the facts to the history, the lamentations to the writer.

7.454 Ἐνταῦθα τῆς ἱστορίας ἡμῖν τὸ πέρας ἐστίν, ἣν ἐπηγγειλάμεθα μετὰ πάσης ἀκριβείας παραδώσειν τοῖς βουλομένοις μαθεῖν, τίνα τρόπον οὗτος ὁ πόλεμος Ῥωμαίοις πρὸς Ἰουδαίους ἐπολεμήθη. **7.455** καὶ πῶς μὲν ἡρμήνευται, τοῖς ἀναγνωσομένοις κρίνειν ἀπολελείφθω, περὶ τῆς ἀληθείας δὲ οὐκ ἂν ὀκνήσαιμι θαρρῶν λέγειν, ὅτι μόνης ταύτης παρὰ πᾶσαν τὴν ἀναγραφὴν ἐστοχασάμην.

7.454 Here is the end of the history by us, which we promised to convey with total accuracy to those wishing to learn how this war by the Romans against the Jews was waged. **7.455** How it has been expressed, let it be left to the readers to judge. But concerning the truth, I would not hesitate to say with confidence that I endeavored after this throughout the entire composition.

First Person Singular in *Antiquities*

1.4 τὸν μὲν γὰρ πρὸς τοὺς Ῥωμαίους πόλεμον ἡμῖν τοῖς Ἰουδαίοις γενόμενον καὶ τὰς ἐν αὐτῷ πράξεις καὶ τὸ τέλος οἷον ἀπέβη πείρᾳ μαθὼν ἐβιάσθην ἐκδιηγήσασθαι διὰ τοὺς ἐν τῷ γράφειν λυμαινομένους τὴν ἀλήθειαν.

For knowing from experience the war that we Jews waged against the Romans, the events in it and what end resulted, I was compelled to describe it in detail because of those who in writing were defiling the truth.

1.5 ταύτην δὲ τὴν ἐνεστῶσαν ἐγκεχείρισμαι πραγματείαν νομίζων ἅπασι φανεῖσθαι τοῖς Ἕλλησιν ἀξίαν σπουδῆς· μέλλει γὰρ περιέξειν ἅπασαν τὴν παρ' ἡμῖν ἀρχαιολογίαν καὶ διάταξιν τοῦ πολιτεύματος ἐκ τῶν Ἑβραϊκῶν μεθηρμηνευμένην γραμμάτων.

I have undertaken this present treatise believing that it will appear to the Greeks worthy of attention, for it shall encompass our whole ancient history and constitution of government, translated from the Hebrew documents.

1.7 ἀλλ' ἐπειδὴ μείζων ἦν ἡ τοῦδε τοῦ λόγου περιβολή, κατ' αὐτὸν ἐκεῖνον χωρίσας ταῖς ἰδίαις ἀρχαῖς αὐτοῦ καὶ τῷ τέλει τὴν γραφὴν συνεμέτρησα· χρόνου δὲ προϊόντος ... ὄκνος μοι καὶ μέλλησις ἐγίνετο τηλικαύτην μετενεγκεῖν ὑπόθεσιν εἰς ἀλλοδαπὴν ἡμῖν καὶ ξένην διαλέκτου συνήθειαν.

But since this project was too large, I limited the work by separating out that volume itself into its own beginning and end. But as time went on ... there was hesitation and delay by me to translate so large a proposal into a custom of language foreign and strange to us.

20.259 Παύσεται δ' ἐνταῦθά μοι τὰ τῆς ἀρχαιολογίας μεθ' ἣν καὶ τὸν πόλεμον ἠρξάμην γράφειν. περιέχει δ' αὕτη τὴν ἀπὸ πρώτης γενέσεως ἀνθρώπου παράδοσιν μέχρι ἔτους δωδεκάτου τῆς Νέρωνος ἡγεμονίας τῶν ἡμῖν συμβεβηκότων τοῖς Ἰουδαίοις κατά τε τὴν Αἴγυπτον καὶ Συρίαν καὶ Παλαιστίνην, **20.260** ὅσα τε πεπόνθαμεν ὑπὸ Ἀσσυρίων τε καὶ Βαβυλωνίων, τίνα τε Πέρσαι καὶ Μακεδόνες διατεθείκασιν ἡμᾶς, καὶ μετ' ἐκείνους Ῥωμαῖοι· πάντα γὰρ οἶμαι μετ' ἀκριβείας συντετάχέναι. 20.259 Here will end my account of ancient history, after which I began to write about the war. This encompasses, from the beginning of humankind's creation up to the twelfth year of Nero's reign, the tradition of the things that have happened to us Jews in Egypt and Syria and Palestine, 20.260 how much we have suffered under the Assyrians and Babylonians, how the Persians and Macedonians have treated us, and after them the Romans. For I believe I have compiled all things with accuracy.

20.268 προῄρημαι δὲ συγγράψαι κατὰ τὰς ἡμετέρας δόξας τῶν Ἰουδαίων ἐν τέσσαρσι βίβλοις περὶ θεοῦ καὶ τῆς οὐσίας αὐτοῦ καὶ περὶ τῶν νόμων, διὰ τί κατ' αὐτοὺς τὰ μὲν ἔξεστιν ἡμῖν ποιεῖν, τὰ δὲ κεκώλυται.

I have proposed to compose a work in four books concerning our opinions as Jews about God and his essence and about the laws, why, in accordance with them, it is possible for us to do some things but others have been prohibited.

10.218 ἐγκαλέσῃ δέ μοι μηδεὶς οὕτως ἕκαστα τούτων ἀπαγέλλοντι διὰ τῆς γραφῆς, ὡς ἐν τοῖς ἀρχαίοις εὑρίσκω βιβλίοις· καὶ γὰρ εὐθὺς ἐν ἀρχῇ τῆς ἱστορίας πρὸς τοὺς ἐπιζητήσοντάς τι περὶ τῶν πραγμάτων ἢ μεμψομένους ἠσφαλισάμην, μόνον τε μεταφράζειν τὰς Ἑβραίων βίβλους εἰπὼν εἰς τὴν Ἑλλάδα γλῶτταν καὶ ταῦτα δηλώσειν μήτε προστιθεὶς τοῖς πράγμασιν αὐτὸς ἰδίᾳ μήτ' ἀφαιρῶν ὑπεσχημένος.

Let no one accuse me for reporting each of these events throughout the document in the way that I find them in the ancient books, for even in the beginning of the history I safeguarded myself against those who would seek or find fault with something about the circumstances, saying that I was only translating the Hebrew books into the Greek tongue and promising to set forth these matters without adding to nor subtracting from the affairs on my own.

First Person Plural in *Antiquities*

14.77 Τούτου τοῦ πάθους τοῖς Ἱεροσολύμοις αἴτιοι κατέστησαν Ὑρκανὸς καὶ Ἀριστόβουλος πρὸς ἀλλήλους στασιάσαντες· τήν τε γὰρ ἐλευθερίαν ἀπεβάλομεν καὶ ὑπήκοοι Ῥωμαίοις κατέστημεν καὶ τὴν χώραν, ἣν τοῖς ὅπλοις ἐκτησάμεθα τοὺς Σύρους ἀφελόμενοι, 14.78 ταύτην ἠναγκάσθημεν ἀποδοῦναι τοῖς Σύροις, καὶ προσέτι πλείω ἢ μύρια τάλαντα Ῥωμαῖοι ἐν βραχεῖ χρόνῳ παρ' ἡμῶν εἰσεπράξαντο. . . .

14.77 Hyrcanus and Aristobulus stood responsible for this suffering in Jerusalem because they were at odds with one another. For we lost our freedom and became subject to the Romans, and the region that we won with weapons, taking it away from the Syrians, 14.78 we were forced to return to the

Syrians, and over and above that the Romans in a short while exacted more than ten thousand talents from us. . . .

3.259 Καὶ περὶ τῶν ζῴων δὲ διέκρινεν ἕκαστον, ὅτι τρέφοιντο καὶ οὐ πάλιν ἀπεχόμενοι διατελοῖεν, περὶ ὧν ἐν οἷς ἂν ἡμῖν ἀφορμὴ τῆς γραφῆς γένηται διελευσόμεθα τὰς αἰτίας προστιθέντες, ἀφ' ὧν κινηθεὶς τὰ μὲν αὐτῶν βρωτὰ ἡμῖν ἐκέλευσεν εἶναι, τῶν δὲ προσέταξεν ἀπέχεσθαι.

And concerning animals, he distinguished each: which may be bred and kept and, on the contrary, from which one ought continue abstaining. Concerning these matters, whenever an occasion for writing comes to us [narrator], we shall recount them in detail, giving as well the reasons because of which he, being driven, proposed to us [narrator and other Jews] that some of them were to be eaten, and from others he ordered to abstain.

Multiple-Person Passages in *Antiquities*

1.25 τοῖς μέντοι βουλομένοις καὶ τὰς αἰτίας ἑκάστου σκοπεῖν πολλὴ γένοιτ' ἂν ἡ θεωρία καὶ λίαν φιλόσοφος, ἣν ἐγὼ νῦν μὲν ὑπερβάλλομαι, θεοῦ δὲ διδόντος ἡμῖν χρόνον πειράσομαι μετὰ ταύτην γράψαι τὴν πραγματείαν.

Nevertheless, for those who wish to contemplate also the motives for each, much would be speculation and exceedingly philosophical. This I now postpone, but if God gives us time, I shall attempt to write about it after this treatise.

16.187 ἡμεῖς δὲ καὶ γένους ὄντες ἀγχοῦ τῶν ἐξ Ἀσαμωναίου βασιλέων καὶ διὰ τοῦτο σὺν τιμῇ τὴν ἱερωσύνην ἔχοντες τὸ ψεύσασθαί τι περὶ αὐτῶν οὐκ εὐπρεπὲς ὑπειληφότες καθαρῶς καὶ δικαίως ἐκτίθεμεν τὰς πράξεις, πολλοὺς μὲν τῶν ἐγγόνων τῶν ἐκείνου καὶ βασιλεύοντας ἔτι δι' ἐντροπῆς ἔχοντες, τὴν δ' ἀλήθειαν πρὸ ἐκείνων τετιμηκότες, ἣν ὅτε δικαίως ἐγίνετο συνέβη τε παρ' αὐτοῖς ἐκείνοις ὀργῇ τυγχάνειν.

But we, being indeed from a family related to the kings from Asamonaios, and because of this having the priesthood together with honor, having assumed it unseemly to lie about anything concerning them, are setting forth the actions honestly and with reason. Although holding in respect many of his descendants who are still reigning, I have honored the truth above them, which, when it was done fairly, happened to meet with anger by those very descendants.

10.151 Ἐπεὶ δὲ τὸ γένος διεξήλθομεν τὸ τῶν βασιλέων καὶ τίνες ἦσαν δεδηλώκαμεν καὶ τοὺς χρόνους αὐτῶν, ἀναγκαῖον ἡγησάμην καὶ τῶν ἀρχιερέων εἰπεῖν τὰ ὀνόματα καὶ τίνες ἦσαν οἱ τὴν ἀρχιερωσύνην καταδείξαντες ἐπὶ τοῖς βασιλεῦσι.

Since we went completely through the house of the kings and have explained who they were and their dates, I believe that it is also necessary to mention the names of the high priests and who they were who, in addition to the kings, introduced the high priesthood.

6.350 ἔτι τούτων πλείω περὶ Σαούλου καὶ τῆς εὐψυχίας λέγειν ἠδυνάμην ὕλην ἡμῖν χορηγησάσης τῆς ὑποθέσεως, ἀλλ' ἵνα μὴ φανῶμεν ἀπειροκάλως αὐτοῦ χρῆσθαι τοῖς ἐπαίνοις, ἐπάνειμι πάλιν ἀφ' ὧν εἰς τούτους ἐξέβην.

I could say still more things about Saul and his courage, which furnishes material to us in abundance for the purpose. But so that we not appear vulgar in declaring his praises, I return from where I digressed into these matters.

1.18 Ἐπειδὴ δὲ πάντα σχεδὸν ἐκ τῆς τοῦ νομοθέτου σοφίας ἡμῖν ἀνήρτηται Μωυσέος, ἀνάγκη μοι βραχέα περὶ ἐκείνου προειπεῖν, ὅπως μή τινες τῶν ἀναγνωσομένων διαπορῶσι, πόθεν ἡμῖν ὁ λόγος περὶ νόμων καὶ πράξεων ἔχων τὴν ἀναγραφὴν ἐπὶ τοσοῦτον φυσιολογίας κεκοινώνηκεν.πειδὴ δὲ πάντα σχεδὸν ἐκ τῆς τοῦ νομοθέτου σοφίας ἡμῖν ἀνήρτηται Μωυσέος, ἀνάγκη μοι βραχέα περὶ ἐκείνου προειπεῖν, ὅπως μή τινες τῶν ἀναγνωσομένων διαπορῶσι, πόθεν ἡμῖν ὁ λόγος περὶ νόμων καὶ πράξεων ἔχων τὴν ἀναγραφὴν ἐπὶ τοσοῦτον φυσιολογίας κεκοινώνηκεν.

Since almost everything depends upon the wisdom of Moses our lawgiver, it is necessary for me to speak briefly about him, lest any of the readers should be at a loss how it can be that the book by us—having in so much of it the description of laws and practices—deals with an inquiry into natural phenomena.

14.265 Πολλὰ μὲν οὖν ἐστιν καὶ ἄλλα τοιαῦτα τῇ συγκλήτῳ καὶ τοῖς αὐτοκράτορσι τοῖς Ῥωμαίων δόγματα πρὸς Ὑρκανὸν καὶ τὸ ἔθνος ἡμῶν γεγενημένα καὶ πόλεσιν ψηφίσματα καὶ γράμματα πρὸς τὰς περὶ τῶν ἡμετέρων δικαίων ἐπιστολὰς ἀντιπεφωνημένα τοῖς ἡγεμόσιν, περὶ ὧν ἁπάντων ἐξ ὧν παρατεθείμεθα πιστεύειν τοῖς ἀναγνωσομένοις οὐ βασκάνως ἡμῶν τὴν γραφὴν πάρεστιν. **14.266** ἐπεὶ γὰρ ἐναργῆ καὶ βλεπόμενα τεκμήρια παρεχόμεθα τῆς πρὸς Ῥωμαίους ἡμῖν φιλίας γενομένης ἐπιδεικνύντες αὐτὰ χαλκαῖς στήλαις καὶ δέλτοις ἐν τῷ Καπετωλίῳ μέχρι νῦν διαμένοντα καὶ διαμενοῦντα, τὴν μὲν πάντων παράθεσιν ὡς περιττήν τε ἅμα καὶ ἀτερπῆ παρῃτησάμην, **14.267** οὐδένα δ' οὕτως ἡγησάμην σκαιόν, ὃς οὐχὶ καὶ περὶ τῆς Ῥωμαίων ἡμῖν πιστεύσει φιλανθρωπίας, ὅτι ταύτην καὶ διὰ πλειόνων ἐπεδείξαντο πρὸς ἡμᾶς δογμάτων, καὶ ἡμᾶς οὐχ ὑπολήψεται περὶ ὧν εἶναί φαμεν ἀληθεύειν ἐξ ὧν ἐπεδείξαμεν. τὴν μὲν οὖν πρὸς Ῥωμαίους φιλίαν καὶ συμμαχίαν κατ' ἐκείνους τοὺς καιροὺς γενομένην δεδηλώκαμεν.

14.265 There are, then, many other such decrees passed by the senate and dictators of the Romans in reference to Hyrcanus and our nation, as well as measures and documents by cities in response to the emperors' letters about our rights, concerning all of which it is easy for those who will read our book without malice to believe from the things we have cited. **14.266** For since we have furnished clear and visible proofs of our friendship with the Romans, pointing out those decrees that remain up to the present time—and will be permanent—on bronze monuments and tablets in the Capitol, I declined the mention of all of them as superfluous and at the same time displeasing. **14.267** And I think that no one is so stupid he will not believe regarding the benevolence of the Romans toward us, inasmuch as they exhibited this benevolence in a majority of the decrees about us, and who will not accept that we are speaking the truth about the things we have said from the facts we have pointed out. We have certainly demonstrated the friendship and alliance that there was with the Romans in those times.

Bibliography

Aichele, George, et al. *The Postmodern Bible*. New Haven: Yale University Press, 1995.

Aland, Kurt. "The Problem of Anonymity and Pseudonymity in Christian Literature of the First Two Centuries." Pages 1–13 in *The Authorship and Integrity of the New Testament*. Theological Collections 4. London: SPCK, 1965. Repr. from *JTS* 12 (1961): 39–49.

Aland, Kurt, and Barbara Aland. *The Text of the New Testament: An Introduction to the Critical Editions and to the Theory and Practice of Modern Textual Criticism*. Revised ed. Grand Rapids: Eerdmans, 1989.

Alexander, Loveday C. A. "Fact, Fiction and the Genre of Acts." *NTS* 44 (1998): 380–99.

————. "Formal Elements and Genre: Which Greco-Roman Prologues Most Closely Parallel the Lukan Prologues?" Pages 9–26 in *Jesus and the Heritage of Israel: Luke's Narrative Claim upon Israel's Legacy*. Edited by David P. Moessner. Luke the Interpreter of Israel Series 1. Harrisburg, Pa.: Trinity, 1999.

————. " 'In Journeying Often': Voyaging in the Acts of the Apostles and in Greek Romance." Pages 17–49 in *Luke's Literary Achievement: Collected Essays*. Edited by Christopher M. Tuckett. JSNTSup 116. Sheffield: Sheffield Academic Press, 1995.

————. "Luke's Preface in the Context of Greek Preface-Writing." *NovT* 28 (1986): 48–74.

————. "Mapping Early Christianity: Acts and the Shape of Early Church History." *Int* 57 (2003): 163–73.

————. "The Preface to Acts and the Historians." Pages 73–103 in *History, Literature, and Society in the Book of Acts*. Edited by Ben Witherington III. Cambridge: Cambridge University Press, 1996.

————. *The Preface to Luke's Gospel: Literary Convention and Social Context in Luke 1:1–4 and Acts 1:1*. SNTSMS 78. Cambridge: Cambridge University Press, 1993.

Alter, Robert. *The Art of Biblical Narrative*. New York: Basic Books, 1981.

Aronica, Joseph J. "Big Mouths." *Legal Times* 29/23 (5 June 2006): n.p. Cited 7 August 2006. Online: http://www.duanemorris.com/articles/static/aronicalegaltimes 060506.pdf.

Arterbury, Andrew E. "The Ancient Custom of Hospitality, the Greek Novels, and Acts 10:1–11:18." *PRSt* 29 (2002): 53–72.

Attridge, Harold W. *The Interpretation of Biblical History in the "Antiquitates Ju-daicae" of Flavius Josephus*. HDR 7. Missoula: Scholars Press, 1976.

Aune, David E. *The New Testament in Its Literary Environment*. LEC 8. Philadelphia: Westminster, 1987.

Bal, Mieke. *Narratology: Introduction to the Theory of Narrative*. Translated by Christine van Boheemen. Toronto: University of Toronto Press, 1985.

————. *On Story-Telling: Essays in Narratology*. Foundations and Facets: Literary Facets. Sonoma, Calif.: Polebridge, 1991.

Balch, David L. "Comments on the Genre and a Political Theme of Luke-Acts: A Preliminary Comparison of Two Hellenistic Historians." Pages 343–61 in *Society of Biblical Literature 1989 Seminar Papers*. SBLSP 28. Atlanta: Scholars Press, 1989.

Barrett, C. K. *A Critical and Exegetical Commentary on the Acts of the Apostles*. 2 vols. ICC. Edinburgh: T&T Clark, 1994–1998.

————. "The End of Acts." Pages 545–55 in *Frühes Christentum*. Edited by Hermann Lichtenberger. Vol. 3 of *Geschichte-Tradition-Reflexion: Festschrift für Martin Hengel zum 70. Geburtstag*. Edited by Hubert Cancik, Hermann Lichtenberger, and Peter Schäfer. Tübingen: Mohr Siebeck, 1996.

————. "Paul Shipwrecked." Pages 51–64 in *Scripture: Meaning and Method: Essays Presented to Anthony Tyrrell Hanson for His Seventieth Birthday*. Edited by Barry P. Thompson. Hull, England: Hull University Press, 1987.

————. "Theologia Crucis—In Acts?" Pages 73–84 in *Theologia Crucis—Signum Crucis: Festschrift für Erich Dinkler zum 70. Geburtstag*. Edited by Carl Andresen and Günter Klein. Tübingen: Mohr Siebeck, 1979.

————. "The Third Gospel as a Preface to Acts? Some Reflections." Pages 1451–66 in vol. 2 of *The Four Gospels 1992: Festschrift Frans Neirynck*. Edited by F. Van Segbroeck et al. Leuven: Leuven University Press, 1992.

Bauckham, Richard. "Barnabas in Galatians." *JSNT* 2 (1979): 61–70.

Bauer, Bruno. *Die Apostelgeschichte: Eine Ausgleichung des Paulinismus und des Judenthums innerhalb der christlichen Kirche*. Berlin: Hempel, 1850.

————. *Kritik der Evangelien und Geschichte ihres Ursprungs*. 3 vols. Berlin: Hempel, 1850–1851.

Baur, F. C. "Die Christuspartei in der korinthischen Gemeinde, der Gegensatz des petrinischen und paulinischen Christenthums in der ältesten Kirche, der Apostel Petrus in Rom." *Tübinger Zeitschrift für Theologie* 4 (1831): 61–206. Repr. as pages 1–146 in *Historisch-kritische Untersuchungen zum Neuen Testament*. Edited by Klaus Scholder. Stuttgart: Frommann, 1963.

————. *The Church History of the First Three Centuries*. Translated by Allen Menzies. 3rd ed. 2 vols. London: Williams & Norgate, 1878–1879.

————. *Paulus, der Apostel Jesu Christi: Sein Leben und Wirken, seine Briefe und seine Lehre*. Stuttgart: Becher & Müller, 1845.

Béchard, Dean P. "The Disputed Case against Paul: A Redaction-Critical Analysis of Acts 21:27–22:29. *CBQ* 65 (2003): 232–50.

Beker, J. Christiaan. *Paul the Apostle: The Triumph of God in Life and Thought*. Philadelphia: Fortress, 1980.

Berger, Klaus. "Hellenistische Gattungen im Neuen Testament." *ANRW* 25.2:1031–432.

Berkowitz, Luci, and Karl Squirtier, eds. *Thesaurus Linguae Graecae: Canon of Greek Authors and Works*. 3rd ed. Oxford: Oxford University Press, 1990.

Berlin, Adele. *Poetics and Interpretation of Biblical Narrative*. Bible and Literature Series 9. Sheffield: Almond, 1983.

Bilde, Per. *Flavius Josephus between Jerusalem and Rome: His Life, His Works, and Their Importance*. JSPSup 2. Sheffield: Sheffield Academic Press, 1988.

Bindemann, Walther. "Verkündiger: Das Paulusbild der Wir-Stücke in der Apostlegeschichte: seine Aufnahme und Bearbeitung durch Lukas." *TLZ* 114 (1989): 705–20.

Black, C. Clifton. "John Mark in the Acts of the Apostles." Pages 101–20 in *Literary Studies in Luke-Acts: Essays in Honor of Joseph B. Tyson*. Edited by Richard P. Thompson and Thomas E. Phillips. Macon, Ga.: Mercer University Press, 1998.

Bolt, Peter G. "Mission and Witness." Pages 191–214 in *Witness to the Gospel: The Theology of Acts*. Edited by I. Howard Marshall and David Peterson. Grand Rapids: Eerdmans, 1998.

Booth, Wayne C. *The Rhetoric of Fiction*. 2nd ed. Chicago: University of Chicago Press, 1983.

———. "Where Is the Authorial Audience in Biblical Narrative—and in Other 'Authoritative' Texts?" *Narrative* 4 (1996): 235–53.

Bovon, François. *Luke the Theologian: Thirty-Three Years of Research (1950–1983)*. Allison Park, Pa.: Pickwick, 1987.

Brawley, Robert L. *Centering on God: Method and Message in Luke-Acts*. Literary Currents in Biblical Interpretation. Louisville: Westminster John Knox, 1990.

———. *Luke-Acts and the Jews: Conflict, Apology, and Conciliation*. SBLMS 33. Atlanta: Scholars Press, 1987.

———. "Paul in Acts: Lucan Apology and Conciliation." Pages 129–47 in *Luke-Acts: New Perspectives from the Society of Biblical Literature Seminar*. Edited by Charles H. Talbert. New York: Crossroad, 1984.

Brock, Sebastian. "Βαρναβας· Υιος Παρακλησεως." *JTS* NS 25 (1974): 93–98.

Brosend, William F. "The Means of Absent Ends." Pages 348–62 in *History, Literature, and Society in the Book of Acts*. Edited by Ben Witherington III. Cambridge: Cambridge University Press, 1996.

Brown, Dan. *Angels and Demons*. New York: Pocket Books, 2000.

———. *The Da Vinci Code*. New York: Doubleday, 2003.

Bruce, F. F. *The Acts of the Apostles: The Greek Text with Introduction and Commentary*. 3rd ed. Grand Rapids: Eerdmans, 1990.

———. *Commentary on the Book of the Acts: The English Text with Introduction, Exposition and Notes*. Rev. ed. NICNT. Grand Rapids: Eerdmans, 1988.

———. *Paul: Apostle of the Heart Set Free*. Grand Rapids: Eerdmans, 1977.

Burchard, Christoph. *Der dreizehnte Zeuge: Traditions- und kompositionsgeschichtliche Untersuchungen zu Lukas' Darstellung der Frühzeit des Paulus*. Göttingen: Vandenhoeck & Ruprecht, 1970.

Burfeind, Carsten. "Paulus muß nach Rom. Zur politischen Dimension der Apostelgeschichte." *NTS* 46 (2000): 75–91.

Burnett, Fred W. "Characterization and Reader Construction of Characters in the Gospels." *Semeia* 63 (1993): 3–28.

Büttner-Wobst, T., ed. *Polybii Historiae*. 4 vols. 1889–1905. Repr., Stuttgart: Teubner, 1962–1967.

Byrskog, Samuel. "History or Story in Acts—A Middle Way? The 'We' Passages, Historical Intertexture, and Oral History." Pages 257–83 in *Contextualizing Acts: Lukan Narrative and Greco-Roman Discourse*. Edited by Todd Penner and Caroline Vander Stichele. SBLSymS 20. Atlanta: Society of Biblical Literature, 2003.

Cadbury, Henry J. *The Book of Acts in History*. London: Black, 1955.

———. "Commentary on the Preface of Luke." Pages 489–510 in *Prolegomena II: Criticism*. Edited by F. J. Foakes Jackson and Kirsopp Lake. Vol. 2 of *The Beginnings of Christianity, Part 1: The Acts of the Apostles*. London: Macmillan, 1922.

———. "The Greek and Jewish Traditions of History Writing." Pages 7–29 in *Prolegomena II: Criticism*. Edited by F. J. Foakes Jackson and Kirsopp Lake. Vol. 2 of *The Beginnings of Christianity, Part 1: The Acts of the Apostles*. London: Macmillan, 1922.

———. "The Knowledge Claimed in Luke's Preface." *Expositor* 24 (1922): 401–20.

———. "Lexical Notes on Luke-Acts: III. Luke's Interest in Lodging." *JBL* 45 (1926): 305–25.

———. "Lexical Notes on Luke-Acts: V. Luke and the Horse-Doctors." *JBL* 52 (1933): 55–65.

———. "Luke's Indebtedness to Josephus." Pages 355–58 in *Prolegomena II: Criticism*. Edited by F. J. Foakes Jackson and Kirsopp Lake. Vol. 2 of *The Beginnings of Christianity, Part 1: The Acts of the Apostles*. London: Macmillan, 1922.

———. "Luke-Translator or Author?" *AJT* 24 (1920): 436–55.

———. *The Making of Luke-Acts*. New York: Macmillan, 1927.

———. "The Purpose Expressed in Luke's Preface." *Expositor* 21 (1921): 431–41.

———. "Questions of Authorship in the New Testament." Pages 376–84 in vol. 4 of *An Outline of Christianity: The Story of Our Civilization*. Edited by Francis J. McConnell. New York: Bethlehem, 1926.

———. "Roman Law and the Trial of Paul." Pages 297–338 in *Additional Notes to the Commentary*. Edited by Kirsopp Lake and Henry J. Cadbury. Vol. 5 of *The Beginnings of Christianity, Part 1: The Acts of the Apostles*. London: Macmillan, 1933.

———. "Some Semitic Personal Names in Luke-Acts." Pages 45–56 in *Amicitiae Corolla*. Edited by H. G. Wood. London: University of London Press, 1933.

———. *The Style and Literary Method of Luke*. Cambridge: Harvard University Press, 1920.

———. "Subsidiary Points." Pages 349–59 in *Prolegomena II: Criticism*. Edited by F. J. Foakes Jackson and Kirsopp Lake. Vol. 2 of *The Beginnings of Christianity, Part 1: The Acts of the Apostles*. London: Macmillan, 1922.

———. "The Tradition." Pages 212–21 in *Prolegomena II: Criticism*. Edited by F. J. Foakes Jackson and Kirsopp Lake. Vol. 2 of *The Beginnings of Christianity, Part 1: The Acts of the Apostles*. London: Macmillan, 1922.

———. " 'We' and 'I' Passages in Luke-Acts." *NTS* 3 (1956–57): 128–32.

Callan, Terrance. "The Preface of Luke-Acts and Historiography." *NTS* 31 (1985): 576–81.

Chatman, Seymour. *Story and Discourse: Narrative Structure in Fiction and Film.* Ithaca, N.Y.: Cornell University Press, 1978.

———. "On the Formalist-Structuralist Theory of Character." *Journal of Literary Semantics* 1 (1972): 57–79.

Clark, Andrew C. "The Role of the Apostles." Pages 169–90 in *Witness to the Gospel: The Theology of Acts.* Edited by I. Howard Marshall and David Peterson. Grand Rapids: Eerdmans, 1998.

Colson, F. H. "Notes on St. Luke's Preface." *JTS* 24 (1923): 300–309.

Conzelmann, Hans. *Acts of the Apostles.* Translated by James Limburg, A. Thomas Kraabel, and Donald H. Juel. Hermeneia. Philadelphia: Fortress, 1987.

———. *History of Primitive Christianity.* Translated by John E. Steely. Nashville: Abingdon, 1973.

———. *The Theology of St. Luke.* Translated by Geoffrey Buswell. New York: Harper, 1961.

Cosgrove, Charles H. "The Divine Δεῖ in Luke-Acts: Investigations into the Lukan Understanding of God's Providence." *NovT* 26 (1984): 168–90.

Creech, R. Robert. "The Most Excellent Narratee: The Significance of Theophilus in Luke-Acts." Pages 107–26 in *With Steadfast Purpose: Essays on Acts in Honor of Henry Jackson Flanders, Jr.* Edited by Naymond H. Keathley. Waco, Tex.: Baylor University Press, 1990.

Crosman, Robert. "Do Readers Make Meaning?" Pages 149–64 in *The Reader in the Text: Essays on Audience and Interpretation.* Edited by Susan R. Suleiman and Inge Crosman. Princeton: Princeton University Press, 1980.

Culler, Jonathan. "Making Sense." *Twentieth Century Studies* 12 (1974): 27–36.

Dahl, Nils A. "The Purpose of Luke-Acts." Pages 87–98 in *Jesus in the Memory of the Church: Essays.* Minneapolis: Augsburg, 1976.

Darr, John A. "Discerning The Lukan Voice: The Narrator as Character in Luke-Acts." Pages 255–65 in *Society of Biblical Literature 1992 Seminar Papers.* SBLSP 31. Atlanta: Scholars Press, 1992.

———. *Herod the Fox: Audience Criticism and Lukan Characterization.* JSNTSup 163. Sheffield: Sheffield Academic Press, 1998.

———. "Narrator as Character: Mapping a Reader-Oriented Approach to Narration in Luke-Acts." *Semeia* 63 (1993): 43–59.

———. *On Character Building: The Reader and the Rhetoric of Characterization in Luke-Acts.* Literary Currents in Biblical Interpretation. Louisville: Westminster John Knox, 1992.

Dawsey, James M. "Characteristics of Folk-Epic in Acts." Pages 317–25 in *Society of Biblical Literature 1989 Seminar Papers.* SBLSP 28. Atlanta: Scholars Press, 1989.

———. *The Lukan Voice: Confusion and Irony in the Gospel of Luke.* Macon, Ga.: Mercer University Press, 1986.

Deissmann, Adolf. *Bible Studies: Contributions Chiefly from Papyri and Inscriptions to the History of the Language, the Literature, and the Religion of Hellenistic Judaism and Primitive Christianity.* Edinburgh: T&T Clark, 1901.

Detweiler, Robert, and Vernon K. Robbins. "From New Criticism to Poststructuralism: Twentieth-Century Hermeneutics." Pages 225–75 in *Reading the Text: Biblical Criticism and Literary Theory.* Edited by Stephen Prickett. Oxford: Blackwell, 1991.

Dibelius, Martin. *From Tradition to Gospel*. Translated by Bertram Woolf. New York: Scribner, 1965.

————. *Studies in the Acts of the Apostles*. Translated by Mary Ling. Edited by Heinrich Greeven. London: SCM, 1956.

Dillon, Richard. "Reviewing Luke's Project from His Prologue (Luke 1:1–4)." *CBQ* 43 (1981): 205–27.

Docherty, Thomas. *Reading (Absent) Character: Toward a Theory of Characterization in Fiction*. Oxford: Clarendon, 1983.

Donaldson, Laura E. "Cyborgs, Ciphers, and Sexuality: Re-theorizing Literary and Biblical Character." *Semeia* 63 (1993): 81–95.

Donfried, Karl P. "1 Thessalonians, Acts and the Early Paul." Pages 3–26 in *The Thessalonian Correspondence*. Edited by Raymond F. Collins. Leuven: Leuven University Press, 1990.

Dunn, James D. G. *The Acts of the Apostles*. Narrative Commentaries. Valley Forge, Pa.: Trinity, 1996.

————. *Unity and Diversity in the New Testament: An Inquiry into the Character of Earliest Christianity*. Philadelphia: Westminster, 1977.

Dupont, Jacques. *The Sources of Acts*. Translated by Kathleen Pond. London: Darton, Longman & Todd, 1964.

Eagleton, Terry. *Literary Theory: An Introduction*. Minneapolis: University of Minnesota Press, 1983.

Edwards, Douglas R. "Acts of the Apostles and the Graeco-Roman World: Narrative Communication in Social Contexts." Pages 362–77 in *Society of Biblical Literature 1989 Seminar Papers*. SBLSP 28. Atlanta: Scholars Press, 1989.

Ehrhardt, Arnold. *The Acts of the Apostles: Ten Lectures*. Manchester: Manchester University Press, 1969.

Esler, Philip Francis. *Community and Gospel in Luke-Acts: The Social and Political Motivations of Lucan Theology*. SNTSMS 57. Cambridge: Cambridge University Press, 1987.

Feldman, Louis H. *Josephus and Modern Scholarship (1937–1980)*. New York: de Gruyter, 1984.

Filson, Floyd V. *Pioneers of the Primitive Church*. New York: Abingdon, 1940.

Finegan, J. "Thessalonica." *IDB* 4:629.

Fitzmyer, Joseph A. *The Acts of the Apostles*. AB 31. New York: Doubleday, 1998.

————. *The Gospel according to Luke*. 2 vols. AB 28–28A. Garden City, N.Y.: Doubleday, 1981–1985.

————. *Luke the Theologian: Aspects of His Teaching*. New York: Paulist, 1989.

Foakes Jackson, F. J. *Josephus and the Jews*. London: SPCK, 1930.

Foakes Jackson, F. J., and Kirsopp Lake, eds. *The Beginnings of Christianity: Part I: The Acts of the Apostles*. 5 vols. London: Macmillan, 1920–1933.

Forster, E. M. *Anonymity: An Enquiry*. Hogarth Essays 12. London: Woolf, 1925. Repr., Folcraft, Pa.: Folcraft, 1976.

————. *Aspects of the Novel*. New York: Harcourt, Brace, 1927. Repr., Harmondsworth, U.K.: Penguin, 1963.

Fowler, Robert M. "Characterizing Character in Biblical Narrative." *Semeia* 63 (1993): 97–104.

———. *Let the Reader Understand: Reader-Response Criticism and the Gospel of Mark.* Minneapolis: Fortress, 1991.

———. "Who Is the 'Reader' in Reader Response Criticism?" *Semeia* 31 (1985): 5–23.

Fusco, Vittorio. "Le Sezioni-Noi Degli Atti Nella Discussione Recente." *BeO* 25 (1983): 73–86.

Garrett, Susan R. *The Demise of the Devil: Magic and the Demonic in Luke's Writings.* Minneapolis: Fortress, 1989.

Gasque, W. Ward. "A Fruitful Field: Recent Study of the Acts of the Apostles." *Int* 42 (1988): 117–31.

———. "The Historical Value of the Book of Acts: An Essay in the History of New Testament Criticism." *EvQ* 41 (1969): 68–88.

———. *A History of the Criticism of the Acts of the Apostles.* Tübingen: Mohr Siebeck, 1975.

Gaventa, Beverly Roberts. *The Acts of the Apostles.* ANTC. Nashville: Abingdon, 2003.

———. *From Darkness to Light: Aspects of Conversion in the New Testament.* OBT. Philadelphia: Fortress, 1986.

———. "Galatians 1 and 2: Autobiography as Paradigm." *NovT* 28 (1986): 309–26.

———. "The Overthrown Enemy: Luke's Portrait of Paul." Pages 439–49 in *Society of Biblical Literature 1985 Seminar Papers.* SBLSP 24. Atlanta: Scholars Press, 1985.

———. "The Peril of Modernizing Henry Joel Cadbury." Pages 7–26 in *Cadbury, Knox, and Talbert: American Contributions to the Study of Acts.* Edited by Mikeal C. Parsons and Joseph B. Tyson. Atlanta: Scholars Press, 1992.

———. "Toward a Theology of Acts." *Int* 42 (1988): 146–57.

Genette, Gérard. *Narrative Discourse: An Essay in Method.* Translated by Jane E. Lewin. Ithaca, N.Y.: Cornell University Press, 1980.

Graham, Susan Lochrie. "On Scripture and Authorial Intent: A Narratological Proposal." *AThR* 77 (1995): 307–20.

Grant, Michael. *The Ancient Historians.* New York: Scribner, 1970.

Grant, Robert M. *Irenaeus of Lyons.* London: Routledge, 1997.

Green, Joel B. *The Gospel of Luke.* NICNT. Grand Rapids: Eerdmans, 1997.

———. "Internal Repetition in Luke-Acts: Contemporary Narratology and Lucan Historiography." Pages 283–99 in *History, Literature, and Society in the Book of Acts.* Edited by Ben Witherington III. Cambridge: Cambridge University Press, 1996.

———, ed. *Hearing the New Testament: Strategies for Interpretation.* Grand Rapids: Eerdmans, 1995.

Hadas-Lebel, Mireille. *Flavius Josephus: Eyewitness to Rome's First-Century Conquest of Judea.* New York: Macmillan, 1993.

Haenchen, Ernst. "Acta 27." Pages 235–54 in *Zeit und Geschichte.* Edited by Erich Dinkler. Tübingen: Mohr Siebeck, 1964.

———. *The Acts of the Apostles.* Translated by Bernard Noble et al. Philadelphia: Westminster, 1971.

———. "The Book of Acts as Source Material for the History of Early Christianity." Pages 258–78 in *Studies in Luke-Acts*. Edited by Leander E. Keck and J. Louis Martyn. Nashville: Abingdon, 1966.

———. "'We' in Acts and the Itinerary." Translated by Jack Wilson. *JTC* 1 (1965): 65–99.

Hannam, Wilfrid L. "The Man Who Saw the Grace of God: A Study of Barnabas." *Religion in Life* 5 (1936): 417–24.

Harnack, Adolf. *Lukas der Arzt: Der Verfasser des Dritten Evangeliums und der Apostelgeschichte*. Vol. 1 of *Beiträge zur Einleitung in das Neue Testament*. Leipzig: Hinrich, 1906.

———. *Neue Untersuchungen zur Apostelgeschichte und zur Abfassungszeit der Synoptischen Evangelien*. Vol. 4 of *Beiträge zur Einleitung in das Neue Testament*. Leipzig: Hinrich, 1906.

Harrisville, Roy A. "Acts 22:6–21." *Int* 42 (1988): 181–85.

Harvey, W. J. *Character and the Novel*. London: Chatto & Windus, 1965.

Hemer, Colin J. *The Book of Acts in the Setting of Hellenistic History*. WUNT 49. Tübingen: Mohr Siebeck, 1989.

———. "First Person Narrative in Acts 27–28." *TynBul* 36 (1985): 79–109.

———. "The Name of Paul." *TynBul* 36 (1985): 179–83.

Hengel, Martin. *Acts and the History of Earliest Christianity*. Translated by John Bowden. Philadelphia: Fortress, 1980.

———. *Between Jesus and Paul: Studies in the Earliest History of Christianity*. Translated by John Bowden. London: SCM, 1983.

———. *The Four Gospels and the One Gospel of Jesus Christ: An Investigation of the Collection and Origin of the Canonical Gospels*. Translated by John Bowden. Harrisburg, Pa.: Trinity, 2000.

———. *Judaism and Hellenism: Studies in Their Encounter in Palestine during the Early Hellenistic Period*. Translated by John Bowden. 2 vols. Minneapolis: Fortress, 1974.

———. *Studies in the Gospel of Mark*. Translated by John Bowden. Philadelphia: Fortress, 1985.

Hilden, Julie. "Should Martha Stewart's Lawyer Have Strongly Advised Her to Testify? Assessing the Defense in the Stewart Case, Part One." *FindLaw Legal News and Commentary* (15 March 2004): n.p. Cited 3 August 2006. Online: http://writ.news.findlaw.com/hilden/20040315.html.

Hilgenfeld, Adolf. *Historisch-kritische Einleitung in das Neue Testament*. Leipzig: Fues, 1875.

Hill, Craig. *Hellenists and Hebrews: Reappraising Division within the Earliest Church*. Minneapolis: Fortress, 1992.

Holtzmann, H. J. *Die Apostelgeschichte*. Vol. 1 of *Hand-Commentar zum Neuen Testament*. 3rd ed. Tübingen: Mohr Siebeck, 1901.

Hur, Ju. *A Dynamic Reading of the Holy Spirit in Luke-Acts*. JSNTSup 211. Sheffield: Sheffield Academic Press, 2001. Repr., London: T&T Clark, 2004.

Jeremias, Joachim. *Jerusalem in the Time of Jesus: An Investigation into Economic and Social Conditions during the New Testament Period*. Translated by F. H. and C. H. Cave. Philadelphia: Fortress, 1969.

Jervell, Jacob. *Luke and the People of God: A New Look at Luke-Acts*. Minneapolis: Augsburg, 1972.

———. *The Theology of the Acts of the Apostles*. New Testament Theology. Cambridge: Cambridge University Press, 1996.

———. *The Unknown Paul: Essays on Luke-Acts and Early Christian History*. Minneapolis: Augsburg, 1984.

Johnson, Luke T. *The Acts of the Apostles*. SP 5. Collegeville, Minn.: Liturgical Press, 1992.

———. *The Gospel of Luke*. SP 3. Collegeville, Minn.: Liturgical Press, 1991.

———. *The Literary Function of Possessions in Luke-Acts*. SBLDS 39. Missoula, Mont.: Scholars Press, 1977.

Johnson, Sherman E. *Paul the Apostle and His Cities*. Wilmington, Del.: Glazier, 1987.

Jones, A. H. M. *The Cities of the Eastern Roman Provinces*. Oxford: Clarendon, 1937.

Jones, Donald L. "The Legacy of Henry Joel Cadbury: Or What He Learned That We Ought to Know." Pages 27–36 in *Cadbury, Knox, and Talbert: American Contributions to the Study of Acts*. Edited by Mikeal C. Parsons and Joseph B. Tyson. Atlanta: Scholars Press, 1992.

Jones, H. S., and J. E. Powell, eds. *Thucydidis Historiae*. 2 vols. Oxford: Clarendon, 1942.

Josephus. Translated by H. St. J. Thackeray et al. 9 vols. LCL. Cambridge: Harvard University Press, 1926–1965.

Juel, Donald. *Luke-Acts: The Promise of History*. Atlanta: John Knox, 1983.

Kaye, Bruce N. "Acts' Portrait of Silas." *NovT* 21 (1979): 13–26.

Keble, John. *Five Books of S. Irenaeus*. Oxford: Parker, 1872.

Keck, Leander E., and J. Louis Martyn, eds. *Studies in Luke-Acts*. Nashville: Abingdon, 1966.

Kee, Howard Clark. *To Every Nation under Heaven: The Acts of the Apostles*. The New Testament in Context. Harrisburg, Pa.: Trinity, 1997.

Kim, Seyoon. *The Origin of Paul's Gospel*. Tübingen: Mohr Siebeck, 1981.

Kissling, Paul J. *Reliable Characters in the Primary History: Profiles of Moses, Joshua, Elijah and Elisha*. Sheffield: Sheffield Academic Press, 1996.

Koch, Dietrich-Alex. "Kollektenbericht, 'Wir'-Bericht und Itinerar: Neue (?) Überlegungen zu einem alten Problem." *NTS* 45 (1999): 367–90.

Kollmann, Bernd. *Joseph Barnabas: Leben und Wirkungsgeschichte*. Stuttgart: Katholisches Bibelwerk, 1998.

Königsmann, Bernhard. "De fontibus commentariorum sacrorum, qui Lucae nomen praeferunt deque eorum consilio et aetate." Pages 215–39 in vol. 3 of *Sylloge Commentationum Theologicarum*. Edited by David J. Pott. Helmstadt: Fleckeisen, 1802.

Krodel, Gerhard A. *Acts*. Proclamation Commentaries: The New Testament Witnesses for Preaching. Philadelphia: Fortress, 1981.

Kümmel, Werner Georg. *The New Testament: The History of the Investigation of Its Problems*. Translated by S. McLean Gilmour and Howard C. Kee. Nashville: Abingdon, 1972.

Kurz, William S. "Effects of Variant Narrators in Acts 10–11." *NTS* 43 (1997): 570–86.

———. "Narrative Approaches to Luke-Acts." *Bib* 68 (1987): 195–220.

———. *Reading Luke-Acts: Dynamics of Biblical Narrative*. Louisville: Westminster John Knox, 1993.

Ladouceur, David. "Hellenistic Preconceptions of Shipwreck and Pollution as a Context for Acts 27–28." *HTR* 73 (1980): 435–49.

Lake, Kirsopp. "The Twelve and the Apostles." Pages 37–59 in *Additional Notes to the Commentary*. Edited by Kirsopp Lake and Henry J. Cadbury. Vol. 5 of *The Beginnings of Christianity, Part 1: The Acts of the Apostles*. London: Macmillan, 1933.

Lake, Kirsopp, and Henry J. Cadbury. *English Translation and Commentary*. Vol. 4 of *The Beginnings of Christianity, Part 1: The Acts of the Apostles*. Edited by F. J. Foakes Jackson and Kirsopp Lake. London: Macmillan, 1933.

Lampe, G. W. H. "The Holy Spirit in the Writings of St. Luke." Pages 159–200 in *Studies in the Gospels: Essays in Memory of R. H. Lightfoot*. Edited by D. E. Nineham. Oxford: Blackwell, 1955.

LaSor, William S. *Great Personalities of the New Testament: Their Lives and Times*. Westwood, N.J.: Revell, 1961.

Légasse, Simon. "Paul's Pre-Christian Career according to Acts." Pages 365–90 in *The Book of Acts in Its Palestinian Setting*. Edited by Richard Bauckham. Vol. 4 of *The Book of Acts in Its First Century Setting*. Edited by Bruce W. Winter. Grand Rapids: Eerdmans, 1995.

Lentz, John C. *Luke's Portrait of Paul*. SNTSMS 77. Cambridge: Cambridge University Press, 1993.

Lohfink, Gerhard. *The Conversion of St. Paul: Narrative and History in Acts*. Chicago: Franciscan, 1976.

Lyons, George. *Pauline Autobiography: Toward a New Understanding*. Atlanta: Scholars Press, 1985.

MacDonald, Dennis R. "The Shipwrecks of Odysseus and Paul." *NTS* 45 (1999): 88–107.

Maddox, Robert. *The Purpose of Luke-Acts*. FRLANT 126. Göttingen: Vandenhoeck & Ruprecht, 1982.

Malas, William H. "The Importance of Acts 19:21–22 for the Literary Structure of the Book of Acts." Paper presented at the Annual Meeting of the AAR/SBL, San Francisco, Calif., November 1997.

Malina, Bruce J. "Reading Theory Perspective: Reading Luke-Acts." Pages 3–23 in *The Social World of Luke-Acts: Models for Interpretation*. Edited by Jerome Neyrey. Peabody, Mass.: Hendrickson, 1991.

Malina, Bruce J., and Jerome H. Neyrey, *Portraits of Paul: An Archaeology of Ancient Personality*. Louisville: Westminster John Knox, 1996.

Marguerat, Daniel. "The Enigma of the Silent Closing of Acts (28:16–31)." Pages 284–304 in *Jesus and the Heritage of Israel: Luke's Narrative Claim upon Israel's Legacy*. Edited by David P. Moessner. Luke the Interpreter of Israel Series 1. Harrisburg, Pa.: Trinity, 1999.

———. *The First Christian Historian: Writing the 'Acts of the Apostles'*. Translated by Ken McKinney, Gregory J. Laughery, and Richard Bauckham. Cambridge: Cambridge University Press, 2002.

———. "Saul's Conversion (Acts 9, 22, 26) and the Multiplication of Narrative in Acts." Pages 127–55 in *Luke's Literary Achievement: Collected Essays*. Edited by Christopher M. Tuckett. JSNTSup 116. Sheffield: Sheffield Academic Press, 1995.

Marshall, I. Howard. "Acts in Current Study." *ExpTim* 115 (2003): 49–52.

———. *The Acts of the Apostles: An Introduction and Commentary*. TNTC. Grand Rapids: Eerdmans, 1980.

Martin, Luther H. "Gods or Ambassadors of God? Barnabas and Paul in Lystra." *NTS* 41 (1995): 152–56.

Martin, Wallace. *Recent Theories of Narrative*. Ithaca, N.Y.: Cornell University Press, 1986.

Mason, Steve. *Josephus and the New Testament*. Peabody, Mass.: Hendrickson, 1992.

Mattill, A. J., and Mary Bedford Mattill. *A Classified Bibliography of Literature on the Acts of the Apostles*. Leiden: Brill, 1966.

Mayeroff, Ernst. "Über den Zweck, die Quellen und den Verfasser der Apostelgeschichte." Pages 1–30 in *Historisch-critische Einleitung in die petrinischen Schriften nebst einer Abhandlung über den Verfasser der Apostelgeschichte*. Hamburg: Perthes, 1835.

McCasland, S. V. "Travel and Communication in the NT." *IDB* 4:690–93.

McGiffert, A. C. "The Historical Criticism of Acts in Germany." Pages 363–95 in *Prolegomena II: Criticism*. Edited by F. J. Foakes Jackson and Kirsopp Lake. Vol. 2 of *The Beginnings of Christianity, Part 1: The Acts of the Apostles*. London: Macmillan, 1922.

McKnight, Edgar V. "A Biblical Criticism for American Biblical Scholarship." Pages 123–34 in *Society of Biblical Literature 1980 Seminar Papers*. SBLSP 19. Chico, Calif.: Scholars Press, 1980.

———. *Meaning in Texts: The Historical Shaping of Narrative Hermeneutics*. Philadelphia: Fortress, 1978.

———. "A Sheep in Wolf's Clothing: An Option in Contemporary New Testament Hermeneutics." Pages 326–47 in *The New Literary Criticism and the New Testament*. Edited by Elizabeth Struthers Malbon and Edgar V. McKnight. Sheffield: Sheffield Academic Press, 1994.

McRay, John. "Greece." *ABD* 2:1092–98.

Meeks, Wayne A., and Robert L. Wilken. *Jews and Christians in Antioch in the First Four Centuries of the Common Era*. SBLSBL 13. Missoula, Mont.: Scholars Press, 1978.

Menzies, Robert P. *The Development of Early Christian Pneumatology with Special Reference to Luke-Acts*. JSNTSup 54. Sheffield: JSOT Press, 1991.

Metzger, Bruce M. "History of Editing the Greek New Testament." *PSB* 8 (1987): 33–45.

———. *A Textual Commentary on the Greek New Testament*. London: United Bible Societies, 1971.

Meyer, Eduard. *Der Papyrusfund von Elephantine: Dokumente einer jüdischen*

Gemeinde aus der Perserzeit und das älteste erhaltene Buch der Weltliteratur. Leipzig: Hinrich, 1912.

Miles, Gary B., and Garry Trompf. "Luke and Antiphon: The Theology of Acts 27–28 in the Light of Pagan Beliefs about Divine Retribution, Pollution, and Shipwreck." *HTR* 69 (1976): 259–67.

Miller, J. Hillis. "Narrative." Pages 66–79 in *Critical Terms for Literary Study.* Edited by Frank Lentricchia and Thomas McLaughlin. Chicago: University of Chicago Press, 1990.

Mills, Watson E. *A Bibliography of the Periodical Literature on the Acts of the Apostles 1962–1984.* Leiden: Brill, 1986.

———, ed. *The Acts of the Apostles.* Vol. 5 of *Bibliographies for Biblical Research: New Testament Series.* Edited by Watson E. Mills. Lewiston, N.Y.: Mellen, 1996.

Minear, Paul. "Dear Theo: The Kerygmatic Intention and Claim of the Book of Acts." *Int* 27 (1973): 131–50.

Mitchell, Margaret M. "New Testament Envoys in the Context of Greco-Roman Diplomatic and Epistolary Conventions: The Example of Timothy and Titus (1 Thess 3:6–10; 2 Cor 7:5–16)." *JBL* 111 (1992): 641–62.

Moessner, David P. "The Appeal and Power of Poetics (Luke 1:1–4): Luke's Superior Credentials (παρηκολουθηκότι), Narrative Sequence (καθεξῆς), and Firmness of Understanding (ἡ ἀσφάλεια) for the Reader." Pages 84–123 in *Jesus and the Heritage of Israel: Luke's Narrative Claim upon Israel's Legacy.* Edited by David P. Moessner. Luke the Interpreter of Israel Series 1. Harrisburg, Pa.: Trinity, 1999.

———. " 'The Christ Must Suffer': New Light on the Jesus-Peter, Stephen, Paul Parallels in Luke-Acts." *NovT* 28 (1986): 220–56.

———. " 'The Christ Must Suffer,' The Church Must Suffer: Rethinking the Theology of the Cross in Luke-Acts." Pages 165–95 in *Society of Biblical Literature 1990 Seminar Papers.* SBLSP 29. Atlanta: Scholars Press, 1990.

———. " 'Eyewitnesses,' 'Informed Contemporaries,' and 'Unknowing Inquirers': Josephus' Criteria for Authentic Historiography and the Meaning of Παρακολουθεω." *NovT* 38 (1996): 105–22.

———. "The Meaning of καθεξῆς in the Lukan Prologue as a Key to the Distinctive Contribution of Luke's Narrative among the 'Many.' " Pages 1513–28 in vol. 2 of *The Four Gospels 1992: Festschrift Frans Neirynck.* Edited by F. Van Segbroeck et al. Leuven: Leuven University Press, 1992.

Moore, John M. *The Manuscript Tradition of Polybius.* Cambridge: Cambridge University Press, 1965.

Moore, Stephen D. "Doing Gospel Criticism as/with a 'Reader.'" *BTB* 19 (1989): 85–93.

———. *Literary Criticism and the Gospels: The Theoretical Challenge.* New Haven: Yale University Press, 1989.

Mortley, Raoul. *The Idea of Universal History from Hellenistic Philosophy to Early Christian Historiography.* Lewiston, N.Y.: Mellen, 1996.

Mount, Christopher. *Pauline Christianity: Luke-Acts and the Legacy of Paul.* NovTSup 104. Leiden: Brill, 2002.

Munck, Johannes. *The Acts of the Apostles*. AB 31. Garden City, N.Y.: Doubleday, 1967.

Neil, William. *Acts*. London: Marshall, Morgan & Scott, 1973. Repr., Grand Rapids: Eerdmans, 1987.

Nelson, Edwin S. "Paul's First Missionary Journey as Paradigm: A Literary-Critical Assessment of Acts 13–14." Ph.D. diss., Boston University, 1982.

Neyrey, Jerome H. "Acts 17, Epicureans, and Theodicy: A Study in Stereotypes." Pages 118–34 in *Greeks, Romans, and Christians: Essays in Honor of Abraham J. Malherbe*. Edited by David L. Balch, Everett Ferguson, and Wayne Meeks. Minneapolis: Fortress, 1990.

Niese, B., ed. *Flavii Josephi Opera*. 7 vols. Berlin: Weidmann, 1885–1895.

Nock, Arthur Darby. "The Book of Acts." Pages 821–32 in vol. 2 of *Arthur Darby Nock: Essays on Religion and the Ancient World*. Edited by Zeph Stewart. Oxford: Clarendon, 1972.

———. *Conversion: The Old and the New in Religion from Alexander the Great to Augustine of Hippo*. Oxford: Oxford University Press, 1933.

Norden, Eduard. *Agnostos Theos: Untersuchungen zur Formengeschichte Religiöser Rede*. Leipzig: Teubner, 1913.

Oberhummer, E. "Kypros." Pages 59–117 in vol. 12.1 of *Paulys Realencyclopädie der classischen Altertumswissenschaft*. Edited by A. F. Pauly, Georg Wissowa, and Wilhelm Kroll. Stuttgart: Metzler, 1924.

Parsons, Mikeal, and Richard Pervo. *Rethinking the Unity of Luke-Acts*. Minneapolis: Fortress, 1993.

Pervo, Richard. "Israel's Heritage and Claims upon the Genre(s) of Luke and Acts: The Problems of a History." Pages 127–43 in *Jesus and the Heritage of Israel: Luke's Narrative Claim upon Israel's Legacy*. Edited by David P. Moessner. Luke the Interpreter of Israel Series 1. Harrisburg, Pa.: Trinity, 1999.

———"Must Luke and Acts Belong to the Same Genre?" Pages 309–15 in *Society of Biblical Literature 1989 Seminar Papers*. SBLSP 28. Atlanta: Scholars Press, 1989.

———. "'On Perilous Things': A Response to Beverly R. Gaventa." Pages 37–43 in *Cadbury, Knox, and Talbert: American Contributions to the Study of Acts*. Edited by Mikeal C. Parsons and Joseph B. Tyson. Atlanta: Scholars Press, 1992.

———. *Profit with Delight: The Literary Genre of the Acts of the Apostles*. Philadelphia: Fortress, 1987.

Petersen, Norman R. "'Point of View' in Mark's Narrative." *Semeia* 12 (1978): 97–121.

Peterson, David. "Luke's Theological Enterprise: Integration and Intent." Pages 521–44 in *Witness to the Gospel: The Theology of Acts*. Edited by I. Howard Marshall and David Peterson. Grand Rapids: Eerdmans, 1998.

——— . "The Motif of Fulfillment and the Purpose of Luke Acts." Pages 83–104 in *The Book of Acts in Its Ancient Literary Setting*. Edited by Bruce W. Winter and Andrew D. Clarke. Vol. 1 of *The Book of Acts in Its First Century Setting*. Edited by Bruce W. Winter. Grand Rapids: Eerdmans, 1993.

Plümacher, Eckhard. *Lukas als hellenistischer Schriftsteller: Studien zur Apostelgeschichte*. SUNT 9. Göttingen: Vandenhoeck & Ruprecht, 1972.

————. "Wirklichkeitserfahrung und Geschichtsschreibung bei Lukas: Erwägungen zu den Wir-Stücken der Apostelgeschichte." *ZNW* 68 (1977): 2–22.

Polybius. *The Histories.* Translated by W. R. Paton. 6 vols. LCL. New York: Putnam, 1922–1927.

————. *The Histories of Polybius.* Translated by Evelyn S. Shuckburgh. 2 vols. New York: Macmillan, 1889.

Porter, Stanley E. *The Paul of Acts: Essays in Literary Criticism, Rhetoric, and Theology.* WUNT 115. Tübingen: Mohr Siebeck, 1999.

————. "The 'We' Passages." Pages 545–74 in *The Book of Acts in Its Graeco-Roman Setting.* Edited by David W. J. Gill and Conrad Gempf. Vol. 2 of *The Book of Acts in Its First Century Setting.* Edited by Bruce W. Winter. Grand Rapids: Eerdmans, 1994.

Powell, Mark. *What Is Narrative Criticism?* GBS. Minneapolis: Fortress, 1990.

Praeder, Susan Marie. "Acts 27:1–28:16: Sea Voyages in Ancient Literature and the Theology of Luke-Acts." *CBQ* 46 (1984): 683–706.

————. "The Narrative Voyage: An Analysis and Interpretation of Acts 27–28." Ph.D. diss., Graduate Theological Union, 1980.

————. "The Problem of First Person Narration in Acts." *NovT* 29 (1987): 193–218.

Pucci Ben Zeev, Miriam. *Jewish Rights in the Roman World: The Greek and Roman Documents Quoted by Josephus Flavius.* TSAJ 74. Tübingen: Mohr Siebeck, 1998.

Rackham, Richard B. *The Acts of the Apostles.* 2nd ed. WC. London: Methuen, 1904.

Ramsay, W. M. *St. Paul the Traveller and the Roman Citizen.* New York: Putnam, 1896.

Ramsey, George. "Is Name-Giving an Act of Domination in Genesis 2:23 and Elsewhere?" *CBQ* 50 (1988): 24–35.

Rapske, Brian. *The Book of Acts and Paul in Roman Custody.* Vol. 3 of *The Book of Acts in Its First Century Setting.* Edited by Bruce W. Winter. Grand Rapids: Eerdmans, 1994.

————. "Opposition to the Plan of God and Persecution." Pages 235–56 in *Witness to the Gospel: The Theology of Acts.* Edited by I. Howard Marshall and David Peterson. Grand Rapids: Eerdmans, 1998.

————. "Acts, Travel and Shipwreck." Pages 1–47 in *The Book of Acts in Its Graeco-Roman Setting.* Edited by David W. J. Gill and Conrad Gempf. Vol. 2 of *The Book of Acts in Its First Century Setting.* Edited by Bruce W. Winter. Grand Rapids: Eerdmans, 1994.

Rashkow, Ilona N. "In Our Image We Create Him, Male and Female We Create Them: The E/Affect of Biblical Characterization." *Semeia* 63 (1993): 105–13.

Ray, Jerry Lynn. *Narrative Irony in Luke-Acts: The Paradoxical Interaction of Prophetic Fulfillment and Jewish Rejection.* Lewiston, N.Y.: Mellen, 1996.

Read-Heimerdinger, Jenny. "Barnabas in Acts: A Study of His Role in the Text of Codex Bezae." *JSNT* 72 (1998): 23–66.

Rehm, Merlin D. "Levites and Priests." *ABD* 4:297–310.

Reinhartz, Adele. *"Why Ask My Name?" Anonymity and Identity in Biblical Narrative.* Oxford: Oxford University Press, 1998.

Renan, Ernest. *Les Apôtres*. Vol. 2 of *Histoire des Origines du Christianisme*. Paris: Lévy, 1866.

Reumann, John. "The 'Itinerary' as a Form in Classical Literature and the Acts of the Apostles." Pages 335–57 in *To Touch the Text: Biblical and Related Studies in Honor of Joseph A. Fitzmyer, S.J.*. Edited by Maurya P. Horgan and Paul J. Kobelski. New York: Crossroad, 1989.

Richard, Earl. *Acts 6:1–8:4: The Author's Method of Composition*. SBLDS 41. Missoula, Mont.: Scholars Press, 1978.

———. "The Divine Purpose: The Jews and the Gentile Mission (Acts 15)." Pages 188–209 in *Luke-Acts: New Perspectives from the Society of Biblical Literature Seminar*. Edited by Charles H. Talbert. New York: Crossroad, 1984.

———. "Pentecost as a Recurrent Theme in Luke-Acts." Pages 133–49 in *New Views on Luke and Acts*. Edited by Earl Richard. Collegeville, Minn.: Liturgical Press, 1990.

Ricoeur, Paul. "Biblical Hermeneutics." *Semeia* 4 (1975): 27–148.

———. "Interpretative Narrative." Pages 237–75 in *The Book and the Text: The Bible and Literary Theory*. Edited by Regina M. Schwartz. Translated by David Pellauer. Cambridge, Mass.: Blackwell, 1990.

Rimmon-Kenan, Shlomith. *Narrative Fiction: Contemporary Poetics*. New York: Methuen, 1983.

Robbins, Vernon K. "By Land and By Sea: The We-Passages and Ancient Sea Voyages." Pages 215–42 in *Perspectives on Luke-Acts*. Edited by Charles Talbert. Danville, Va.: Association of Baptist Professors of Religion, 1978.

———. "Prefaces in Greco-Roman Biography and Luke-Acts." Pages 193–207 in vol. 2 of *Society of Biblical Literature 1978 Seminar Papers*. SBLSP 17. Missoula, Mont.: Scholars Press, 1978.

———. "The We-Passages in Acts and Ancient Sea Voyages." *BR* 20 (1975): 5–18.

———. "The Social Location of the Implied Author of Luke-Acts." Pages 305–32 in *The Social World of Luke-Acts: Models for Interpretation*. Edited by Jerome Neyrey. Peabody, Mass.: Hendrickson, 1991.

Roloff, Jürgen. *Die Apostelgeschichte*. Göttingen: Vandenhoeck & Ruprecht, 1981.

Rolston, Holmes. *Personalities around Paul: Men and Women Who Helped or Hindered the Apostle Paul*. Richmond, Va.: John Knox, 1954.

Root, Michael. "The Narrative Structure of Soteriology." *Modern Theology* 2 (1986): 145–57.

Root, Robert L., Jr. "Naming Nonfiction (a Polyptych)." *College English* 65 (2003): 242–56.

Ropes, James H. "St. Luke's Preface: ασφαλεια and παρακολουθειν." *JTS* 25 (1924): 67–71.

Rosenblatt, Marie-Eloise. *Paul the Accused: His Portrait in the Acts of the Apostles*. Zacchaeus Studies: New Testament. Collegeville, Minn.: Liturgical Press, 1995.

———. "Under Interrogation: Paul as Witness in Juridical Contexts in Acts and the Implied Spirituality for Luke's Community." Ph.D. diss., Graduate Theological Union, 1976.

Rousseau, Adelin, and Louis Doutreleau. *Irénée di Lyon Contre Les Hérésies, Livre III*. Paris: Cerf, 1974.

Sanders, E. P. *Judaism: Practice and Belief, 63 BCE to 66 CE*. London: SCM, 1992.

Schmidt, Daryl D. "Rhetorical Influences and Genre: Luke's Preface and the Rhetoric of Hellenistic Historiography." Pages 27–60 in *Jesus and the Heritage of Israel: Luke's Narrative Claim upon Israel's Legacy*. Edited by David P. Moessner. Luke the Interpreter of Israel Series 1. Harrisburg, Pa.: Trinity, 1999.

———. "Syntactical Style in the 'We'-Sections of Acts: How Lukan Is It?" Pages 300–307 in *Society of Biblical Literature 1989 Seminar Papers*. SBLSP 28. Atlanta: Scholars Press, 1989.

Schmithals, Walter. *The Office of Apostle in the Early Church*. London: SPCK, 1971.

Scholes, Robert, and Robert Kellogg. *The Nature of Narrative*. Oxford: Oxford University Press, 1966.

Schubert, Paul. "The Place of the Areopagus Speech in the Composition of Acts." Pages 235–61 in *Transitions in Biblical Scholarship*. Edited by J. Rylaarsdam. Chicago: University of Chicago Press, 1968.

———. "The Structure and Significance of Luke 24." Pages 165–86 in *Neutestamentlich Studien für Rudolf Bultmann*. Edited by Walther Estester. Berlin: Töpelmann, 1954.

Schwanbeck, Eugen Alexis. *Über die Quellen der Apostelgeschichte*. Vol. 1 of *Über die Quellen der Schriften des Lukas*. Darmstadt: Leske, 1847.

Schwartz, Regina M. "Introduction: On Biblical Criticism." Pages 1–15 in *The Book and the Text: The Bible and Literary Theory*. Edited by Regina M. Schwartz. Cambridge, Mass.: Blackwell, 1990.

Schweitzer, Albert. *The Quest of the Historical Jesus: A Critical Study of Its Progress from Reimarus to Wrede*. 2nd ed. London: Black, 1911.

Scrivener, Frederick H., ed. *Bezae Codex Cantabrigiensis*. 1864. Repr., Pittsburgh: Pickwick, 1978.

Seekings, Herbert S. *The Men of the Pauline Circle*. London: Kelly, 1914.

Sheeley, Steven M. "Getting into the Act(s): Narrative Presence in the 'We' Sections." *PRSt* 26 (1999): 203–20.

———. *Narrative Asides in Luke-Acts*. JSNTSup 72. Sheffield: JSOT Press, 1992.

Shepherd, William H. *The Narrative Function of the Holy Spirit as a Character in Luke-Acts*. SBLDS 147. Atlanta: Scholars Press, 1994.

Sherwin-White, A. N. *Roman Society and Roman Law in the New Testament*. Oxford: Oxford University Press, 1963. Repr., Grand Rapids: Baker, 1978.

Skinner, Matthew L. *Locating Paul: Places of Custody as Narrative Settings in Acts 21–28*. SBLAcBib 13. Atlanta: Society of Biblical Literature, 2003.

Smith, T. C. "The Sources of Acts." Pages 56–75 in *With Steadfast Purpose: Essays on Acts in Honor of Henry Jackson Flanders, Jr.*. Edited by Naymond H. Keathley. Waco, Tex.: Baylor University, 1990.

Soards, Marion L. *The Speeches in Acts: Their Content, Context, and Concerns*. Louisville: Westminster John Knox, 1994.

Spencer, F. Scott. *Acts*. Readings: A New Biblical Commentary. Sheffield: Sheffield Academic Press, 1997.

———. "Acts and Modern Literary Approaches." Pages 381–414 in *The Book of Acts in Its Ancient Literary Setting*. Edited by Bruce W. Winter and Andrew D. Clarke. Vol. 1 of *The Book of Acts in Its First Century Setting*. Edited by Bruce W. Winter. Grand Rapids: Eerdmans, 1993.

————. *The Portrait of Philip in Acts: A Study of Roles and Relations.* JSNTSup 67. Sheffield: JSOT Press, 1992.

Squires, John T. *The Plan of God in Luke-Acts.* SNTSMS 76. Cambridge: Cambridge University Press, 1993.

————. "The Plan of God in the Acts of the Apostles." Pages 19–39 in *Witness to the Gospel: The Theology of Acts.* Edited by I. Howard Marshall and David Peterson. Grand Rapids: Eerdmans, 1998.

Stagg, Frank. "Textual Criticism for Luke-Acts." *PRSt* 5 (1978): 152–65.

Stendahl, Krister. *Paul among Jews and Gentiles and Other Essays.* Philadelphia: Fortress, 1976.

Sterling, Gregory E. *Historiography and Self-Definition: Josephos, Luke-Acts and Apologetic Historiography.* NovTSup 64. Leiden: Brill, 1992.

————. "Luke-Acts and Apologetic Historiography." Pages 326–41 in *Society of Biblical Literature 1989 Seminar Papers.* SBLSP 28. Atlanta: Scholars Press, 1989.

Sternberg, Meir. *The Poetics of Biblical Narrative: Ideological Literature and the Drama of Reading.* Bloomington: Indiana University Press, 1985.

————. "Time and Space in Biblical (Hi)story Telling: The Grand Chronology." Pages 81–145 in *The Book and the Text: The Bible and Literary Theory.* Edited by Regina M. Schwartz. Cambridge, Mass.: Blackwell, 1990.

Stonehouse, N. B. *The Witness of Luke to Christ.* London: Tyndale, 1951.

Stout, Jeffrey. "What Is the Meaning of a Text?" *New Literary History* 14 (1982): 1–12.

Suleiman, Susan R. "Introduction: Varieties of Audience-Oriented Criticism." Pages 3–45 in *The Reader in the Text: Essays on Audience and Interpretation.* Edited by Susan R. Suleiman and Inge Crosman. Princeton: Princeton University Press, 1980.

Sutcliffe, Andrea J., et al., eds. *The New York Public Library Writer's Guide to Style and Usage.* New York: HarperCollins, 1994.

Sutherland, A. "The Call and Ordination of Barnabas and Saul to Missionary Work." *Methodist Review* 75 (1893): 562–75.

Tajra, Harry W. *The Trial of St. Paul: A Juridical Exegesis of the Second Half of the Acts of the Apostles.* WUNT 35. Tübingen: Mohr Siebeck, 1989.

Talbert, Charles H. *Literary Patterns, Theological Themes, and the Genre of Luke-Acts.* SBLMS 20. Missoula, Mont.: Scholars Press, 1974.

————. "Luke-Acts." Pages 297–320 in *The New Testament and Its Modern Interpreters.* Edited by Eldon Jay Epp and George W. MacRae. Philadelphia: Fortress, 1989.

————. *Reading Luke: A Literary and Theological Commentary on the Third Gospel.* Reading the New Testament. New York: Crossroad, 1982.

Talbert, Charles H., and J. H. Hayes. "A Theology of Sea Storms in Luke-Acts." Pages 321–36 in *Society of Biblical Literature 1995 Seminar Papers.* SBLSP 34. Atlanta: Scholars Press, 1995.

Tannehill, Robert C. *Luke.* ANTC. Nashville: Abingdon, 1996.

————. *The Narrative Unity of Luke-Acts: A Literary Interpretation.* 2 vols. Minneapolis: Fortress, 1986–1990.

————. "Rejection by Jews and Turning to Gentiles: The Pattern of Paul's Mission in Acts." Pages 130–41 in *Society of Biblical Literature 1986 Seminar Papers*. SBLSP 25. Atlanta: Scholars Press, 1986.

Thesaurus Linguae Graecae. Version D. Irvine: University of California, 1992. Online: http://www.tlg.uci.edu.

Thornton, Claus-Jürgen. *Der Zeuge des Zeugen: Lukas als Historiker der Paulusreisen*. WUNT 56. Tübingen: Mohr Siebeck, 1991.

Thucydides. *History of the Peloponnesian War*. Translated by C. Forster Smith. 4 vols. LCL. New York: Putnam, 1919–1923.

Todorov, Tzvetan. "Reading as Construction." Pages 67–82 in *The Reader in the Text: Essays on Audience and Interpretation*. Edited by Susan R. Suleiman and Inge Crosman. Princeton: Princeton University Press, 1980.

Trible, Phyllis. *God and the Rhetoric of Sexuality*. OBT. Philadelphia: Fortress, 1978.

Trompf, Garry W. "On Why Luke Declined to Recount the Death of Paul: Acts 27–28 and Beyond." Pages 225–39 in *Luke-Acts: New Perspectives from the Society of Biblical Literature Seminar*. Edited by Charles Talbert. New York: Crossroad, 1984.

Unnik, W. C. van. "Der Befehl an Philippus." *ZNW* 47 (1956): 181–91.

———. "The 'Book of Acts' The Confirmation of the Gospel." *NovT* 4 (1960): 26–59.

———. "Luke-Acts, A Storm Center in Contemporary Scholarship." Pages 15–32 in *Studies in Luke-Acts*. Edited by Leander Keck and J. Louis Martyn. Nashville: Abingdon, 1966.

———. "Once More St. Luke's Prologue." *Neot* 7 (1973): 7–26.

Vanhoozer, K. J. "The Hermeneutics of I-Witness Testimony: John 21.20–24 and the 'Death' of the 'Author.'" Pages 366–87 in *Understanding Poets and Prophets: Essays in Honour of George Wishart Anderson*. Edited by A. Graeme Auld. JSOTSup 152. Sheffield: Sheffield Academic Press, 1993.

Vielhauer, Philipp. "On the 'Paulinism' of Acts." Pages 33–50 in *Studies in Luke-Acts*. Edited by Leander E. Keck and J. Louis Martyn. Nashville: Abingdon, 1966.

Vos, Craig S. de. "Finding a Charge That Fits: The Accusation against Paul and Silas at Philippi (Acts 16.19–21)." *JSNT* 74 (1999): 51–63.

Walasky, Paul W. *Acts*. Westminster Bible Companion. Louisville: Westminster John Knox, 1998.

Walbank, F. W. *A Historical Commentary on Polybius*. 3 vols. Oxford: Clarendon, 1957–1979.

Walworth, Allen J. "The Narrator of Acts." Ph.D. diss., Southern Baptist Theological Seminary, 1984.

Wedderburn, Alexander J. M. "The 'We'-Passages: On the Horns of a Dilemma." *ZNW* 93 (2002): 78–98.

Wehnert, Jürgen. *Die Wir-Passagen der Apostelgeschichte: Ein lukanisches Stilmittel aus jüdischer Tradition*. GTA 40. Göttingen: Vandenhoeck & Ruprecht, 1989.

Wellhausen, Julius. *Kritische Analyse der Apostelgeschichte*. Berlin: Weidmann, 1914.

———. "Noten zur Apostelgeschichte." Pages 1–21 in *Nachrichten von der königlichen Gesellschaft der Wissenschaften zu Göttingen: Philologisch-historische Klasse aus dem Jahre 1907*. Berlin: Weidmann, 1907.

Wette, W. M. L. de. *An Historico-Critical Introduction to the Canonical Books of the New Testament*. Translated by Frederick Frothingham. Boston: Crosby, Nichols, 1858.

——. *Lehrbuch der historisch kritischen Einleitung in die kanonischen Bücher des Neuen Testaments*. Berlin: Reimer, 1826. 5th ed. Berlin: Reimer, 1848.

White, L. Michael. "Visualizing the 'Real' World of Acts 16: Toward Construction of a Social Index." Pages 234–61 in *The Social World of the First Christians: Essays in Honor of Wayne A. Meeks*. Edited by L. Michael White and O. Larry Yarbrough. Minneapolis: Fortress, 1995.

Wilder, Terry L. *Pseudonymity, the New Testament, and Deception: An Inquiry into Intention and Reception*. Lanham, Md.: University Press of America, 2004.

Wilson, Stephen G. *The Gentiles and the Gentile Mission in Luke-Acts*. SNTSMS 23. Cambridge: Cambridge University Press, 1973.

Wineland, John. "Adramyttium." *ABD* 1:80.

Witherington, Ben, III. *The Acts of the Apostles: A Socio-rhetorical Commentary*. Grand Rapids: Eerdmans, 1998.

Yamauchi, Edwin. "Troas." *ABD* 6:666–67.

——. "Tyrannus." *ABD* 6:686.

Zahn, Theodor. *Die Apostelgeschichte des Lucas*. 2 vols. Vol. 5 of *Kommentar zum Neuen Testament*. Leipzig: Deichert, 1919.

Zeller, Eduard. *The Contents and Origin of the Acts of the Apostles Critically Investigated*. Translated by Joseph Dare. 2 vols. London: Williams & Norgate, 1875–1876.

Index of Names

Index of Ancient Sources

LaVergne, TN USA
02 November 2009
162593LV00002B/20/A